Social Work Evaluation

Also Available from Lyceum Books, Inc.

Social Work Evaluation: Enhancing What We Do

James R. Dudley
University of North Carolina Charlotte

LYCEUM
BOOKS, INC.

Chicago, Illinois

© Lyceum Books, Inc., 2009

Published by

LYCEUM BOOKS, INC.
5758 S. Blackstone Ave.
Chicago, Illinois 60637
773+643-1903 (Fax)
773+643-1902 (Phone)
lyceum@lyceumbooks.com
http://www.lyceumbooks.com

6 5 4 3 2   10 11 12

ISBN 978-0-925065-72-8

Library of Congress Cataloging-in-Publication Data

Dudley, James R.
    Social work evaluation : enhancing what we do / James R. Dudley.
       p. cm.
    Includes bibliographical references.
    ISBN 978-0-925065-72-8
    1. Social service—Evaluation. 2. Evaluation research (Social action programs)
I. Title.
    HV41.D83   2008
    361.3072—dc22
                                                    2008016806

I dedicate this book to my current and former students, who have inspired and encouraged me over many years. Thank you so much!

Contents

Preface

Every social worker is expected to know how to conduct an evaluation of his or her practice. Growing numbers of social workers will also be assuming a program evaluator role at some point in their careers because of the increasing demands for program accountability. Ironically, most social workers are still inadequately prepared to design and implement such evaluations. *Social Work Evaluation: Enhancing What We Do* introduces social workers and other human service workers to a broad array of knowledge about evaluations that they can conduct. The book also prepares them with the insights, knowledge, and skills needed to conduct a range of evaluations.

The book is organized around a three-stage model of evaluation. The stages divide evaluation into activities during the planning of an intervention, its implementation, and the measuring of its impact on recipients. In addition, the text describes seven general steps to follow in conducting evaluations. These steps offer a flexible set of guidelines to follow in implementing an evaluation with all of its practicalities. Specific tools in the form of questions to ask, designs, techniques, and practical skills are described for readers to be able to take and use them. Both quantitative and qualitative methods as well as mixed research methods are used in the evaluations covered in this book.

This book can be used for several research and practice courses in both bachelor of social work (BSW) and master of social work (MSW) programs. It is designed for primary use in a one-semester evaluation course in MSW programs. It can also be a primary text for a two-course research sequence in BSW programs. The book can also be very useful as a secondary text in BSW and MSW practice courses at all system levels. Further, it is an excellent handbook for professionals of several disciplines to use in conducting evaluations.

Special Features of the Book

Social Work Evaluation: Enhancing What We Do has several distinct features. First, both program and practice evaluation are discussed throughout the book. Evaluations at both levels have much in common. In addition, there is frequently a need to distinguish the two levels of evaluation. In these instances, separate sections are provided on both program and practice evaluations that explain their differences and how each can be implemented.

Both qualitative and quantitative methods of evaluation are also described and highlighted throughout the book. Although quantitative evaluations are especially pertinent to summative evaluations, qualitative methods are presented as especially relevant to many types of formative evaluations. Criteria are offered for when to use qualitative evaluations and when to use quantitative ones, and examples of both are provided. Mixed methods are also often encouraged.

The book presents evaluation material in a form that is easily understandable and especially relevant to social work students. Research is among the most difficult content areas for social work students to comprehend. This is largely because it is difficult to see the applicability of research to social work practice. The statistical and other technical aspects of research content also tend to be alien to students and difficult to comprehend. This book is especially designed to overcome these and other types of barriers more than other social work evaluation texts do because it continually discusses evaluation in the context of social work programs and practice and uses numerous pertinent examples.

Another feature of the text is that it directly addresses all of the current accreditation standards of the Council on Social Work Education (CSWE), the national accrediting organization for social workers. The CSWE promulgates minimum curriculum standards for all BSW and MSW programs, including research and evaluation content. This book devotes an entire chapter to several issues related to evaluation with a special focus on evaluation's links to three other foundational areas: ethics, diversity, and social and economic justice. Because of the importance of these three foundational areas, they are highlighted in numerous examples and exercises throughout the book. In addition, practice, a central foundational area of the social work curriculum is often highlighted as it relates to evaluation. Evaluation is described throughout the book as a vital and necessary component of practice at both the MSW and the BSW levels.

Although a social work perspective is emphasized that helps in understanding the connections of evaluation with practice, ethics, diversity issues, and commitments to social justice, other human service professionals will also find these topics pertinent. Professionals in psychology, family and individual therapy, child welfare, health, mental health, criminal justice, school counseling, special education, substance abuse, and others will find this text to be a very useful handbook.

Another distinguishing aspect of this book is the extensive use of case examples. Specific evaluation studies from professional journals, Web sites, and books are frequently highlighted to illustrate concepts, findings, data analyses, and other issues. It has been the author's experience that students' learning is enhanced when they can immediately see the application of abstract concepts to human service situations. Exemplary evaluation activities of social work students and practitioners are also generously included.

These illustrations reflect what students will often find in the field agencies and social agencies that will hire them. The book also contains a glossary of terms, discussion questions at the end of each chapter, and other visual aids.

In addition, the book is user-friendly for faculty who teach evaluation courses. Sometimes social work educators who do not have the time to conduct their own evaluations teach research courses. Such faculty may often feel less than qualified to teach an evaluation course. This text is understandable to both inexperienced and experienced faculty. Also, discussion questions included at the end of each chapter can serve as a focus for class discussions, quizzes, and tests. In addition, a teacher's guide is available from Lyceum Books that elaborates on how the content of the book can be used and suggests helpful ways to involve students in understanding and using it.

Moreover, the evaluation process is described, when possible, as a collaborative effort that encourages the participation of the clients and other stakeholders in some of the steps. A periodic focus on the principles of participant action research is highlighted in some sections to emphasize how evaluation can be used to promote client involvement, empowerment, and social change.

Finally, knowledge and technology skills are infused throughout the text. Social work practitioners must know how to use various electronic tools like e-mail, Listservs, the World Wide Web, data analysis programs like SPSS, bulletin boards, and chat rooms. The text often includes electronic exercises and other assignments that involve the students in using such tools. Emphasis is given to electronic skills that help students obtain access to the latest information on client populations, practice and program interventions, information from professional organizations, relevant articles, and helpful Listservs.

Organization of the Book

The book is organized into six parts. Part I, the first chapter, provides an introduction to evaluation and how it is described and defined in the book. The chapter begins with a persuasive rationale for why social workers should be proficient in evaluation. Definitions of program and practice evaluation, their characteristics and aims, and the larger social contexts for evaluations are introduced. The misuses of the term *evaluation* are also pointed out.

Part II is an orientation to the bigger picture about evaluations. Chapter 2 highlights key historical events that have shaped current ways of conducting evaluations. Also, six different theoretical perspectives on evaluation are introduced to remind readers that evaluation is not a monolithic enterprise; to the contrary, its purposes vary widely depending on who is conducting the evaluation and what he or she is attempting to accomplish. Aspects of almost all of these perspectives contribute to the concept of evaluation covered here. Chapter 3 focuses on the ethics of evaluation, drawing on the Code of Ethics of the National Association of Social Workers (NASW) and the ethical principles of the American Evaluation Association. The chapter explains how the accreditation standards of the CSWE can be implemented, including the ethics of social work and the importance of diversity and social and economic justice. Chapter 4 introduces readers to several models of program and practice evaluation that are commonly practiced in the settings in which social workers and other human service workers are employed. These models are identified in this chapter to help readers identify and search them out in various settings. These models range from client satisfaction studies to outcome studies, licensing of professionals and programs, quality assurance, and judicial decisions.

Part III focuses on the first of three stages of evaluation activities, the planning stage, when a program or practice area is being conceptualized. The planning stage is presented as a critical time for evaluation activities, especially to document the need for a new intervention. Chapter 5 offers guidelines for focusing an evaluation and presents a tool that can be used to craft a focus for a variety of evaluation purposes. Chapter 6 is devoted to conducting needs assessments, especially during the planning stage. The chapter explains why needs assessments are so important, describes a variety of assessment tools, and describes the steps involved in conducting a needs assessment. Crafting goals and objectives for a new program or practice intervention are highlighted in chapter 7. Characteristics of goals, limitations of goals, and the importance of measurable objectives are highlighted. A practical approach to crafting measurable objectives is described with several examples and exercises to ensure that readers are able to understand how to craft objectives for their own interventions.

Part IV, consisting of chapter 8, focuses on the second of three stages, the implementation stage, when numerous evaluation activities can occur. Implementation or process evaluations can address a wide variety of important issues, and this chapter describes the central ones. The chapter explores an array of evaluations, including testing an intervention against the logic model; determining whether the actual intervention is what it was initially intended to be; and determining quality, accessibility, and client satisfaction at both the program and the practice levels.

Part V, consisting of chapter 9, covers the third of the three stages, the outcome stage, when evaluations are initiated to determine how an intervention has affected the clients. The chapter portrays outcomes as multidimensional and complex. Criteria are offered for choosing outcome measures. Also, the enormous challenge of adequately documenting that an intervention is the cause of any improvement in the clients' lives is explained in some detail. Several outcome designs are introduced for evaluating both program and practice interventions, and the advantages and limitations of each design are highlighted. These designs are presented in a practical way so that readers can easily implement them. Ethical issues in selecting designs are also discussed.

Part VI discusses the final steps in conducting an evaluation. Data analysis is an important step to understand and implement as discussed in chapter 10. The chapter discusses the many options available for analyzing both qualitative and quantitative data. Several statistical tools are described for analyzing data for quantitative evaluations, and three different approaches are offered for analyzing data from qualitative evaluations. Although the principles of data analysis in an evaluation are similar to those used in a research study, several differences are also evident and noted in this chapter. Most important, analysis of evaluation data begins and ends with questions of who needs to know what, when, and why.

Chapter 11 addresses the final steps of an evaluation, preparation and dissemination of the report of the findings. The chapter recommends beginning by planning the report with stakeholders and discussing their needs. Several options for report formats are explored. Finally, several strategies are offered to both prepare a report and disseminate it to stakeholders and others.

The Author's Background

The author, Jim Dudley, has extensive experience in both teaching and conducting program and practice evaluations. He has developed and taught program and practice evaluation courses in two different MSW programs over a fifteen-year period and has taught research methods courses at both the BSW and the MSW levels for more than twenty-five years. He has also taught BSW and MSW practice courses at all system levels (micro, mezzo, macro) during the same period. Dudley has conducted evaluations large and small. These evaluations have been widely varied in topic, purpose, and methodology, and several of them are briefly described in various parts of the book as illustrations of concepts and methods. He has also supervised the evaluation projects of hundreds of graduate students that have been conducted in the students' field agencies as major course assignments, and he has conducted several evaluations involving student assistance as well.

Acknowledgments

Numerous people have graciously assisted in the preparation of this text. Tom Meenahan and Carl Brun contributed significantly to the organization and conceptualization of the book. I also thank David Moxley for a thoughtful and thorough review of the manuscript. Scott Wilson, Israel Colon, Cy Rosenthal, Dennis Brunn, and Bill Perry, former colleagues at Temple University, initially introduced me to the complex enterprise of evaluation and its relevance to social work and social change. Several colleagues at the

University of North Carolina at Charlotte provided support along the way, particularly at times when it was most needed. Among them, Dennis Long generously assisted with material resources needed to attend conferences and obtain editorial assistance. Frada Mozenter helped retrieve several Web sites and other resources, always in amazingly supportive ways. Lynn Ahlgrim-Delzell and Jeff Shears contributed to the writing of one of the chapters. Nohra Núñez and Cynthia Stasiewski made themselves available to help in countless ways.

My MSW social work students from seven years at UNC Charlotte and another eight years at Temple University gave invaluable feedback and support while I taught program and practice evaluation courses over these years. They consistently assured me that these evaluation courses were useful and valuable to their professional development, and they gave me the initial encouragement to develop a textbook reflecting the multifaceted content areas covered in the courses.

David Follmer, my editor, was an invaluable catalyst for writing the text and broadening its focus to the larger community of professional evaluators. He supported me throughout the writing period, which often seemed endless. Appreciation also goes to Katherine Faydash, Lyn Rosen, and Nina Nguyen.

Part I

Introduction

Chapter 1

Evaluation and Social Work: A Logical Connection

Introduction

Is evaluation an important part of social work?
Is the evaluator role a central one for social workers?
How can evaluations help social work interventions work better?

Let's begin with these three important questions. They may be your questions as you begin to read this book. They are questions that many social work students and practitioners are pondering. The book's responses to the first two questions, in brief, will be no surprise to you. Yes, evaluation *is* an important part of social work. Also, the evaluator role is an important role for every social worker to assume. Some social workers will be evaluators of programs, and virtually every social worker will be an evaluator of his or her practice. It's like asking why social workers need to know whether they are doing a good job, or asking them if they know whether their interventions are the most effective ones for helping their clients. The third question, asking how evaluation can help social work interventions work better is the focus of this text.

The underlying theme driving the book is that evaluation is a vital element of any social work approach and is critical for ensuring that social work actually *works*! A reassuring theme is that evaluation is a practice area that BSW and MSW students and practitioners alike can learn. Social workers and students wanting to maximize their impact on their jobs will find that the perspective, knowledge, ethics, and skills of evaluations covered in this book can be a central component of practice and provide a much greater impact on clients.

This book provides the needed preparation for evaluation in both a comprehensive and a readable format. The primary emphasis is on the various kinds of small and midrange formative evaluations that are often implemented at the local agency level more than the large, complex national and regional studies that may draw the most coverage under the title *evaluation*. These smaller formative evaluations are also the critical ones that social work students and graduates either are assigned or should consider taking on in their field placements and employment agencies.

Example of a Small, Formative Evaluation

An agency that provides an anger management program to perpetrators of domestic violence offers a series of ten psycho-educational group sessions to help them manage their anger. The agency also conducts an evaluation of this program that is integral to the program. An anger management scale is used to measure changes that occur in the participants' anger after they have completed all ten sessions of a group program. Throughout the series, the specific items of the anger management scale (e.g., being respectful, having self-control, being self-aware, learning alternatives to violent behavior) identify some of the key discussion topics of the group sessions. In this way, practice and evaluation go hand in hand in helping practitioners and clients partner to meet the goals of the program.

Evaluation is a multifaceted approach that addresses some of the most vital questions and issues facing programs and practice, including the following:

- Who are the clients that need the program most?
- What kinds of intervention do they need?
- How are the interventions to be implemented?
- What will the intervention achieve?

In other words, evaluations can address important issues at all stages of development of a program or practice area:

- **Program planning**, when a vision is created for a program and developed into a proposal or plan
- **Program implementation**, when the plan is actually carried out
- **Outcome observation**, when the clients' outcomes or affected behaviors are measured during a post-program period

Evaluation is important to consider for both the services of each practitioner and the program itself. At the practice level, an evaluation can investigate inputs, or what the practitioner needs to develop or construct an intervention; the processes the practitioner uses to implement the intervention; and the outcomes, or client accomplishments of the practitioner's interventions. At the program level, an evaluation can investigate the same stages (inputs, processes, and outcomes) of a complex interplay of many interventions, typically provided by several practitioners.

Practice Is Embedded in a Program

Programs and individual practice are closely intertwined. Practice is, at times, a microcosm of a program. For example, a small program can comprise a set of interventions of a few practitioners (e.g., a family counseling program) or a set of interrelated interventions provided by a team of practitioners from different disciplines (e.g., an intake team at a mental hospital). Furthermore, a major thesis of this book is that practice is almost always embedded in a program, and the program is or can be instrumental in informing, shaping, and directing the definition of practice. Practice is not an entity to be developed in a vacuum or at the whim of a practitioner or supervisor, as often can happen in reality.

Social work practitioners, once they graduate, usually have a good beginning sense of an overall approach to helping clients. However, it is an approach that is still mostly understood in the abstract, on the basis of practice theories being taught in a professional program along with some opportunities for testing the theories in field practicum experiences.

However, when practitioners begin work at an agency, there are numerous new variables that come into play. The client population is one of them. Who are the clients? What kinds of problems and needs do they have? What kinds of interventions do they need the most? In addition, the agency typically has an approach (or approaches) that it uses to help clients, and the agency expects its practitioners to know this approach and become competent in using it. The approach may be explicit and detailed or quite vague and mostly abstract. Practitioners new to an agency need to ask how they can learn and implement this agency approach, hopefully with assistance from a supervisor. Later on, new practitioners also come to realize and face growing challenges as they become aware of the subtle variations in the application of the agency approach to the various and unique needs of each client.

An agency's approach is usually embedded in its programs. Therefore, a new practitioner's practice is naturally embedded in a program context as well. This program context provides many important clues about what a social worker's practice will look like. Because this book is about both programs and practice, and their relationship, it offers numerous insights into the vital link between professional practice and its program context. In this light, this book includes several objectives for practitioners to consider throughout the chapters:

- Realize that your practice is embedded in a program context.
- Recognize how your program works and informs your practice.
- Understand the bigger picture of the agency, its environment, and the stakeholders, and how they affect your practice.
- Realize that program evaluations usually have valuable implications for improving your practice.
- Know what is important to evaluate in your practice, taking into account the program context.
- Consider using some of the strategies of program evaluations when evaluating your practice.

Common Characteristics of Evaluations

To fully understand the nature of an evaluation, we need to understand some of its common characteristics. These characteristics include account-ability, scientific research methods, stakeholders, political processes, an eth-ical code, and critical thinking. As figure 1.1 depicts, these characteristics continually interact with and influence one another.

FIGURE 1.1   Common Characteristics of Evaluations

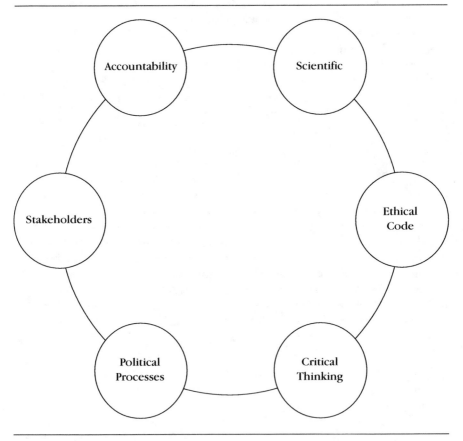

Being Accountable

If there is one overall concept that explains why evaluations are so im-portant, it is accountability. Partially because of past failings of social pro-grams, governmental and most privately funded agencies now require that all agencies be held accountable for how they use their funds and what they achieve for clients. Evaluations have become one of the most reliable mechanisms incorporated into program proposals for ensuring such accountability. Agency accountability is now inherent in the jurisdiction of virtually all funding and regulatory agencies, and it has become a key job expectation of agency and program administrators.

These funding, regulatory, and administrative roles require accountability to address questions such as the following:

- Is the intervention focusing on the target population with the greatest need?
- Is the intervention designed to meet the specified needs of the target population?
- Is the intervention being implemented in the way that it was designed and proposed?
- Is the intervention being implemented with high standards?
- How satisfied are clients and their families with the program?
- Is the intervention achieving its goals and objectives?
- Is the intervention cost-effective?

Ultimately, it is also important for program sponsors to be accountable to the clients they serve. Because of the power imbalance between an agency and clients, special attention is needed to bring more balance to these two entities in the form of greater power and protection for clients. In addition, agencies need to be accountable to the communities intrinsically connected to clients, such as their family members and the immediate neighbors surrounding residential programs. Accountability to clients and relevant communities often requires the introduction of empowerment strategies, such as client satisfaction surveys and client representation on agency boards. Another strategy is to encourage agencies to involve client groups as participants in program evaluations and to share the results of their evaluations with them. Chapter 2 further elaborates on other empowerment strategies.

Social workers who work in such programs must also be accountable not only to the agency employing them but also to their own professional groups, such as the National Association of Social Workers (NASW), Political Action for Candidate Election (PACE, a political arm of NASW), and their state professional licensing boards. In these instances, accountability refers to such things as the ethical conduct of social workers, their commitments to clients' dignity and well-being, their advocating for social justice, and their provision of sound and evidence-based professional practice.

Using Scientific Research Methods

Evaluation activities are scientific and use a wide range of research methodologies (e.g., Dudley, 2005). Scientific research has long-standing values and principles that distinguish it from other types of information gathering. Many of these principles are evident in evaluations, including:

- The search from a particular viewpoint to discover a truth or something that exists rather than something that is desired
- Use of a methodology that minimizes the influence of biases and involves a systematic set of steps or procedures that can be flexibly employed
- The abiding by a special code of ethical conduct that includes a commitment to neutrality in conducting research and a demonstration of concern to protect the people studied
- Assumption of a universal stance in the evaluation's interests, such that it represents the concerns of all society, even though it may focus on a few subgroups of people or a narrow topic
- Accurate reporting of findings despite whether they are consistent with the researcher's viewpoints

Although these principles of scientific research are ideals that should be fulfilled to the greatest extent possible in all scientific studies, in reality they are evident in evaluation studies to varying degrees and along a continuum of quality. The more an evaluation rigorously fulfills these ideals, the more confident one can be that it is considered "good" science.

Involving Stakeholders and a Political Process

Although basic research is often considered apolitical, evaluations involve a political process. Historical events and current political considerations need to be considered when discussing, planning, and implementing an evaluation. Indeed, an evaluation is a special type of research that incorporates political considerations into its execution. An evaluation may have several different stakeholders, and each could have special interests that compete with one another. When talking about an evaluation, political issues almost always come into play, whether explicitly or implicitly. Political processes might be involved in any of the following types of questions that agency administrators raise:

- How can we help those with the greatest need?
- How can an evaluation help our program survive?
- How can an evaluation improve the chances of obtaining funding to expand my program?
- How can the results of an evaluation be used to enhance our program's identity in the larger network of agencies in our field?
- How can we use negative findings from an evaluation without jeopardizing our program's existence?

Example of a Political Consideration

A graduate student conducted an evaluation of staff morale at her field agency. She gave the staff members a questionnaire to fill out, asking them how important they perceived each of several different issues that affected their morale. The issues included salaries, medical benefits, size of caseloads, hours of work, supervision (its quality and frequency), and openness of administration to staff concerns. The findings revealed that their major concerns about morale related to their problems with supervisors and administration. Because the administration of the agency was taken by surprise and unprepared to seriously address these issues, they decided to ignore them and instructed the graduate student to withhold her findings from the staff members.

Stakeholders of an evaluation have different interests. Stakeholders often include agency administrators, governmental funding and regulatory agencies, foundations, elected officials, board members, staff members, citizens, clients, advocacy groups, accountants and auditors, and the surrounding community. A funding agency, for example, might ask the following questions:

- How can I be sure that this program is fulfilling its responsibilities?
- How can I determine whether this program is more or less important than another program that we fund?
- How can I get the most fiscal value out of this program?
- I like this program and its director, but how can I justify funding them when the proposal falls short of what we want?

Political considerations such as these must be taken into account at all stages of evaluating interventions, including planning, implementation, and outcome observations. An approach to identify and analyze these contextual forces within and outside an agency is elaborated on later. In general, though, this approach can help evaluators consider the political issues and questions that they may need to address or avert in conducting an evaluation before they become serious problems or ethical dilemmas. The approach identifies a wide range of possible constraints that can create conflicts for an evaluation and considers a range of potential resources that can help in conducting the evaluation. The identification of potential constraints and resources before implementation of an evaluation helps address both its feasibility and its ethical standing.

Abiding by an Ethical Code

Ethical issues are extremely important to identify when addressing political issues. Actually, the way in which decisions are made or not made should be partially based on an ethical code such as the NASW Code of Ethics (www.naswdc.org) and the ethical principles of the American Evaluation Association (AEA; www.eval.org). As social workers and other human service professionals know, those who participate in research and evaluation are obligated to follow an ethical code. The NASW Code of Ethics is a basic code required of all social workers. It obligates an evaluator to be well informed about ethical issues and well versed in how to implement a variety of measures intended to prevent ethical problems from occurring. The ethical principles of the AEA are designed for professional evaluators specifically conducting evaluation studies. These principles are valuable to consult because they are directed toward dilemmas essential for a professional evaluator to follow (the AEA ethical principles are located in appendix A).

Ethical problems include such things as physical and psychological harm to research participants, invasion of privacy, and misrepresentation of published study findings. Evaluators are obligated to prevent such ethical problems by implementing a variety of ethical safeguards, including an informed consent protocol, confidentiality, and selection of evaluators with appropriate credentials and objectivity. Chapter 3 focuses on an extensive introduction to many of the ethical concerns that are evident in evaluations and how to address these problems. It examines the NASW Code of Ethics and portions of the ethical principles of the AEA, particularly as they pertain to social workers' ethical obligations related to evaluations.

Thinking Critically

Another important characteristic of evaluations is critical thinking. Critical thinkers are natural skeptics about how well an evaluation is conducted, whether it is someone else's evaluation or one's own. Gibbs and Gambrill (1996) identify several types of problems that program providers experience when they fail to be critical thinkers:

- Overlooking the people who may need the services of a program the most
- Not understanding the larger social forces that influence the ways clients behave
- Misclassifying or misdiagnosing clients and their problems
- Focusing on irrelevant factors that are not important in helping clients make progress
- Selecting interventions that are weak or inappropriate
- Arranging for interventions to continue either too long or not long enough

The Council on Social Work Education (CSWE) views critical thinking as essential to the practice of every social worker. Because of the importance of critical thinking, CSWE mandates that it be one of the basic tenets of the professional foundation of every accredited social work education program at both the BSW and the MSW levels. One of the core program objectives required of the curricula of all programs and to be infused into every course is to "apply critical thinking skills within the context of professional social work."

Defining the Aims of Evaluation

Overall, evaluations of programs and practice are concerned with many purposes, including efficiency, quality, effectiveness, effort, and relevance. Martin and Kettner (1996), among others, stress the importance of efficiency, quality, and effectiveness. Efficiency is concerned with channeling available resources to the target problems. Misdirected and wasted resources are to be avoided or minimized. Efficiency is important because resources for health and human service programs are always likely to be limited or even scarce, and the more efficiently that programs and practices are delivered, the more clients can be helped.

Quality refers to services being delivered as intended and done very well or at a high standard. Sometimes this high standard has been referred to as best practices. Quality is obviously important because a program or practice delivered well will have the greatest positive impact on the recipients; the higher the quality, the greater is the likely impact. For example, a social worker who is not adequately prepared to provide intensive counseling to emancipated adolescents about to be released from foster care will fall short of helping them enough to function on their own.

Also, interventions have to be effective or lead to effectiveness. If interventions do not successfully work to bring about the anticipated changes in clients' lives, the interventions should be reevaluated or the social worker will risk losing funding. All three of these areas—efficiency, quality, and effectiveness—are extremely important to evaluations. One cannot be preferred over the other two, as all three are required to ensure that a program or practice intervention works well.

In addition to these three common qualities of programs and practice, two more are also crucial: evidence of effort and relevance to the clients and community. Evidence of effort is important regardless of the achievements of a program. Effort refers to what staff members, volunteers, and administrators put into a program and practice. Effort especially refers to what happens when the interventions are implemented. How much time was spent in the helping process? How many visits or sessions occurred? What happened in these sessions? Most important, was the effort commensurate with the expectations of the funding agency, the program director, and clients?

Relevance is another fundamental quality of any intervention. Relevance of the intervention to the clients' needs and the larger social problems that clients experience is the most important aspect of relevance. A program intervention can be carried out in a high-quality way that uses resources efficiently and achieves program goals, but if it is not directly relevant to what the clients need, then it is incomplete and/or misguided. The concept of relevance is related to the seeking of social justice for client populations and a diversity in the client population that reflects the larger population that needs the interventions. Both of these efforts, social justice and diversity, as well as other important issues of relevance, are covered extensively in this text.

Both the NASW Code of Ethics and the AEA Code highlight these issues and the responsibilities of evaluators to take into account the diversity of general and public interests and to be mindful of the rights and needs of all pertinent groups.

Defining Important Terms

Several important terms need to be defined before going further. They are relevant to answering numerous basic questions like, What is a program and how is it different from services? What distinguishes programs from the practice of individual workers? What are program evaluations and practice evaluations? How are they similar and different? Let's take a look at the basic terms: *program, services, professional practice, intervention, program evaluation*, and *practice evaluation*.

A *program* is a subunit of a social agency that provides a set of goods and/or services with common goals. These goods and services are typically provided to a particular population of clients who either voluntarily seek them or are required to seek them. A program typically employs more than one and usually several staff members to provide goods and services.

Chen (1990) expands on this definition by developing the notion of program theory. Program theory is expected to encompass two important sets of documentation. First, it provides a descriptive documentation of the goals, outcomes, and interventions of the program based on the perspectives of various stakeholders. Second, program theory documents the nature of the causal relationship between the program interventions and the desired outcomes for the target group of recipients. It does this by offering research evidence that the proposed program model has been effective in helping in the past a group of clients with a particular set of characteristics. Practice theory can easily be described in a similar way.

Services are the activities that programs or one practitioner offer. Services focus mostly on the processes that help clients reach their program goals. They are the means to the ends, not ends in themselves. These helping processes are the major focus of practice courses of professional social work programs and draw from a broad range of practice theories, such as generalist problem solving; locality development; and cognitive behavioral, person-centered, and solution-focused treatments. In addition, in-service training programs periodically provide helpful updates on such knowledge and helping skills.

Example of a Program and Services of a Home Health Agency

A home health agency often sponsors one overall program, the goals of which are to help medically indigent clients remain in their own homes independently and prevent placement in a residential program such as an assisted living facility. Such a program offers several services to clients who are homebound, including counseling and referrals, nursing, physical therapy, and occupational therapy. These services, provided by a team of social workers, nurses, physical and occupational therapists, and others, exist to help the program meet its goals. Home health programs also offer goods, such as medical supplies and incontinence products.

Distinguishing between programs and services is important. For example, if you were to describe a program to someone unfamiliar with what you do, you would likely begin by referring to its goals and what it attempts to accomplish for clients. In contrast, if you begin by describing the services of the program, your explanation may appear incomplete and beg for an explanation of why these services exist or what they intend to accomplish. Note the difference between saying, "Our program is designed to help prevent teenagers from participating in unsafe sex," and, "Our services include individual counseling and psycho-educational groups for teenagers."

Professional practices are the interventions of a human service worker in helping a client system. Professional practice can be offered to one individual, a family, a small group of clients, an organization, an institution, a social policy area, or a larger community. It is important to distinguish between the professional practice of one individual and the services of a program, which encompass the practices of all staff members within a program.

Because this book balances emphasis on programs and the practice of an individual practitioner, the term *intervention* is often used to refer either to the services and goods of programs or to an individual worker's practice. As an example, interventions are evident both in the recovery programs of a substance abuse agency and in the clinical practice that one social worker offers to a client's family.

Using working definitions of these key concepts (programs, services, professional practice, and interventions), we can define program evaluations and practice evaluations. A *program evaluation* is a study of a social program that uses the principles and methods of scientific research. It concerns itself with the practical needs of an organization, not theoretical issues, and it abides by a professional ethical code. The primary purposes of a program evaluation are to provide accountability to its various stakeholders and to improve what the program can accomplish.

A *practice evaluation* is a study of a professional practitioner's interventions with a client system, which can be at several different system levels (e.g., individual, group, neighborhood). Like a program evaluation, a practice evaluation uses the principles and methods of scientific research. Unlike a program evaluation, it focuses on only one practitioner's practice at a time. Its primary purposes are to increase the effectiveness of a practitioner's interventions and to determine whether the interventions successfully help clients reach their goals.

Although these definitions of program and practice evaluations are meant to be fairly distinct, at times they are blurred. For example, if we decided to evaluate an agency's group services, would it be a program or practice evaluation? Two issues need to be considered before this question can be answered: (1) Does the group service comprise the groups of only one worker or of several different workers? and (2) Is the purpose of the evaluation to examine the effectiveness of an individual practitioner's interventions or the group services of the entire program?

In our example, if only one staff member provided the group service, it could be both a program and a practice evaluation. Therefore, it is important to clarify at the outset what kind of evaluation is intended. For example, is it a practice evaluation intended to evaluate the interventions of individual staff members, or is it a program evaluation concerned with agencywide issues, such as the goals of the group service generally or the use of limited resources.

What Program Evaluation Is Not

Considering what a program evaluation is not can also be helpful in understanding these key concepts. Program evaluations are not evaluations of individual clients; instead, program evaluations typically aim to provide useful information about cohorts of clients. In this case, the emphasis is on the impact of the entire program on the cohort that it serves. Program evaluations usually have an informed consent protocol that clarifies that the client's personal identity is not to be revealed in association with any of his or her specific responses. However, a program evaluation occasionally could become an evaluation of individual clients under special circumstances. In this case, the ethical thing to do would be to notify the clients as to why the change is occurring before implementation of the policy change. This preparatory step allows clients the opportunity to withdraw from the study if they wish.

Example of a Change from a Program Evaluation to Evaluation of Individual Clients

The state of North Carolina was successfully sued in a federal district court for failing to provide adequate services and physical safety to a selected group of people with mental illness and mental retardation in state mental hospitals (Dudley & Ahlgrim-Delzell, 2002). For four years, a university sponsor of a longitudinal evaluation of the class members reported only to a state agency on the aggregate data, using a set of statewide indicators of client progress or success. Then the state agency's needs shifted and it decided to begin requesting information on individual participants in these programs. The original informed consent letter of the academic sponsor of the evaluation specified that data would be released only in aggregate form without identifying individuals. Therefore, a change in informed consent was needed. As a matter of policy, the longitudinal research team provided each class member and his or her guardian or family member with a letter informing of the change in policy. The letter explained the purpose of the study, outlined the type of data that would be collected, and how the data would be obtained and released to the state on an individual basis. This letter also provided the recipient with the opportunity to withdraw from the study at any time without repercussions. Surprisingly, no one withdrew from the study.

Program evaluations do not evaluate the performance of individual staff members. Although evaluations of staff effort and performance are necessary, it would be confusing and a mistake to mix the purposes of a program evaluation and an evaluation of individual staff members. Such an initiative would not only confuse the participants in a study but also would likely instill distrust in the evaluation and discourage full cooperation of staff members. It may even encourage staff participants to manipulate their response in their favor or sabotage the study by boycotting it.

Program evaluations are not public relations projects. A public relations project could be falsely presented as a program evaluation and used to promote the agency's programs in annual reports and other material disseminated to the public. In this case, the purpose would be misleading and dishonest, as it gives the impression that a genuine evaluation is going on. Although the results or portions of the results of an evaluation may be useful and appropriate to display in public relations materials that promote the agency once an independent evaluation is completed, having a public relations emphasis built into an evaluation could bias the study toward a distorted positive outcome. In this case, some of the dramatic positive findings could end up being used in a report prepared for a funding agency while the neutral or less dramatic findings are disregarded and forgotten.

Example of a Program Evaluation with Potentially Conflicting Purposes

A student was asked to conduct an evaluation for a family agency of two different sets of groups of formerly incarcerated women. In designing the study, the student was told by her supervisor that the agency wanted to use the data in part to determine whether one staff member's group practice was less effective than the others. After some discussion, the supervisor agreed to remove this concern, a personnel matter, as one of the agency's study questions, so as not to confuse the study's intent and to maximize staff cooperation.

What Practice Evaluation Is Not

What practice evaluation is not is similar to the points made about a program evaluation. For example, practice evaluations do not evaluate the performance of the individual staff members. As mentioned previously, evaluations of staff performance are needed, but it would be confusing to mix such evaluations with a practice evaluation. Mixing these two different types of evaluation can easily instill distrust and resistance in staff members. Furthermore, they are likely to be influenced to manipulate the results in their favor if success with a client can be translated into a favorable performance review of their work.

Practice evaluations are not measures of the effectiveness of a program. Although one practitioner in a program may effectively help his or her clients on the basis of the results of a practice evaluation, it is not logical to conclude that the program is therefore effective. A practice evaluation does not take into account other components of the program, including the services that other staff members offer.

It is also important to note that although it would be unethical to refer to any of these activities as an evaluation of a program or practice, this can still happen. As mentioned earlier, the politics of evaluations could lead some agencies into considering such things if it could be viewed as beneficial to the agency and its programs. Evaluators always need to be ready to confront any ethical dilemmas that can surface, and their obligation is to do the most ethical thing.

Understanding the Larger Context of a Program

A program does not exist or operate in a vacuum. It is part of a larger dynamic system of many forces and factors, such as administrative leadership styles, staff and administrative communication patterns, perceptions of clients, and financial issues, all of which must be taken into consideration when conducting a program evaluation. Figure 1.2 provides a sketch of many of these factors.

All of these factors and their dynamic interplay can have a major influence on an evaluation conducted by the agency. One illustration of this dynamic interplay is the leadership style of the administrators. Administrators can assume many styles, including autocrat, collaborator, and delegator. Administrators who are primarily collaborative, for example, are likely to have

FIGURE 1.2   Contextual Factors in Evaluations

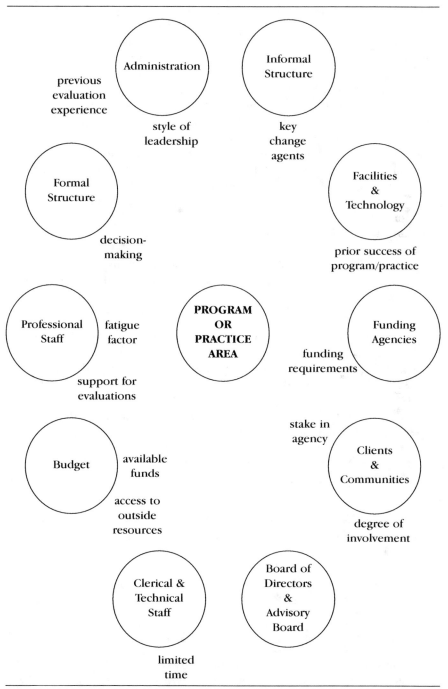

a different kind of influence on staff members when conducting an evaluation from that of an autocratic administrator.

Also, organizational structures, both informal and formal, are important factors with respect to their interplay with decision making (Weissman, Epstein, & Savage, 1983). In this case, while it is usually a good idea to consult everyone in an organization who is interested in and affected by an evaluation, some players will be more important to identify, including the administrators who formally oversee the program in question and those who have informal influence regardless of their formal title. These informal players could be instrumental in supporting or undermining an agency's formal structure. They could be, for example, lower-ranked employees, such as a highly invested secretary or a popular and outspoken staff member. All in all, evaluators can commit a serious and possibly fatal error in evaluation if they overlook stakeholders who may be potentially central to the success of an evaluation but are excluded from evaluation discussions.

Many other contextual factors are also directly relevant to an evaluation. For example, is the agency leadership a knowledgeable supporter and instigator of evaluations? Or does it comprise novices who may be cautious and reluctant to pursue a study that may be risky. What is the agency's track record in this regard? Some fairly standard questions of this sort could be asked at the outset:

- What kinds of expertise does the agency have for conducting a variety of evaluations?
- How cooperative are staff members, both professional and support staff, in taking on additional responsibilities such as filling out questionnaires or searching for client records?
- What's in it for the administration and staff? Are all of the motives openly known and transparent or do some appear to be covert or hidden?
- Are there reasons staff members may be suspicious of the motives for an evaluation or reluctant to participate for fear of jeopardizing their jobs?

Several contextual factors could also influence the extent to which the agency will disseminate the findings of an evaluation and implement its recommendations, including whether there are adequate resources, degree of desire to bring about a change in direction, and openness to risk the program's future. More attention will be given to these various forces in later chapters within the context of specific topics and steps of an evaluation.

Steps in Conducting an Evaluation

A general approach for conducting an evaluation is introduced here and elaborated on throughout the book. The steps of this approach apply to both program and practice evaluations. The generic term *intervention* is used to describe both program and practice activities. The approach involves seven general steps based on a modified version of the steps identified in other evaluation models (e.g., Posavac & Carey, 1997).

Step 1: Identify the Problem or Concern to Be Evaluated

During step 1, the evaluator becomes familiar with the problem or concern that an evaluation will examine. Some general questions include the following: What is to be evaluated? Is the program working well or are there some problems that are manifesting? On the practice level, is my intervention with my client working well? Why or why not?

During this step it is also important to begin gathering information about the program or practice context of the problem. It would be helpful to find out more about some of the pertinent components of the program or practice intervention. A description of the intervention could include identifying the client population that is served, the problems and needs that the intervention addresses, and the goals of the intervention. The services and goods that are provided to reach these goals are also important to identify and understand.

Step 2: Identify and Explore Ways to Involve Stakeholders

A concurrent step with the information gathering of step 1 is to identify and explore ways to involve the stakeholders of the program. Stakeholders are the people who are invested in the intervention in some way, such as representatives of the funding and regulatory groups that finance and set standards for the intervention or the administrators and board members of the agency sponsoring the program and those who direct the program. Some stakeholders, especially program directors, are likely to be evaluated on the basis of the intervention's performance, so they have an obvious stake in what happens.

Staff members who deliver the goods and services have an obvious stake in the intervention as well. Their jobs depend on the program's survival, and their careers, currently and in the future, may also be entwined in the intervention's outcome. In addition, clients who receive the intervention and their family members have a vital stake in what happens to the intervention, as their daily functioning and very survival may depend on how well it performs. Stakeholders are likely to be different for program and practice interventions. Program interventions tend to primarily have macro stakeholders, such as members of a board of directors, community advisory boards, and others in the public sector, while the main stakeholders of practice interventions are often supervisors, practitioners, and client advocates.

Step 3: Determine the Purpose of the Evaluation

Once the evaluator is familiar with the program or practice intervention to be evaluated and the problems or concerns, and has developed a relationship with all stakeholders, more information needs to be gathered about who wants the evaluation and why. These discussions can help the evaluator find out how much the stakeholders know about evaluations, their views and past experiences with them, and whether they have a narrow or broad understanding of what an evaluation can be. These discussions should be used to highlight the potential contributions of an evaluation, such as program improvements, the creation of new opportunities to help and/or understand clients, or assistance to the agency in making an important decision.

These discussions can also uncover any apprehensions or doubts of stakeholders about evaluations generally. For example, could an evaluation be risky for some reason? Too costly? Take too much time? Interfere with program or practice operations? During this step, it is also important to help the stakeholders identify both the resources available to support them and the evaluation and the real or potential constraints.

Possible Resources and Constraints to Consider in Initiating a Program Evaluation

Possible resources

- Expressed concerns are highly relevant to clients' well-being
- Considerable interest in an evaluation
- Financial support
- Awareness of a problem with a program
- Openness to examine a problem further
- Some understanding and respect for evaluation
- Openness to the evaluator as a resource
- Staff support

Possible constraints or resistant forces

- Limited time
- Costs too high
- Payoff is risky
- Evaluation focus can be too subjective
- May open up the need to change
- Limits to what can change
- Politics of the system
- Evaluator lacks expertise
- Problem of access to clients
- No need to justify such an evaluation to funding agency
- Lack of creativity

This step becomes complete when all stakeholders and the evaluator have agreed on the general purpose of an evaluation. If a commonly agreed-on purpose for an evaluation cannot be identified, negotiations would likely discontinue or be delayed until a purpose could be identified. The purpose of a program evaluation could lead to keeping, expanding, or eliminating a program, whereas a practice evaluation may lead to varying an approach with some types of clients.

Step 4: Plan the Evaluation

Once a general purpose for an evaluation is agreed on, a plan for conducting an evaluation follows. As background work, a literature review is often needed to find out more about the problems that face the evaluation team and to identify reports on research methodologies, pertinent practice approaches, and studies on which to base the evaluation. Then several aspects of a research design need to be developed, including a set of study questions and/or hypotheses to explore or test, a source (e.g., clients, staff members) from whom the data are to be gathered, a specific data collection method, and a data analysis plan. A plan to protect human participants of the study is also an important task to complete for approval.

All of these aspects of a plan should be discussed and involve the stakeholders so that there is strong support for a specific evaluation plan. When appropriate, the plan should be prepared as a readable written proposal and/or oral presentation understandable to all stakeholders. With practice evaluations, attention needs to be given to engaging the clients in understanding and participating in the evaluation. For example, a goal attainment scale (GAS) may be used in a practice evaluation to measure the clients' progress on their outcomes. In this case, the scale should be described to the clients initially, and clients should be encouraged to help define the specific outcome measures that fit their circumstances. Goal attainment scales and the role that clients can play in developing them are described more fully in chapter 9.

Step 5: Implement the Evaluation

The plan that has been developed for an evaluation, often referred to as the evaluation design, is now ready to be implemented. Often its implementation may involve several people in an agency, such as secretaries searching for client case material, staff members who might interview clients individually or in focus groups, and a questionnaire that staff members might need to hand out to clients. In a practice evaluation, staff members are likely to implement one form or another of a single-system design. Along with implementing the data collection effort, collected data are coded, entered into computer programs, and analyzed, sometimes over and over again.

Step 6: Prepare a Written or Oral Report

Once the study has been completed, preparation of a report of the results follows. Such reports are designed to address the major questions of stakeholders, usually reflected in the initial purpose worked out in step 3. The report can be oral, written, or both. Report preparation involves several steps, including organizing, analyzing, and interpreting the findings so that they are understandable; developing conclusions and recommendations that are useful and practical; and exploring the use of visual aids, such as tables and graphs, to assist in communication. Reports of program evaluations are usually prepared for different stakeholders (e.g., funding agencies, administrators, boards of directors, community groups) from those of practice evaluations (e.g., supervisors, program coordinators, clients).

Step 7: Disseminate the Results

The last step of an evaluation is to disseminate the results to stakeholders and others. Unfortunately, this step is often overlooked or its importance minimized. The results are likely to be disseminated to several different types of stakeholders, some of which are obvious, such as the funding and regulatory agencies and agency administration. Other stakeholders may be easily overlooked but are also important, including former and current clients and relevant community groups. A report can be communicated in many forms—including oral or written, comprehensive or brief—and in varied formats, such as a technical report, a public meeting, a staff workshop, a series of discussions, a one-page summary for clients and their families, or other formats.

What's Next?

The chapters in part II focus on the bigger picture of evaluations, including various evaluation perspectives in chapter 2, professional ethics relevant to evaluations in chapter 3, and some common models of evaluations evident in agencies in chapter 4. These chapters are intended to provide a general background of relevant information for the chapters that follow them.

Key Terms
Accountability
Critical thinking
Ethical codes
Intervention
Practice evaluation
Professional practice
Program
Program evaluation

Scientific research methods
Services
Stages of program development
Stakeholders

Discussion Questions and Assignments

1. Prepare an agency information sheet about your field or employment agency. Answer all or some of the following questions to learn more about the agency.
   a. What programs does your agency provide?
   b. What have you discovered so far to be the views, attitudes, and knowledge of administrators and staff in your agency about program and practice evaluation?
   c. What types of program and practice evaluations are conducted in your agency?
   d. Who in your agency, if anyone, is involved and interested in evaluations? Have you been involved in any evaluation activities?
   e. What aspects of programs or professional practice in your field agency need to be evaluated, in your opinion?
   f. List the key funding and regulatory agencies, professional associations, consumer groups, and other organizations to which you think your agency should be accountable.
2. Assume that you are employed at the agency mentioned in the chapter that provides psycho-educational group services to perpetrators of domestic violence. After the study was completed, the executive director of the agency decides to use the results of the study to evaluate the performance of individual staff members who are group leaders. What are the ethical issues that the executive director needs to consider before proceeding? What would you recommend that the agency do or not do related to evaluating the performance of staff members?
3. Review the elements that make up the larger context of a program in figure 1.2. In your opinion, which elements are essential for the effective functioning of a program? Which are optional? Give reasons for your answers.
4. Select three different types of stakeholders of interest to you. Then identify the kinds of informational needs of each stakeholder. How are their needs different? How might they result in conflicting views about the purpose of an evaluation?
5. Interview a staff member who was (or currently is) involved in conducting an evaluation at your agency and/or read the final report of such an evaluation. In what ways, if at all, do you see the five common characteristics of evaluations (accountability, use of scientific research methods, stakeholders and a political process, an ethical code, and thinking critically)?

References

Chen, H. (1990). *Theory-driven evaluations*. Newbury Park, CA: Sage Publications.

Dudley, J. R. (2005). *Research methods for social work: Becoming consumers and producers of research*. Boston: Allyn & Bacon.

Dudley, J., & Ahlgrim-Delzell, L. (2002). From lawsuit to quality improvement. In J. Dudley, M. L. Calhoun, & L. Ahlgrim-Delzell (Eds.), *Lessons learned from a lawsuit: Creating services for people with mental illness and mental retardation* (pp. 99–107). Kingston, NY: National Association for the Dually Diagnosed Press.

Gibbs, L., & Gambrill, E. (1996). *Critical thinking for social workers: A workbook*. Thousand Oaks, CA: Pine Forge Press.

Martin, L. L., & Kettner, P. M. (1996). *Measuring performance of human service programs*. Thousand Oaks, CA: Sage Publications.

Posavac, E. J., & Carey, R. G. (1997). *Program evaluation: Methods and case studies*. Upper Saddle River, NJ: Prentice Hall.

Weissman, H., Epstein, I., & Savage, A. (1983). *Agency-based social work: Neglected aspects of clinical practice*. Philadelphia: Temple University Press.

Part II

Orientation to the Bigger Picture of Evaluations

Chapter 2

The Context for an Evaluation

What are the motivating factors for conducting an evaluation?

The evaluation enterprise is by no means driven by one monolithic or standardized philosophy or approach. It has been influenced by many different philosophies, practical approaches, and some key historical events. Moreover, evaluations have been used to obtain many different kinds of results. In this sense, they are similar to research in general. Evaluation studies can vary from small exploratory case studies to large explanatory studies involving representative samples and well-tested measurement instruments. Evaluation philosophies can range from inductive to deductive, qualitative to quantitative, and local to global.

This chapter provides a better understanding of the widely varied intentions of evaluators from several different disciplines, including social work. The chapter addresses several important historical events and many theoretical notions that have influenced what evaluations are all about. The chapter begins by highlighting some pertinent historical events that have greatly influenced the evolution of evaluations in recent decades, followed by a description of several philosophical approaches and perspectives on program evaluation. The chapter closes with a synthesis of the many perspectives and an introduction to how these forces have contributed to the concept of evaluation developed in the text.

Relevant Events in History

Program Evaluations

Evaluations have emerged through a long and tumultuous history of experimentation with social programs. Several historical events have been instrumental in ensuring that social programs are increasingly accountable to the larger society and to the funding and regulatory agencies that oversee their activities. Social workers function within these programs, and they too have been confronted with increasing responsibility to be accountable for what they do.

Program evaluations have not always been a central concern in the functioning of social programs. However, even social programs operating during the settlement movement and within charity organization societies in the early part of the past century were mindful that their programs must work.

But their costs were relatively low, they often depended on volunteers, and they operated at the local level with little governmental assistance or regulation. Perhaps this local control and management ensured that those who oversaw the early programs kept a close watch on their volunteers and activities. Further, they most likely used common sense to determine that they were making headway in accomplishing their goals.

Since then, social programs have become much more complex and expensive. And they have expanded to serve almost infinitely more people. The New Deal legislation ushered in the beginning of national involvement in social programs by establishing old-age pensions and public assistance. The public assistance program, for example, was intended to provide temporary relief to poor people who could not find employment. The emphasis was on helping limited numbers and only during the Great Depression. Yet, as we know in retrospect, public assistance programs developed into a huge, burgeoning system of programs that provided permanent, not temporary, relief.

Social programs boomed in the 1960s. Historical events of that decade resulted in major changes in social policies, particularly in the areas of civil rights, poverty, and deinstitutionalization of people with mental illnesses and mental retardation. President Johnson's Great Society and War on Poverty were instrumental in creating numerous programs, including local community action councils, Job Corps, Neighborhood Youth Corp, community legal services, and Head Start among others. But the War on Poverty promised much more than it could deliver, and it pursued broad goals like eliminating poverty and building community control.

Further, the 1962 and 1967 Social Security amendments instituted new initiatives such as services for welfare recipients in addition to financial support. Rehabilitation became the mantra that replaced relief, and training people for useful work became the goal for addressing prolonged dependency. The 1967 amendments separated eligibility and social services functions in the hope of affecting family disorganization and conflicts. These new social service functions were to be filled by professionals with advanced degrees who would help poor people strengthen their family ties and become employed, educated, and ultimately self-sufficient. All of these initiatives not only promised more than they could even begin to deliver but also required runaway federal funding to pay for them.

All of these and other events moved program evaluation to the top of the list of solutions for legislators, funding agencies, and program providers. The pie-in-the-sky promises and expanding federal budgets devoted to social programs created an environment in which a rising social movement of fiscal conservatives demanded more emphasis on financial cutbacks and fiscal management, program accountability, and evaluations.

After the euphoric reform days of the 1960s, social programs began to face major problems in the 1970s and 1980s. Such programs, particularly those funded by governmental agencies, were no longer popular and came under attack. Accountability was still lacking for many of the programs, which left them exposed to growing criticism. Their ambitious agendas sought too much, including overcoming dependency on government and eliminating poverty. Ironically, the opposite seemed to be happening as the number of recipients in public programs soared and costs to the public exploded.

The growing clamor for social program accountability culminated in the passage of the Government Performance and Results Act of 1993. The act required strategic planning by all governmental agencies focusing on client outcomes and especially required definitions of how their outcomes would be achieved. The act gave the U.S. Congress tools to hold all governmental programs and those receiving governmental funds accountable. From here on, the federal government intended to base budget decisions on the agencies' reports of performance and success in achieving their intended outcomes. This federal act was so important to social work that it became a focus of an article in the journal *Social Work* (Kautz, Netting, Huber, Borders, & Davis, 1997).

From this point on, programs would be expected to develop annual performance plans with clear goals and objectives for their programs and employees, quantifiable measurements of these goals, strategies for achieving goals and objectives, a description of the program evaluations that they would use, and a presentation of the results demonstrating the extent to which they had reached their identified goals. These new policies were implemented in 1997. By the end of that year, almost one hundred federal agencies delivered their plans to Congress as required. However, the new act helped federal overseers realize that evaluation plans did not offer an easy or quick fix. Performance goals and measures were not as results oriented as expected, and some goals were found to be not objective or measurable. Further, these goals and objectives were not always linked to the individual programs and day-to-day agency activities intended to effect them. Nevertheless, the Government Performance and Results Act has become a key catalyst in an ongoing social movement aimed to hold social programs accountable for documenting their achievements. Amazingly, virtually every program proposal submitted to a funding agency today requires an evaluation.

Today, the development of program and practice evaluations has become more and more professional. Professions like social work, education, and other disciplines have formed professional associations to promulgate standards for high-quality, acceptable evaluations and a conference context for sharing ideas and experiences in implementing evaluations. These types of activities occur in professional associations like the National Association of Social Workers (NASW) and the Council on Social Work Education (CSWE). In particular, the CSWE gives major emphasis to evaluating BSW and MSW social work programs as part of its accreditation standards. Multidisciplinary organizations like the American Evaluation Association are also actively involved in promoting similar purposes, and there are at least eight professional journals that focus exclusively on evaluation (see chapter 6).

Practice Evaluations

Prominent social workers and government officials have challenged that social workers need to be accountable for their practice effectiveness. In 1973, Joel Fischer wrote a landmark article in *Social Work* titled "Is Casework Effective? A Review," in which he examined all of the studies that he could find to determine whether social casework (i.e., practice with individuals) was effective. Fischer assumed that effectiveness could be determined only using a classic experimental design with a control group that did not receive social casework services. He found seventy studies that he had to discard because they did not have a control group. Only eleven studies met this criterion and were reviewed. Unfortunately, Fischer found no evidence from the eleven studies that social casework worked; in some cases, clients actually deteriorated.

Numerous evaluations and meta-analyses have been published since Fischer's study that focus on the effectiveness of specific interventions in helping a variety of client populations (for an example of such a meta-analysis, see chapter 8; Harding & Higginson, 2003). In brief, this meta-analysis uncovered findings not too dissimilar from Fischer's: of twenty-two evaluations of interventions to help cancer and palliative care patients, few used experimental and quasi-experimental designs to evaluate effectiveness.

The social work profession has been involved in a long, arduous, and impressive search for new ways to examine how to scrutinize social work interventions to ensure that they worked for clients. This examination has continued, sometimes in dramatic ways, up to the present. Many of the efforts have come from social work authors. Gibbs and Gambrill (1996) have made major contributions to the development of critical-thinking principles that practitioners can use. Gibbs (2003), O'Hare (2005), and many others have expanded on the concept and practice of evidence-based practice. O'Hare, in particular, provides evidence-based concepts that apply to specific conditions like schizophrenia, depression, personality disorders, and child abuse and neglect. Finally, Fischer himself and colleagues (e.g., Bloom, Fischer, & Orme, 2003) have helped develop more sophisticated practice evaluation tools, especially additional ways to apply a single-system design to evaluating practice.

Perspectives on and Approaches to Evaluation

Although the various theoretical perspectives and approaches existing in the evaluation field are too many to cover in this short introduction, some are highlighted next. This sampling is intended to acquaint readers with those that are most pertinent to social work and to highlight some useful concepts, principles, and skills for new evaluators to incorporate into their own evolving eclectic approaches to evaluation. These theoretical perspectives and approaches include the following:

- Results-oriented model
- Feminist model
- Empowerment model
- Experimental models
- Fourth-generation evaluation
- Evaluations evolving within particular fields of practice

Results-Oriented Model

The results-oriented model focuses on performance, outcomes, and accountability. Evidence-based program and practice approaches and outcome evaluations fit here as well. This model has emerged as a public necessity because social programs have often fallen short of meeting their goals or have had difficulty communicating how they were achieving their goals (Wholey, 1999). Advocates of the results-oriented model believe that it is important to convince a variety of stakeholders that the outcomes they achieve are the ultimate reason why they are in business. In this regard, Wholey (1999) presents this three-step process: (1) development of agreement from stakeholders on goals and strategies, (2) regular measurement and evaluation of performance goals, and (3) use of performance results to improve programs and enhance accountability to stakeholders and the public. This model gives most of its attention to the ultimate point of a program's existence: socially desirable outcomes for clients.

As mentioned in chapter 1, Martin and Kettner (1996) give primary attention to performance and its measurement based on elements such as the efficiency and effectiveness of a social program. Efficiency involves calculating the amount of service provided and the number of clients who complete the program (program outputs) and comparing the outputs to the costs involved (program inputs). Effectiveness, another element of performance measurement, focuses on outcomes of social programs or results, impact, or accomplishments. Examples could include the number of parents who stop abusing their children as the result of a parenting-skills training program or the number of an adoption agency's successfully placed adoptions. The concepts of program inputs, outputs, and outcomes are developed further in chapter 3.

Feminist Models

Feminist evaluations are defined by the substantive areas that such researchers choose to study. Feminist models are likely to aim to conduct evaluations that increase social justice for the oppressed, especially but not exclusively for oppressed women. They are inclined to focus on the relative positions and experiences of women in relation to men and the effects that gender issues have on both sexes (Deem, 2002). Examples in agency organizations include gender discrimination in hiring and promotion, the low representation of women in administrative and other leadership roles, salary inequities based on gender, and family-supportive policies of employers. Other feminist topics could include the roles of men and women in parenting children and assuming household tasks, enforcement of child support, the earning power of single-parent households, and the availability of quality day care for low-income families.

An Example of a Feminist Study: Women's Salaries

Gibelman (2003) examined the issue of men's and women's salaries in the human services by analyzing existing data from the Bureau of Labor Statistics. She found that salary disparities continue to exist. She attributes these disparities to discrimination patterns. Gibelman recommended several strategies to combat such discrimination, including public and professional education and advocacy. She also pointed out that the gender discrimination experienced by social workers is paralleled among some client groups.

In addition, feminist evaluations can be partially defined by the research methods that they prefer. Most feminist researchers prefer qualitative over quantitative methods because of the flexibility built into this method and the value that it places on uncovering new knowledge about and insight into interventions at deeper levels of meaning. In addition, some suggest that similar principles guide both feminist studies and qualitative methods (Skeggs, 2001). Both feminist and qualitative methodologists are sensitive to a power differential between evaluators and participants in evaluations, and both are concerned that the participants gain something from their involvement in an evaluation. Both feminist and qualitative methodologists are also likely to assume an accountability to the wider community as well as to the participants. Many feminist evaluators also attempt to use principles of the participatory action approach, such as involvement of participants in as many of the steps of planning and implementing an evaluation as possible.

Many authors have covered feminist perspectives and social work practice (e.g., Bricker-Jenkins, Hooyman, & Gottlieb, 1991). Their practice perspectives have focused on person-centered approaches, inclusiveness, collaboration with clients, and empowerment. These qualities would also tend to be highlighted in practice evaluations that encourage clients to become as fully involved as possible in evaluations to benefit clients' welfare.

Empowerment Models

Empowerment is a familiar action word in social work. It refers to promoting increased power for clients and helping equip them to assume greater control over their lives. Empowerment models advocate for both client rights and client responsibilities in their lives. An empowerment philosophy is especially important to evaluation activities, as is evident in the empowerment evaluation approach that Fetterman, Kaftarian, and Wandersman (1996) articulate. The value orientation of their approach is to help people help themselves and to improve their programs using self-evaluation and self-reflection techniques. Fetterman (2003) describes a simple, logical, and systematic approach to facilitating self-evaluation. Program participants are helped to conduct their own evaluations, and they use outside evaluators and other experts as coaches. Evaluation concepts, techniques, and findings are used to help specific oppressed groups or communities develop their self-determining capacity and improve their programs. Such evaluators typically play the roles of coach, facilitator, expert consultant, and critical friend.

Fetterman et al. (1996) distinguish between empowering processes and empowering outcomes. Empowering processes help people develop the skills needed for them to become independent problem solvers and decision makers (Zimmerman, 2000). These processes are critical in providing people with a particular stake in gaining control over their future, obtaining needed resources, and critically understanding their social environment. Empowered outcomes, in some contrast, are the consequences that empowerment processes seek. Examples include creating or strengthening organizational networks, creating greater accessibility to community resources, and greater citizen control over community decision making.

Inclusive evaluation, developed by Mertens (2003), is similar to the empowerment approach; she advocates for a deliberate inclusion of groups and communities that have been historically discriminated against on the basis of race, ethnicity, culture, gender, social class, sexual orientation, and disability. This perspective aims to redress power imbalances in society by involving stakeholders and taking seriously and accurately their views and needs. This perspective promotes social justice outcomes and takes issue with deficit models that blame those affected by a problem.

Participatory action research (PAR) is a practical type of empowerment model that can be used in evaluations. Sometimes referred to as participant action research or critical action research, PAR is readily familiar to social work research (DePoy, Hartman, & Haslett, 1999). As its perspective PAR has an interest in actively involving research participants in all or most steps of the process. Some of the key PAR principles are the following:

- Collaborate with those affected by the problem to clearly articulate the problem, its scope, and all stakeholders.

- Articulate the purpose of the change that the research is designed to accomplish.
- Have both professional and lay researchers on the team.
- Train the lay researchers in how to design, conduct, and use appropriate research methods.
- Report findings in accessible formats for all stakeholder groups.

Implementation of PAR can occur in all or some steps of an evaluation. For example, if involving community stakeholders at every step is not realistic, they can be involved in some steps. Client and community stakeholders can be particularly important in the first step of helping articulate program issues that need to be addressed and in the last step of assisting in dissemination of evaluation results to various community groups and getting feedback and greater community involvement.

An Example of an Evaluation with PAR Principles to Support Social Action

Reese, Ahern, Nair, O'Faire, and Warren (1999) initiated a program evaluation using PAR principles that resulted in improved access to hospice services for African Americans. Collaboration occurred with research participants and practitioners throughout the study. The evaluators' activities began with a small qualitative study with African American pastors. The pilot study was followed by a larger quantitative study of African American hospice patients that documented their access barriers to hospice. Finally a social action effort was initiated to engage local health-care providers in addressing these access barriers. The findings of their studies were used to facilitate this social action effort.

Experimental Models

Supporters of experimental models believe that experimental and quasi-experimental designs are superior to other designs because they deliver scientifically credible evidence of the impact of programs on clients' welfare (Cook & Campbell, 1979). They argue that experimental designs and randomized samples are feasible and ethical. Further, the features of these designs are the only way to rule out the influence of other factors, such as other means of helping clients and the maturity process for participants that inevitably occurs over the time of an experiment.

Philosophies deriving from this traditional scientific research paradigm are reviewed only briefly in this section, as readers are expected to be well acquainted with this paradigm from research methods courses in professional degree programs. Also, chapter 9 is partially devoted to experimental and quasi-experimental designs used in program and practice outcome evaluations.

Fourth-Generation Evaluation

Lincoln (2003) advocates for a fourth-generation approach for this millennium that strives to redress power imbalances and expand the repertoire of data-gathering and data analysis methods used in evaluations. She argues that we must move beyond the modernist and Eurocentric philosophies that tend to believe that rational, orderly investigations and deductions in the social sciences will help us arrive at social truth, as in the physical sciences. A postmodernist would argue that no single method or design can produce anything more than a partial truth. A postmodernist distrusts all methods equally and recognizes and admits the situational limitations of the knower, whether based in science, literature, or another vantage point. Lincoln views politics as a major voice of influence in her inquiries, and her perspective takes into account the needs of global society, not just Western society. This global perspective particularly seeks to hear and value the often-unheard indigenous voices of other societies.

Lincoln (2003) also advocates for the use of naturalistic inquiries with the more traditional quantitative methodologies in evaluations. Her writings offer qualitative methodologies and techniques in many forms for evaluation purposes. In terms of the practical aspects of evaluation, she warns that evaluators who fail to pay attention to the growing number of pluralistic voices in social life will find these voices in a chorus of opposition to any evaluation with a single method of inquiry. Several sections of this book describe qualitative methods for evaluation, including client and staff satisfaction studies in chapter 8 and data analysis in chapter 11.

Evaluations Evolving within Particular Fields of Practice

The various program evaluation texts currently available reveal that many evaluation approaches are tailored to particular fields of practice and specific client populations. Health care is a good example. Evaluation is an integral part of health-care programs, for example, in the special emphasis on health maintenance organizations, diagnostic treatment groups, and the growing importance of managed care. As health-care technologies expand, the costs continue to soar, as growing numbers of people can benefit from these technologies. Thus, cost-benefit analyses are critical. Other special interests in health-care evaluation include risk management, quality improvement, patient and consumer communications, safety and security needs for evaluation in long-term care, AIDS treatment, and other areas (Kavaler & Spiegel, 2003).

Child welfare is another example of a field that has an extensive evaluation literature. Briar-Lawson and Zlotnik (2002), for example, have edited a collection of articles that focus on the necessity of clear and relevant child welfare outcomes in programs for children. They stress recruiting and retaining social workers who have special preparation in child welfare in the public sector.

Other examples of fields of practice that emphasize a particular evaluation approach include teacher and staff performance in school settings, dignity and normalization for people with developmental disabilities, child-custody evaluations in family court, and evaluations of various community organization models.

Synthesis of the Different Evaluation Perspectives

Some authors have provided a fuller understanding of the different perspectives driving evaluations and what each values in their classification. These classifying efforts have been useful in synthesizing several distinct perspectives and in revealing the strengths and limitations of each one.

First, Patton (2002) offers his understanding of different evaluation perspectives by identifying five distinct paradigms. Each paradigm, in part, captures elements of the types of evaluations that are pertinent to social service agencies, schools, and institutions that employ human service workers:

1. **Traditional scientific paradigm:** the traditional social science paradigm emphasizes objectivity and the independence of the evaluator from the group studied, and it minimizes investigators' bias. It also pays close attention to validity, reliability, generalizability, and a marked preference for quantitative measurement and experimental designs. This paradigm is expanded in the work of Rossi, Freeman, and Lipsey (1999).

2. **Social construction and constructionist:** this paradigm asserts the inevitability of subjectivity, uses multiple perspectives, favors qualitative inquiry, and offers alternative criteria to validity and reliability for judging methodological quality (e.g., trustworthiness, authenticity, and gathering findings that enhance and deepen understanding). Responding to multiple stakeholder perspectives is a hallmark of constructionist evaluation. This paradigm is expanded in the work of Guba and Lincoln (1989) and Greene (2000).

3. **Artistic and evocative paradigm:** this paradigm, while not yet widely used in evaluations, uses role-playing and dramatic techniques, poetry, and other literary forms to gather and present data, as well as short stories and narrative techniques to report findings. The criteria for judging artistic and evocative evaluations include creativity, aesthetic quality, and interpretive vitality. The findings of such studies can open the program world to the evaluation audience

through literary and dramatic devices and offer a deep sense of the lived experience of program participants. Eisner's (1991) work models this paradigm.

4. **Pragmatic and utilitarian paradigm:** this paradigm emphasizes the specific practical, informative needs of users of an evaluation. Criteria include responsiveness to the needs of stakeholders, situational adaptability, attending to interactive engagement between the evaluator and stakeholders, methodological flexibility, and preparation of findings such that they respond to stakeholders' needs. Utilization-focused evaluations highlight this paradigm (Patton, 1997).

5. **Critical change paradigm:** in this paradigm, evaluators are involved in evaluations primarily as change agents by bringing a critical change orientation and explicit agenda to uncover political, economic, and social inequalities; to raise people's consciousness; and to strive to change the balance of power in favor of the less powerful. An underlying purpose of such evaluations is to increase social justice, and to increase the ability of the oppressed to represent their own interests through the evaluation and follow up with action. Critical change criteria undergird empowerment evaluations (Fetterman, 2003), diversity-inclusive evaluations (Mertens, 2003), and those aspects of deliberative democratic evaluation that involve values-based advocacy for democracy (House & Howe, 2000).

Social workers need the objectivity and methodical rigor of the traditional scientific research paradigm described extensively in later chapters. The social constructionist paradigm is also useful, because social work evaluators are increasingly using qualitative and quantitative methods to describe and define a growing number of unfamiliar concepts and are committed to addressing the concerns of multiple stakeholders, especially program recipients. In addition, social work, a very practical profession, stresses a utilitarian perspective similar to the pragmatic and utilitarian paradigm, as social work evaluations must be relevant, practical, and responsive to the evolving program needs in social agencies. Also among the ethical priorities of a social work evaluator is the persistent concern for social justice; therefore, social work evaluators gravitate toward evaluations that can bring about social change beneficial to clients, in keeping with the critical change paradigm. As noted previously, the evaluation enterprise is by no means monolithic or uniform in its theoretical perspective. It has been driven by many different perspectives and can generate many different benefits for social program development and program recipients.

Brun's Typology

Carl Brun (2005), a social work educator and experienced program evaluator, offers another helpful way to look at the various evaluation perspectives. He conceptualizes evaluation as driven by five overall factors: (1) decisions that have to be made, (2) the involvement of stakeholders, (3) the following of values, (4) application of theory, and (5) use of appropriate data-collection methods. Although he states that all five factors are evident in all evaluations, one of these five factors usually has the greatest influence. Decision-making evaluations emphasize the gathering of data to address specific decisions that have to be made about a program. Involvement of stakeholders gives the most attention to the processes of identifying stakeholders critical to the evaluation and how they can become involved as fully as possible. Values-driven evaluations give greatest emphasis to the underlying values of the evaluation. For example, social work values stress the importance of the strengths of participants, their cultural context, and empowerment of oppressed client groups. Theory-driven evaluations begin with theoretical explorations and commitments and a desire to link the causes of the participants' problems with how the interventions can address such causes. Data-driven evaluations emphasize the types of data needed and the preferred methodologies to obtain them, such as a preference for a qualitative or quantitative method, with all decisions revolving around the methodological commitment. According to Brun, all five factors, and their emphases, are important.

All five of Brun's emphases—making decisions, involving stakeholders, following values, applying theory, and choosing research methods—are important in evaluations. They all compete for resources and influence in most evaluations, so Brun's framework is helpful in sorting out all of their contributions and the frequent need to set priorities. In this instance, an evaluation that pays extensive attention to identifying and involving a range of stakeholders, including client groups, has the potential to be in tension with theory-driven evaluations. For example, all the stakeholders would need to be adequately trained in the theories undergirding a program, which could require considerable time, collaboration, and cost.

Formative and Summative Evaluations

Finally, an important way to distinguish evaluations is to ask whether they are formative or summative. This is the traditional way in which evaluations are distinguished in many program evaluation texts. Formative evaluations focus on planning for a program and improving its delivery of services. Program processes are important to examine, correct, and enhance because of the direct impact they have on the outcomes for program recipients. These evaluations tend to be exploratory and utilitarian in that their findings can be immediately channeled back into enhancing a program, solving a problem, or filling an obvious omission in a program. The agency sponsoring the program usually initiates and conducts such evaluations; the agency staff or outside consultants internally drive the evaluation.

Summative evaluations focus on the outcomes of programs and attempt to answer the ultimate question: did the intervention reach its goals or make a real difference in the lives of recipients? These evaluations have a finality to them in that they attempt to measure whether a program was effective. An external agent, such as an independent evaluator or governmental agency typically conducts such evaluations to ensure that they are objective. They primarily use a narrower set of research design options, such as experimental and single system. The results of these studies can be decisive in determining whether a program continues, expands, or terminates. Funding and regulatory agencies are most interested in summative evaluations because they provide the kinds of information that they need to make major decisions about future funding.

These two distinct types of evaluations, formative and summative, are somewhat similar to the distinction in research between exploratory and explanatory studies. Exploratory studies are conducted to learn more about a phenomenon when not much is currently known. Exploratory studies identify general research questions to answer. Explanatory studies are conducted to find support for theoretical explanations that the researcher has already crafted. Explanatory studies usually identify hypotheses to confirm or refute. Formative evaluations are like exploratory studies in that they are exploratory in nature and not intended to provide results that can help make major decisions about a program. Summative evaluations are like explanatory studies in that they are used to bring finality to a program's future; either it did or it did not have a significant impact on recipients (see table 2.1).

In formative studies, the intent is to learn more about how the program is functioning and to consider whether the program is instrumental in helping clients meet their predetermined goals. Such studies mostly involve the asking of general study questions that will produce more information about the program so that it can be improved or enhanced. Formative studies often have up to four or five general study questions. The audience for such

TABLE 2.1   Characteristics of Formative and Summative Studies

Formative studies	*Summative studies*
Intent: How is the program or practice intervention functioning?	Intent: Is the program or practice intervention reaching its goals?
Focus provided by general research questions	Focus provided by hypotheses: How much does the intervention have an impact on the recipients' lives?
Use of both qualitative and quantitative methods	Use of quantitative methods
Audience: Stakeholders are mostly affiliated with the agency sponsoring the intervention	Audience: Stakeholders include the funding and regulatory agencies

studies is usually affiliated with the agency sponsor, such as administrators, board members, advisory board members, staff, clients, and others. In contrast, in summative studies, the intent is to determine whether the program is actually effective in reaching its goals. Instead of study questions, explanatory evaluations usually test hypotheses to determine whether the intervention had a positive influence on client outcome measures. Summative studies may have as many as three or four explanatory statements or hypotheses to be tested.

However, these two types of evaluations, formative and summative, are helpful only to a limited extent. Most evaluations that social workers in social agencies conduct will be formative. Summative evaluations are less likely to be initiated by an agency. Nevertheless, the purposes of summative evaluations are important to understand, as they have a vital role in decisions about a program's future. Research designs used in summative evaluations are a focus of chapter 9 and are illustrated in other parts of the book.

Evidence-Based Interventions

Regardless of the specific perspective selected to conduct an evaluation, it should attempt to be as evidence-based as possible. Evidence-based interventions have been defined in medicine as the "integration of the best research evidence with clinical expertise and patient values (Sackett, Richardson, Rosenburg, & Haynes, 2000, p. 1). Gambrill (1999, p. 346), a social worker, adds that "it involves integrating individual practice expertise with the best available external evidence from systematic research as well as considering the values and expectations of clients." Evidence-based interventions use the best available external evidence that the interventions are effective. Evidence comes mostly from practice experience and research studies with quasi-experimental or experimental designs. It is important that evidence-based sources are consistent with the values and expectations of the clients who receive such interventions.

The words *evidence* and *evidence-based* are often used throughout this book. Evidence is something observed firsthand with some or all of the senses (sight, hearing, taste, touch, smell). Evidence documenting the effectiveness of a program or practice needs to be empirical or to reflect some form of reality in the world. When evidence of a phenomenon is not directly observable, then a secondhand source needs to be found that is reliable and valid. Agency case records and questionnaire responses are examples of secondhand sources of evidence.

The NASW Code of Ethics stresses the importance of evidence as an ethical issue: "social workers should . . . use evaluation and research *evidence* in their professional practice." Evidence also has a wider range of implications beyond evaluations. For example, a participant's signature on an informed consent form provides *evidence* of consent; needs assessments provide evidence of clients' specific problems, clinical diagnoses, or medical conditions; evidence is required for outcome studies to document outcome measures.

Example of Evidence-Based Interventions

Harding and Higginson (2003) systematically reviewed articles from several relevant professional journals to identify interventions for helping noninstitutionalized cancer and palliative care patients and their caregivers. They found twenty-two relevant interventions. Overall, they concluded from their review that one-to-one interventions are a means of providing support, education, and building problem-solving and coping skills. However, they are time consuming, costly, and may be unacceptable to many caregivers. Group work interventions, in contrast, were reported to be widely used for support and education for both caregivers and patients.

Empirical evidence of a phenomenon could be illustrated in an outcome study in which the frequency of contact between a client with mental illness and other people is an outcome measure of social adaptation. How can this be determined empirically? Theoretically, it can be observed firsthand if someone were available to observe the interactions of a client all day long without interfering with the contacts in any way. However, it is not realistic or ethically sound to obtain such information in this way. A secondhand source of such information, such as a relative, friend, or the self-reporting of the client, is subjective and likely inaccurate. Moreover, secondhand sources could be biased, so the challenge is to make sure that such reports are as accurate as possible. One way to increase this possibility is to obtain multiple sources, such as reports from two or more people.

A Unique International Source of Evidence-Based Information

The Collaboration (C2; www.campbellcollaboration.org) is an international source of evidence-based information for programs and practice. It is "an independent, international, non-profit organization that provides decision-makers with evidence-based information to empower them to make well-informed decisions about the effects of interventions in the social, behavioral and educational arenas." C2 has a strategic network of renowned scholars and practitioners worldwide who can provide evidence-based information in two ways: (1) by preparing, maintaining, and disseminating systematic reviews of existing social science evidence, and (2) by random controlled trials using their own databases. C2's vision is to promote positive social change and to improve programs and services across the world.

Best practices is a frequently heard term in agencies these days, and is also relevant to the discussion of evidenced-based interventions. Best practices are the "best" or most effective programs or practices known to work in helping people overcome their problems. For this reason, evidence-based practices, in many ways, are strongly correlated with best practices; for example, best practices could be the best evidence-based practices known to exist for a particular client group.

Summary of Perspectives

This review of several types of perspectives and approaches in conducting evaluations reveals some fairly common and overlapping elements. Those that seem most compatible with the evaluation approach described herein include the following:

- Importance of science, neutrality, and objective methods
- Use of critical-thinking skills
- Recognition that achieving socially acceptable outcomes is an essential program expectation
- Recognition that the purpose of an evaluation varies widely and dictates what is to be done
- Importance of working closely with stakeholders and accountability to them
- The following of a professional ethical code
- Flexibility in the use of various methodologies, including qualitative and possibly artistic ones
- Affirmation and promotion of diversity
- Commitment to social and economic justice

Introduction of the Three-Stage Approach

When discussing all of these evaluation perspectives and approaches, it is important to remember that a social program or a practice area is the focal point of an evaluation. Programs and professional practice are dynamic and, in some ways, are similar to a human beings: they are conceived, evolve in an embryolike form, are birthed, grow up, mature, and ultimately decline and end. For programs and practice, these stages are referred to as follows:

- Planning stage, when a program or practice is conceived and developed into a proposal or plan
- Implementation stage, when the program or practice is implemented
- Outcome stage, when the impact of the program or practice on client outcomes is the major focus

The book is organized around these three developmental stages of programs and practice referred to as the three-stage approach. As mentioned in chapter 1, evaluations address important issues at all these stages. However, it is noteworthy that these stages may not always occur in sequential order. To the contrary, they often overlap. For example, during the planning of an intervention, the same intervention may also be implemented as a pilot project for a small group of clients, to explore its potential on a larger scale and to identify the necessary resources. Or after the implementation of an intervention, a process evaluation may be initiated to determine whether the intervention is moving in the right direction toward its goals. The results of such a study could lead to a decision to start over, make major corrections, or move ahead with few or no changes.

Programs

Important program elements that are pertinent to an evaluation need to be identified at each stage. Input elements, such as potential target population and hiring needs, are identified during the planning stage (see figure 2.1). During the implementation stage, such elements are referred to as process elements. Examples include the theoretical underpinnings of the program and the technologies being used. The outcome stage elements are referred to as output and outcome elements and include, for example, the number of clients who complete the program or measures of client progress in reaching their goals (e.g., a client obtaining a stable, well-paying job after completing a job-training program).

FIGURE 2.1   Three-Stage Approach

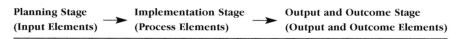

Planning Stage (Input Elements)	→	Implementation Stage (Process Elements)	→	Output and Outcome Stage (Output and Outcome Elements)

Practice

Let's look more closely at how these stages are evident in practice evaluations. At the practice level, an evaluation can investigate the input elements before the implementation of practice interventions. Some important input elements in practice are the credentials that practitioners bring to their position, such as a professional degree, work experience, and other special skills. Other input elements are the criteria used to select prospective clients and the characteristics of those clients (e.g., ethnicity, age, gender). The chosen practice approaches are another example of an input element.

During the implementation of a practice intervention, important process elements can include how the practice approach and its specific techniques are actually being implemented. The outcome stage takes into account other sets of elements, such as the total number of sessions provided to a client (output element) and measures of client progress (outcome element).

Client Satisfaction with Various Practice Approaches

The client satisfaction study by Baker, Zucker, and Gross (1998) sought, among other things, to determine the perceptions of five groups of inpatient mental health clients who were receiving different treatment modalities and services in five different facilities. The evaluator assumed that the clients with severe mental illness "know what's good for them[selves]." Practice approaches varied across facilities. For example, one facility offered extensive assistance with daily activities, while another offered training groups in psychosocial skills and a third emphasized case management, family services, and individual counseling. No overall pattern of client satisfaction was found across the widely varied approaches, though some approaches received lower ratings.

In conclusion, the stages of program and practice development and the elements important to consider in each stage provide a major organizational framework for the book. This organizational framework is helpful in informing you as to how to focus an evaluation before you proceed to implement it.

Key Terms

Empowerment models
Evaluations evolving within particular fields of practice
Evidence-based interventions
Experimental models
Feminist models
Formative and summative evaluations
Fourth-generation evaluation
Participatory action approach
Results-oriented models

Discussion Questions and Assignments

1. In small groups, choose one of the historical events listed below, review what is summarized about the event in the chapter, and find an additional source of information related to evaluation. Discuss within your small groups what you learned about the event and its importance in shaping evaluations. Then share what you have learned with the class.

   • President Johnson's Great Society and War on Poverty, which were instrumental in creating programs such as local community action councils, Job Corps, Neighborhood Youth Corp, community legal services, and Head Start.

- The 1962 Social Security amendments, which instituted initiatives such as services for welfare recipients, rehabilitation, and training for useful work to overcome prolonged dependency.
- The passage of the Government Performance and Results Act of 1993, which requires all governmental agencies to focus on client outcomes and define how they are to be achieved.
- Joel Fischer's article "Is Casework Effective? A Review."

2. Select *one* of the six evaluation perspectives. Find out more about this perspective by reading about it in an evaluation text. Then find one evaluation study in a professional journal that is an example of this perspective.

3. What is your view of the role of empowerment in evaluation? How can an evaluator promote empowerment through an evaluation? What are your views about the limits of empowerment in evaluation, if any?

4. Develop a program evaluation that could be conducted at your agency. What is the overall purpose of the evaluation? What could be accomplished by conducting this evaluation? Which perspectives described in the chapter would have the most impact on how you would conduct this evaluation? Why?

5. Why is it important to know the philosophical orientation of an evaluator? Pick one of the six perspectives described in the chapter and discuss how it can affect, both positively and negatively, how an evaluator conducts a study.

References

Baker, L., Zucker, P., & Gross, M. (1998). Using client satisfaction surveys to evaluate and improve services in locked and unlocked adult inpatient facilities. *Journal of Behavioral Health Services Research, 25*(1), 51–68.

Bloom, M., Fischer, J., & Orme, J. G. (2003). *Evaluating practice: Guidelines for the accountable professional.* Boston: Allyn & Bacon.

Briar-Lawson, K., & Zlotnik, J. L. (Eds.). (2002). *Evaluation research in child welfare: Improving outcomes through university-public agency partnerships.* Binghamton, NY: Haworth Press.

Bricker-Jenkins, M., Hooyman, N. R., & Gottlieb, N. (Eds.). (1991). *Feminist social work practice in clinical settings.* Thousand Oaks, CA: Sage Publications.

Brun, C. F. (2005). *A practical guide to social service evaluation.* Chicago: Lyceum Books.

Cook, T. D., & Campbell, D. T. (1979). *Quasi-experimentation: Design and analysis issues for field settings.* Skokie, IL: Rand McNally.

Deem, R. (2002). Talking to manager-academics: Methodological dilemmas and feminist research strategies. *Sociology, 36*(4), 835–856.

DePoy, E., Hartman, A., & Haslett, D. (1999). Critical action research: A model for social work knowing. *Social Work, 44*(6), 560–569.

Eisner, E. (1991). *The enlightened eye.* New York: Macmillan.

Fetterman, D. (2003). Empowerment evaluation strikes a responsive chord. In S. I. Donaldson & M. Scriven (Eds.), *Evaluating social programs and problems: Visions for the new millennium* (pp. 63–76). Mahwah, NJ: Lawrence Erlbaum Associates.

Fetterman, D. M., Kaftarian, S. J., & Wandersman, A. (Eds.). (1996). *Empowerment evaluation: Knowledge and tools for self-assessment and accountability*. Thousand Oaks, CA: Sage Publications.

Fischer, J. (1973). Is casework effective? A review. *Social Work, 18*, 5–21.

Gambrill, E. (1999). Evidence-based practice: An alternative to authority-based practice. *Families in Society, 80*(4), 341–350.

Gibelman, M. (2003). So how far have we come? Pestilent and persistent gender gap in pay. *Social Work, 48*(1), 22–32.

Gibbs, L. (2003). *Evidence-based practice for the helping professions: A practical guide with integrated multimedia*. Pacific Grove, CA: Thomson.

Gibbs, L., & Gambrill, E. (1996). *Critical thinking for social workers: A workbook*. Thousand Oaks, CA: Pine Forge Press.

Greene, J. C. (2000). Understanding social programs through evaluation. In N. K. Denzin and Y. S. Lincoln (Eds.), *Handbook of qualitative research* (2nd ed., pp. 981–999). Thousand Oaks, CA: Sage Publications.

Guba, E., & Lincoln, Y. (1989). *Fourth generation evaluation*. Thousand Oaks, CA: Sage Publications.

Harding, R., & Higginson, I. J. (2003). What is the best way to help caregivers in cancer and palliative care? A systematic literature review of interventions and their effectiveness. *Palliative Medicine, 17*, 63–74.

House, E. R., & Howe, K. R. (2000). Deliberative democratic evaluation. *New Directions for Evaluation, 85*, 3–12.

Kautz, J. R., Netting, F. E., Huber, R., Borders, K., & Davis, T. S. (1997). The Government Performance and Results Act of 1993: Implications for social work practice. *Social Work, 42*(4), 364–373.

Kavaler, F., & Spiegel, A. (2003). *Risk management in health care institutions: A strategic approach*. Sudbury, MA: Jones & Bartlett Publishers.

Lincoln, Y. S. (2003). Fourth generation evaluation in the new millennium. In S. I. Donaldson & M. Scriven (Eds.), *Evaluating social programs and problems: Visions for the new millennium* (pp. 77–90). Mahwah, NJ: Lawrence Erlbaum Associates.

Martin, L. L., & Kettner, P. M. (1996). *Measuring the performance of human service programs*. Thousand Oaks, CA: Sage Publications.

Mertens, D. M. (2003). The inclusive view of evaluation: Visions for the new millennium. In S. I. Donaldson & M. Scriven (Eds.), *Evaluating social programs and problems: Visions for the new millennium* (pp. 91–107). Mahwah, NJ: Lawrence Erlbaum Associates.

O'Hare, T. (2005). *Evidence-based practices for social workers: An interdisciplinary approach*. Chicago: Lyceum Books.

Patton, M. Q. (1997). *Utilization-focused evaluation* (3rd ed.). Thousand Oaks, CA: Sage Publications.

Patton, M. Q. (2002). Feminist, yes, but is it evaluation? *New Directions for Evaluation, 96*(Winter), 97–108.

Reese, D., Ahern, R., Nair, S., O'Faire, J., & Warren, C. (1999). Hospice access and use by African Americans: Addressing cultural and institutional barriers through participatory action research. *Social Work, 44*(6), 549–559.

Rossi, P., Freeman, H., & Lipsey, M. (1999). *Evaluation: A systematic approach* (6th ed.). Thousand Oaks, CA: Sage Publications.

Sackett, D. L., Richardson, W. S., Rosenburg, W., & Haynes, R. R. (2000). *Evidence-based medicine: How to practice and teach E.M.* (2nd ed.). New York: Churchill-Livingston.

Skeggs, B. (2001). Feminist ethnography. In P. Atkinson, A. Coffey, & S. Delamont (Eds.), *Encyclopaedia of ethnography* (pp. 426–442). London: Sage Publications.

Wholey, J. S. (1999). Quality control: Assessing the accuracy and usefulness of performance measurement systems. In H. P. Hatry (Ed.), *Performance measurement: Getting results* (pp. 217–239). Washington, DC: The Urban Institute.

Zimmerman, M. A. (2000). Empowerment theory: Psychological, organizational, and community levels of analysis. In J. Rappaport & E. Seldman (Eds.), *Handbook of community psychology* (pp. 43–63). New York: Plenum.

Chapter 3

The Role of Ethics in Evaluations

What are our ethical obligations as evaluators?

Ethics plays a crucial role in both program and practice evaluations. This chapter describes the most important ethical issues to be considered when conducting evaluations. Because much of this material is largely a review of the ethics material covered in a basic research methods course, it is condensed here. A research methods text can be a helpful supplement to this chapter for those who want more information on ethics (e.g., Dudley, 2005; Marlow, 2005).

This chapter primarily reviews the ethical standards of three professional associations: the National Association of Social Workers (NASW), the American Evaluation Association (AEA), and the Council on Social Work Education (CSWE).

Ethical concerns for evaluations are similar to those for research studies generally. They are so important to social work evaluations, that the section "Evaluation and Research Standards" of the NASW's (1999) Code of Ethics covers ethical concerns specifically.

Because social work has many functions, and evaluation is only one of them, it is valuable to consult an ethical code of a group such as the AEA, which focuses exclusively on evaluation activities. The five major principles of AEA evaluators are the following:

1. **Systematic inquiry:** A commitment to systematic inquiries that use the highest technical standards and a commitment to communicate the inquiries as clearly as possible to all stakeholders and other parties.
2. **Competence:** Evaluators are expected to provide competent performance to stakeholders, which includes an appropriate educational background, skills, and experiences, as well as cultural competence to conduct an evaluation effectively in terms of race, ethnicity, gender, religion, socioeconomic factors, and others.
3. **Integrity and honesty:** Evaluators are to display honesty and integrity in their own behavior and attempt to ensure honesty and integrity throughout the entire evaluation process, including disclosing conflicts of interest and not misrepresenting their procedures, findings, or interpretations.

4. **Respect for all people:** Evaluators are to respect the security, dignity, and self-worth of evaluation participants, clients, and other evaluation stakeholders. They are to prevent risks of harm and invasion of privacy for participants and assure participants of any benefits they can accrue from an evaluation.
5. **Responsibilities for general and public welfare:** Evaluators are to articulate and take into account the diversity of general and public interests and values that may be related to the evaluation, and to be mindful of the rights and needs of all pertinent groups.

Ethics important to conducting evaluations are also promulgated in the accreditation standards of the CSWE, including recognizing the importance of diversity, promoting social and economic justice, and abiding by the values and ethics of professional social work.

Ethics for Conducting Evaluations

Having an entire section of the NASW Code of Ethics devoted exclusively to social workers' ethical obligations to research and evaluation clearly indicates the importance of ethics. Section 5.02, titled "Evaluation and Research," can be found at the NASW's Web site (www.naswdc.org). Some of the section's specific principles are reviewed below along with selected AEA principles.

Promote and Facilitate Evaluations and Research

This introductory statement of Section 5.02[b] of the NASW Code of Ethics reminds social workers that they have an ethical obligation to promote and facilitate evaluation studies and other types of research. This suggests that social workers should be supportive of others who conduct evaluations in their employment agencies. However, to do this, they need to be familiar with the ethical standards of research and other ethical standards of social work so that they can become gatekeepers, both to encourage new evaluations that meet the ethical standards of the profession and to discourage evaluations that do not.

Consult Appropriate Institutional Review Boards

Institutional review boards (IRBs) are groups of people at an institution who have been designated to promulgate ethical standards and to approve and monitor the ethical provisions of all studies sponsored by the institution. Virtually all universities and governmental agencies have an IRB. Evaluators and other researchers are required to submit a formal statement to the IRB that describes their study, its procedures, its benefits, and how it protects research participants from risks of harm and invasion of privacy (Section 5.02[d] of the NASW Code of Ethics). In addition, IRBs can serve as training centers to inform researchers of specific requirements of informed consent.

Many social agencies also have an IRB or a similar ad hoc group. Social agencies that sponsor research and do not have an IRB should institute a formal way to establish ethical standards and procedures, to protect research participants, and to prevent ethical problems. Using the guidelines herein, you can create a new structure for your agency to carefully review any new studies before they are approved.

Create Your Own IRB

1. Select a group of five to seven agency staff members who represent different programs, disciplines, and positions in the agency.
2. Orient the staff representatives to the ethical problems and safeguards that an IRB typically considers. Introduce them to the various functions of an IRB. Ask experts on these subjects from other agencies and institutions to speak about them to your new IRB members.
3. Role-play three or four typical scenarios involving evaluation studies that have ethical omissions or problems.
4. When reviewing the first two or three cases, step back and examine the process that you used in arriving at your decisions as well as the decisions themselves. You may also want to ask a more experienced IRB to review your deliberations and decisions.
5. Consider combining your IRB with a human rights committee if you have one. However, be sure to distinguish how the review process for approving an evaluation and the process of reviewing a client human rights case are different.
6. Make sure that the IRB is formally accountable to someone in the agency in an authority position, such as the executive director or an assistant director. Make sure this person is assigned with the responsibility for overseeing the training and operation of the IRB and a budget necessary to meet the resource needs of the IRB.

Conduct Your Own Evaluations

The NASW Code also encourages social workers to conduct their own evaluations within agencies or to assist others in doing so (Sections 5.02[a] and [c]). Social workers are encouraged to "monitor and evaluate policies, the implementation of programs, and our practice interventions."

At this point, you may have questions, such as, "What if I don't have an interest in conducting evaluation studies?" The Code of Ethics encourages everyone to participate in evaluation studies. Despite whether someone wants to conduct an evaluation, as a professional, social workers are obligated to do so. If they do not, evaluations conducted without their input and leadership will likely overlook the particular perspectives and experiences they have as a result of direct contact with clients. The NASW Code also states, "Social workers should critically examine and keep current with emerging knowledge relevant to social work and fully use evaluation and research evidence in their professional practice." This is the ultimate reason for us to both support and facilitate evaluation studies by others and to conduct them ourselves. We have an ethical obligation to learn about the most up-to-date knowledge and skills available in our specific fields of practice.

Protect Participants of Evaluation Studies

The NASW Code indicates that it is essential that we protect the research participants, who are usually our clients, from any adverse consequences of an evaluation study (Section 5.02[d] and [j]). Such problems often occur inadvertently because the evaluator has not given enough forethought to consequences or may have decided that the potential contributions from a study outweigh the potential problems that participants experience.

Several types of ethical problems could adversely affect participants of a study, including physical harm, psychological harm, invasion of privacy, or deception. There have been many studies known to harm participants. The Tuskegee Institute study, conducted in the 1930s to determine the adverse effects of untreated syphilis, is a classic example. In that study, African American men were deliberately deceived and effective treatment was deliberately withheld. By the time the study's ethical violations were exposed, twenty-eight men had died from syphilis, one hundred others had died of related complications, at least forty of the men's wives were infected, and nineteen of their children had contracted the disease at birth.

Although such studies are no longer conducted in the United States (thanks to regulations enacted by governmental agencies, universities, and other groups), evaluation studies can still result in physical harm today, even if that harm is not as horrific as in the Tuskegee Institute study. Examples of harm include asking vulnerable people unnecessary sensitive questions or withholding essential services from a client assigned to a control group.

Some evaluation studies also have the potential to cause psychological harm. Although psychological harm is likely to be less tangible and more difficult to detect than physical harm, it can have an equally damaging impact on participants. Evaluations can cause psychological harm, for example, particularly in investigations of sexually abusive experiences of children or adolescents or the dreams of someone with psychosis. The issue of psychological harm is complicated because the harm can manifest immediately after participation in a study or several months or years later.

Evaluation studies can also unnecessarily invade participants' privacy, and they are considered unethical if the possibility of such an invasion of privacy is not pointed out to participants beforehand. It is best to avoid such evaluations unless there is a strong justification to the contrary. People who have difficulty saying no to requests to participate in studies are among the most likely to be susceptible to invasion of privacy. Examples of evaluation study topics likely to invade some people's privacy are those that ask about alcohol or drug practices, sexual orientation, or clinical diagnoses. These evaluation topics are still legitimate if participants provide informed consent, if support is made available to them, and if there is adequate justification to explore these topics.

Deceiving a person into participating in an evaluation can also be harmful. Evaluators can have good reasons to deceive participants, such as minimizing a reactive effect from sharing too many details about the study's purpose or hypotheses. Nevertheless, such deception still can have ethical implications. The *60 Minutes II* undercover episode described subsequently is an example of the administration and staff of a psychiatric facility being deceived. Yet the investigation led to the reform of a facility that was harming its patients. The dilemma embedded in the example is obvious. Although the use of deception in an investigation is wrong, so are unsound professional practices. A decision had to be made about whether the intent of the study and the deception involved outweighed the professional agency's right to privacy. What do you think?

Example of Deception

The former television news-magazine program *60 Minutes II* hired a social worker as an undercover investigator to observe life in a psychiatric facility (O'Neill, 1999). The social worker concealed a videotape recorder in his shirt and a camera in his unusually thick eyeglasses while working as a mental health technician at a private psychiatric hospital. The CBS network was motivated to initiate the story after hearing of the death of a sixteen-year-old boy who had been restrained at a facility owned by the same company. The investigation documented many appalling conditions at the institution, including fraudulent and sometimes bogus case reporting, an understaffed facility, neglect in giving potentially dangerous drugs, and the restraint of juveniles by staff without training. Two facilities owned by the company were closed after the airing of the episode. The episode also led to renewed activities by Congress and mental health advocates to monitor and reform options available for using restraints.

Obtain Voluntary Informed Consent from Evaluation Participants

An informed consent protocol can be designed to address many of the concerns raised about potential ethical problems of studies, including physical and psychological harm, invasion of privacy, and deception. Informed consent means that the participants of a study are thoroughly informed about the study before they agree to participate (American Evaluation Association, 2007; NASW, 1999). Evaluation participants should give informed consent before they are encouraged to participate in any study. The information provided with informed consent is to be clearly communicated and presented at the level of the participants' understanding. It has been suggested that informed consent documentation be written at no higher than a sixth-grade reading level to ensure that it is simple enough to understand. Several types of information should be explicitly covered in an informed consent protocol including (Dudley, 2005):

- The general purpose of the evaluation
- The evaluator's qualifications and agency affiliation
- The expectations of the participant (e.g., number and length of interviews, location and time of interviews, types of questions)
- Assurance of confidentiality; when participants cannot be assured of confidentiality, participants must be told about how their identities will be revealed and to whom
- Identification of any potential negative effects of the evaluation on participants
- Identification of any potential benefits to participants as a result of their participation
- A reminder that participants can leave the study at any time without negative consequences, such as loss of client services (NASW, 1999, Section 5.02[h])
- A name and phone number of someone at the agency who can respond to participants' questions or concerns

An Ethics Exercise

Assume that you work for a family services agency that provides various services. In discussing your caseload with other social workers, you discover that many of your cases include children whose father is not present. You want to conduct a needs assessment to find out whether the children have any contact with their father and how the absence affects them. You decide to ask the children several personal questions and want to consider any possible negative effects of the questions. Answer the following exercise questions:

- What ethical issues are evident as you prepare for the study?
- How will you address these issues?

- What types of questions, if any, would you decide not to ask the children to protect them?
- Would you ask questions of children of all ages or just some age groups? How would your questions be different depending on the child's age?

It is also important to consider the ethical principles of the AEA (2007) for informed consent protocol. For example, while the purpose of the evaluation needs to be explained, a balance of information is recommended. Giving too much information about the evaluation could create a reactive effect in which the participants respond with what they perceive the evaluator wants to hear. Yet, giving too little information could be perceived as being deceptive and unethical.

Preferably, informed consent is provided to participants in written form. The advantages of written informed consent are important; for example, participants can easily review the forms, which makes them easier to understand, and participants can keep a copy of the form for their records. Also, information provided by the evaluator in writing cannot be easily questioned at a later time, particularly if any legal issues arise. A participant's signature on the informed consent form is clear evidence of consent. Most universities and social agencies require written consent for many of these reasons.

There are some limitations to written informed consent. For example, it is still possible that participants misunderstand some aspects of the evaluation. Therefore, a written explanation of the study should also be provided to participants and discussed with them to make sure that they fully understand. Such a discussion is particularly helpful with people who have limited cognitive skills or distorted thinking processes as a result of mental illness. It is also important to fully inform involuntary clients, who may need to hear more than once that participation is voluntary.

Evaluation studies with questionnaires involve special circumstances. The informed consent information can be included in a cover letter or in the introductory paragraphs of the questionnaire. In this case, no one is usually available to answer any questions, so the informed consent must be fully self-explanatory. Participants usually are not asked to sign their names for consent in order to keep the questionnaire anonymous. Instead, the evaluator assumes that participants who voluntarily fill out the questionnaire and return it accept the informed consent provisions.

Steps to Follow in Constructing and Using an Informed Consent Form

1. Check to see what your agency requires to protect evaluation participants.
2. Find out whether the agency has an IRB to approve studies; if not, propose that an ad hoc IRB be set up for this purpose.

3. Consider all of the following information in your efforts to inform the participants about the study:
   - Purpose of the study
   - How the results will be used
   - What will be expected of the participant
   - Your affiliation with a social agency
   - Any possible harmful effects from participating in the study
   - Possible benefits of participation
   - Confidentiality
   - Optional participation and ability to withdraw at any time
   - Contact information for someone who can answer questions and concerns
4. Find out if there are any mechanisms in place to assist participants if they experience any harmful effects (e.g., dealing with difficult emotions).
5. If children are participants, decide how you will inform and involve their parents. If other clients have guardians, decide how you will involve them as well.
6. With all the information that you have collected so far, prepare a draft of the informed consent forms or statements.
7. Get feedback from your IRB or ad hoc committee on the adequacy of the informed consent form.
8. Decide how you will protect the privacy and confidentiality of participants during data collection and the presentation of findings?
9. Describe your plans to store and protect the data, including informed consent forms. Also indicate when you will destroy the data if the agency has no further use for it.
10. Seek agency approval of your study.

Address Participants Who Are Incapable of Giving Informed Consent

In the special case of evaluation studies that involve children or clients with legal guardians, the parents or guardians must give informed consent in their place (NASW, 1999, Standard 5.02[f]). Although this extra step may seem a complication or inconvenience, legal guardians must make the decision on participation. In addition, even though the children and other clients without guardianship are not legally responsible, they should be treated with equal respect and given a thorough explanation of the study and the option to not participate. An assent form with all the information about the study, the same as is covered in the informed consent form, should be prepared for the children and others with guardians to sign. Thus, two informed consent procedures are needed.

Protect the Confidentiality of Participants

The NASW Code mentions several ways to protect the confidentiality of the participants (Sections 5.02[k]–[m]). As indicated earlier, participants' confidentiality or anonymity should be protected, and participants should be informed of the specific measures taken to ensure confidentiality and of when their responses will be destroyed. Exceptions to confidentiality should also be explained, such as if participants respond in a way that indicates that they or another person is at risk of harm.

Participants should be informed that their responses will not be associated in any way with their name or any other identifying information. Sometimes a funding agency, such as a state agency, may require identifying information in connection with responses. In such instances, it is important to explain to participants why they will be identified and to whom they will be identified (e.g., specific groups or officials). Such an exception should be stated in the initial informed consent with an explanation of why it is required. At that time, participants should also be told that they can voluntarily withdraw from the evaluation without penalization.

Finally, measures must be taken to ensure that the information that participants share in an evaluation will only be discussed for professional purposes and only with people professionally concerned with this information. Such results are not to be shared casually or as an outlet for casual conversation or entertainment.

Participants' Access to Support Services

Evaluators also have a responsibility to protect participants by providing access to support services when negative effects of participation in the evaluation do occur (NASW 1999, Section 5.02[i]). This is particularly important if participants are vulnerable in some way or if their participation could result in any physical or psychological harm. Support services could be offered by the agency sponsoring the evaluation or by a referral agency that can provide treatment or other assistance.

In the case of the needs assessment of the children of an absent father cited earlier, the social workers or counselors assigned to serve these children can be alerted to the sensitivity of the questions so that they can explore any troubling feelings that the children reveal (e.g., hurt, abandonment, guilt). The social workers counseling the children could also take the initiative to ask the residential parent to fill out a questionnaire periodically to uncover any problems in adjustment. Once the study is over, the agency could even consider offering a program of older males as mentors or friends with whom the children can spend time.

Evaluations and Evaluators without a Conflict of Interest

Professionals chosen to conduct evaluations should be free of any conflicts of relationships (AEA, 2007; NASW, 1999). They should avoid and be alert to dual relationships with study participants and other stakeholders. For example, evaluators should not oversee programs or client services at the same time that they conduct an evaluation of the programs and clients because of the possible role conflicts.

One way for the evaluator to avoid conflicts of interest is to hire qualified outside evaluators who have no stake in the study results. If agency-based evaluators, for example, obtain results that are negative or potentially damaging to the agency, they should not be pressured to minimize or ignore such results in their presentations.

Misrepresentation of the findings of a study and other actions that compromise the study's integrity and safety of the participants must also be addressed (NASW 1999, Section 5.02[n]). For similar reasons, agency staff members who conduct evaluations may be inclined to manipulate findings, such as by omitting certain results or falsifying findings that could be counterproductive to an agency and its programs. The hiring of qualified outside evaluators ensures that they have the autonomy and freedom to report all significant findings, similar in some ways to a journal's peer-review panel of experienced professionals, which is a valuable safeguard in preventing the publication of misrepresented findings.

Checklist of Questions to Consider in Hiring an Outside Evaluator (Fitzpatrick, Sanders, & Worthen, 2004)

1. Does the evaluator have the ability to use the methodologies and techniques that may be required in the study?
2. Does the evaluator have the ability to help articulate the appropriate focus for the study?
3. Does the evaluator have the management skills to carry out the study?
4. Will the evaluator maintain appropriate ethical standards?
5. Will the evaluator be interested in and able to communicate results to desired stakeholders in such a way that they will be used?

Diversity and Social Justice

The CSWE mandates that every BSW and MSW program prepare its students with understanding, respect, and methods to help people from diverse backgrounds, those experiencing social injustice, and populations that are at risk. Because social workers typically work with a diverse population of clients that are often oppressed and at risk, this mandate is critical to meet the needs of people in a culturally competent way (CSWE, 2002a). This, of course, means being responsive to these issues when conducting program and practice evaluations.

Diversity and Its Importance to Evaluation

When we fully consider the term *diversity*, we are talking about an almost unlimited number of characteristics that distinguish people. The NASW Code of Ethics (1999) highlights several characteristics of diversity that are particularly important in preparing social workers with cultural competence and sensitivity to social diversity: "Social workers should obtain education about and seek to understand the nature of social diversity and oppression with respect to race, ethnicity, national origin, color, sex, sexual orientation, age, marital status, political belief, religion, and mental or physical disability."

Although the code has helped narrow the list of characteristics of diversity considerably, the list is still rather long. We know that often these areas of diversity comprise minority groups or groups that are more vulnerable than others, such as people with serious needs, hardships, and diseases and people experiencing various forms of oppression.

So what does it mean to give special attention to diversity in evaluation? Fortunately, diversity has become a normative aspect of social work research in recent years. Evaluations conducted by social workers typically include participants who are women; people of color; and people of different social classes, sexual orientations, disabilities, and age. Also, theoretical perspectives in social work have expanded to include feminism and Afrocentrism, and to a lesser extent perspectives emphasizing the cultural needs of Latinos, Asian Americans, and recent immigrant groups; gays and lesbians; disability groups; and others (Anderson & Carter, 2003). International issues are also becoming more important as we increasingly realize that we live in a global community and depend on a global economy. However, many of these exciting developments are in an early formative stage and need to be expanded.

Diversity issues are important to consider in evaluations during all stages: conceptualization, planning, and implementation. For example, some possible diversity issues to consider when planning an evaluation study include the following:

- Are the participants able to read?
- Are there any language barriers?
- Are face-to-face interviews conducted in a location that feels safe and is easily accessible for the interviewee?
- Will some important groups be inadvertently excluded in a phone interview study?

- Will any group have discomfort or difficulty participating in an interview study?
- Will some groups choose to be excluded if an observational approach is used?
- How will difficult-to-reach groups such as racial minorities, people with very low incomes, undocumented workers, and those who do not speak English be recruited and involved?

A growing number of journals have recently sprung up that focus on issues of diversity and international issues. Many of their articles report on evaluations of some type. The journals include *Affilia: The Journal of Women and Social Work, Ethnic and Racial Studies, Indian Journal of Social Work, Journal of Gay and Lesbian Social Services, Journal of Gerontological Social Work, Hispanic Journal of Behavioral Sciences, Human Services in the Rural Environment, Journal of Multicultural Social Work, International Social Work, Journal of Immigrant and Refugee Services,* and *European Journal of Social Work.*

Example of Chinese Hospice Patients

Mak (2002) interviewed thirty-three Chinese patients in a hospice program to investigate how they perceived features of a "good death." The qualitative study uncovered seven elements or themes that can be helpful to hospice interventions: being aware of dying, maintaining hope, being free from pain and suffering, experiencing personal control, maintaining connectedness to others, preparing to depart, and accepting the timing of one's death. Acceptance of the timing of death was reported to be easier in four circumstances: if the person had completed his or her social roles (e.g., parenting), if the person had reached an old age, if the person had a religious faith to help facilitate a hope in a better life after death, and if the person had experienced a meaningful life.

Although the general diversity characteristics proposed by CSWE (e.g., race, ethnicity, social class, gender) are vitally important in conducting evaluations, additional types of diversity are also important within specific client groups (Dudley, 2005). For example, if an evaluator is investigating the impact of mental health, substance abuse, or developmental disabilities programs, some aspects of those clients' diversity could be overlooked. Programs for people with developmental disabilities could have varying degrees of impact given the different levels of disability (mild, moderate, severe, and profound) or the different causal or etiological factors (e.g., Down's syndrome, cerebral palsy, environmental factors). Evaluations of programs for people with mental illness should consider the wide range of diagnoses of mental illnesses as well as whether they are acute or chronic. Programs for people who have survived physical and psychological abuse can have varying impact given current family arrangements, who the perpetrators were, environmental circumstances, and a history of abuse in family members' own family of origin. In summary, evaluations must consider the impact of programs with respect to the various characteristics of diversity that affect clients. Ultimately, it is up to the evaluator to be sensitive to and identify the various effects of interventions as a result of clients' diversity.

Example of a Needs Assessment That Addresses Diversity in Homelessness

Two social workers conducted a needs assessment of homeless people in St. Louis (North & Smith, 1994) to investigate and document the varied ways that white and minority men and women were thought to experience homelessness. The sensitivity of the authors to diversity issues was commendable in that they broke down all of their results by race and gender. Essentially, they compared the circumstances of four subgroups (i.e., nonwhite men, white men, nonwhite women, white women). On the negative side, they grouped all people of color together under the category of "nonwhite" and neglected to differentiate among African Americans, Latinos, and Native Americans.

Social and Economic Justice and Their Relevance to Evaluation

Another special mandate promulgated by the CSWE is that social work programs give special emphasis to issues of social and economic justice. One section of the CSWE (2002a) educational policy describes three objectives for graduates in fulfilling this mandate. Social workers are expected to

- "Practice without discrimination and with respect, knowledge, and skills related to clients' age, class, color, culture, disability, ethnicity, family structure, gender, marital status, national origin, race, religion, and sexual orientation."
- "Understand the forms and mechanisms of oppression and discrimination and apply strategies of advocacy and social change that advance social and economic justice."
- "Function within the structure of organizations and service delivery systems and seek necessary organizational change."

These mandates are important to address in program and practice evaluation activities as well as in social work practice. According to the values and ethics of the profession, social workers are encouraged to develop knowledge that promotes the welfare of all people and especially of disadvantaged groups. In other words, evaluations can be an empowering process for social work clients.

There are several ways to conduct program evaluations with a social justice dimension or emphasis. Some of the subsequent examples suggest that the entire focus of a program evaluation can be on a social justice issue, while others may include only a social justice component.

- Evaluating the effectiveness of job-training and employment programs for people with disabilities on the basis of whether they gain better employment in the competitive job market
- Documenting the ways that people with disabilities are discriminated against in hiring practices
- Evaluating programs for homeless people by investigating how the programs help them obtain improved jobs, jobs with longevity, and higher incomes that can sustain them
- Executing a needs assessment of homeless people that documents the extent to which those who are employed cannot afford decent housing
- Eliciting the viewpoints of client groups such as those with AIDS, schizophrenia, gays or lesbians, teenage parents, or former inmates to explore the extent to which the programs they use perpetrate their problems with stigma
- Any evaluation that interviews difficult-to-reach clients rather than relies on more accessible secondary sources, such as a family member or someone in a social support network

A Practitioner's Thinking Outside of the Box

A social worker, Sharon Galusky, naturally reveals her understanding of the connections between evaluation and social justice when she describes the various ways she evaluates her practice as a case manager helping people with developmental disabilities. First, she describes the regulations that Medicaid, the funding agency, requires that she address in her agency documentation to receive reimbursement for her services. She then explains that she has additional criteria that she feels compelled to use to evaluate the effectiveness of her work as a case manager. She knows that one of her major goals with her clients is to help them reach a higher quality of life, so she and her clients have devised additional individualized criteria for each client, such as helping one find a higher-paying job and finding another a volunteer position in which he can offer advice about saving money while grocery shopping (Sharon Galusky, MSW social worker at Open Doors Inc., Charlotte, NC, personal communication, July 2007).

Incorporating Diversity and Social Justice into Evaluations

There are numerous specific ways to incorporate perspectives on diversity and promotion of social and economic justice into evaluations. First, it is important to identify and invite involvement from a diverse group of stakeholders, including people who represent the clients that the agency serves. Second, several initiatives can be considered at each step of the evaluation process.

During step 1 (identify a problem to be evaluated) and step 2 (identify and explore ways to involve stakeholders), several potential stakeholders from the client population, former clients, and the local community can be asked along with other stakeholders to offer their views about a program-related problem or concern that requires evaluation. Because they will not know the perspectives of the agency administrators and staff members, they will likely benefit from an orientation to such information. However, their unique perspectives as clients and family members of clients need to be explored with questions such as the following:

- What programs have you or your family members used?
- How would you describe the agency and its programs and services given your experiences?
- What stands out to you as particularly helpful? What stands out as weak or problematic?

Having discussions with some of these stakeholders in step 1 will be helpful in revealing who they are, their particular positions, how their views vary, and their skills and confidence in effectively communicating what they think. Among such a group of potential stakeholders, a few can be selected to assist in an evaluation. One approach to working with stakeholders is to create an advisory committee or collaborative team of stakeholders, including clients and community members, to assist and support the evaluators in the subsequent steps of the evaluation. Another approach is to periodically consult various stakeholders on an individual basis at a time and place convenient to them.

Step 3 (determine the purpose of the evaluation) focuses the evaluation on a particular problem or concern. This step is a critical one for considering diversity and social justice issues. All stakeholder groups, particularly those representing the client population, can be encouraged to give input on the purpose of the evaluation and the social change that the evaluation could accomplish. Some of the questions that could be posed to the client stakeholders include the following:

- What interventions have been particularly useful to you and others that you know? Which ones have not helped?
- In your opinion, what seem to be the most important ingredients in an effective approach to helping clients like yourself?

- How have the interventions assisted you in reaching your personal goals over time?
- What would you like for the interventions to do differently to help bring positive change into your life?
- What difficulties have you or your family members experienced, if any, in receiving services from these programs and practice areas?

Step 4 (plan the evaluation) can raise many design issues, such as which single-system design to use, who to interview, what questions to ask, and how large a sample should be. Both professionals and lay stakeholders will need some training to participate, in an informed way, in such decisions. Some of the design questions have a diversity or social justice component; for example:

- Have we considered all important demographic characteristics in selecting the sample?
- What are some of the ways to reach a former client when we do not have a forwarding address or phone number?
- How can we formulate specific questions to encourage accurate answers?
- How does a program intervention further social justice for clients?
- How does an intervention strengthen clients rights and responsibilities?

Example of an Evaluation Exploring Diversity

An evaluation (Dudley, 1986) revealed that a community organization was established in a multiethnic community experiencing interracial strife in a large city. Approximately one hundred Southeast Asian (Hmong and Cambodian) people had been relocated from their native countries to this neighborhood. The neighborhood had mostly comprised African Americans and Puerto Ricans before the relocation. The organization initiated several programs over two years to address the multiethnic strife, including a series of cultural events in which each group shared its customs, food, arts, leisure activities, and so on, with the larger community. Two years later, seventeen of the Southeast Asian residents were interviewed to explore the impact of events on their attitudes and intergroup exchanges. The respondents recalled fairly accurately the events that they had attended, and fourteen admitted having learned something from the events. Five volunteered that the events improved their multiethnic understanding. When asked if they had developed any intergroup friendships, eleven of the seventeen indicated having made friends of a different nationality. Although most relationships were rather limited, almost all were with African American or Puerto Rican neighbors.

Step 5 (implement the evaluation) involves carrying out the plans and procedures worked out in step 4. Orientation could be provided to assist stakeholders in becoming involved in contributing to this step in an informed way. Stakeholders could be useful in carrying out many aspects of this step, such as by suggesting strategies to find and engage participants who are difficult to contact or interview, contacting community and civic organizations to help identify participants for the study and offer a site for data collection, and assisting in data collection.

Step 6 (prepare a written or oral report) is one of the most important steps in which to involve stakeholders, as the findings are intended to inform them and help them take action. Report findings should be in a format accessible to all stakeholder groups. Client and community stakeholders in particular are often overlooked when preparing an evaluation report. To overcome this omission, evaluators would be remiss if they did not prepare a report that was relevant to clients and made available to them in some form. Formats that may be most helpful to these stakeholders may be fliers on a bulletin board, brief reports in agency and community newsletters, and informal presentations during client sessions.

Finally, step 7 (disseminate the results) is another critical step for stakeholders because they know a lot about how and when to disseminate evaluation findings in a manner that is relevant and useful to constituents. Evaluation findings can be disseminated in numerous creative ways. For example, evaluation findings intended to inform people and elicit feedback include community forums, regular civic and other neighborhood meetings, church gatherings, and community fairs. Further, stakeholders are valuable as resources in disseminating the results of an evaluation and receiving feedback on proposed next steps for an agency.

Example of an Evaluation Focusing on Empowerment Issues in Practice

Linhorst, Hamilton, Young, and Eckert (2002) reviewed existing documents and conducted focus groups with clients and staff of a public psychiatric hospital to identify barriers to client empowerment. They attempted to identify the conditions necessary for empowerment to occur, especially in getting clients to participate in their own treatment planning. The results revealed several empowerment issues, including the need to prepare clients with decision-making skills, to provide a range of treatment options, to ensure enough time for client participation in the planning process, and to promote staff attitudes that are respectful of clients' ability and potential to participate in treatment planning.

Overall, diversity and social justice concerns can be infused in all or most steps of the evaluation process. The suggestions herein are flexible and apply to numerous types of evaluations. The main point of the discussion in this part has been to make serious efforts to involve stakeholders most likely to be affected by the problem being addressed in the evaluation.

Key Terms

Confidentiality
Diversity issues
Ethical principles of the AEA
Informed consent
Informed consent form
Institutional review board (IRB)
Section 5.02 of the NASW Code of Ethics
Social justice issues

Discussion Questions and Assignments

1. Have groups of three to five people to work on each of the following scenarios of ethical issues in evaluation.

Scenario 1: You have been assigned to conduct an assessment of the needs of older adults in a community surrounding your agency, a senior center. You want to know whether the older adults would use some of your center's existing services and new services that you are considering, including exercise groups, conversation groups, lunches, and nutritional workshops. You plan to conduct a phone interview and will call a representative sample of households in the community.

Questions:
1. What will you say/do to provide informed consent? What will you do if someone does not want to respond to phone interviews or wants to know more about your legitimacy?
2. What will you do if the person who answers the phone only speaks Spanish or another non-English language?
3. If the person who answers the phone is not an older adult but the household has older adults living there, how will you proceed? For example, what if the older adult is hesitant to speak, or the person answering the phone is determined to respond for her or him? What can you do to ensure that the older adult's voice is heard?

Scenario 2: You are a supervisor and you want to evaluate the impact of counseling groups on their members or clients. You want a noninvolved social worker to observe the group, but you are concerned that this evaluation could disrupt the group leader or inhibit participation of group members.

Questions:
1. What ethical issues may need to be considered in this observational study? How would you address them?

2. What will you say and/or do with the group leader and group members to gain informed consent?

3. How can you minimize disruptions in the group process during an observation?

2. A social worker informs you that she is providing a unique sexual counseling program to several clients with cognitive challenges. No one else in her agency or any other agency that she knows about is offering such a program. In addition, her agency administrator is not asking her to evaluate her program; the administrator is just pleased that she is offering her services. This social worker consults you to ask what she should do. Should she continue providing her services without an evaluation plan? Or should she devise an evaluation? What specific suggestions would you have for her in conducting an evaluation?

3. Assume that you conducted a study three months ago in which you asked a group of clients to complete a questionnaire that measured their progress in improving communication skills since they had first received services from the agency. At the beginning of the program, they were told that the findings would be kept strictly confidential and their names would not be included with any responses. However, now the agency wants to use the findings to evaluate the individual progress of each client. You have the original data and information on who filled out each questionnaire. What ethical issues are involved in this situation? What should you do?

4. What are two advantages and disadvantages of using an outside evaluator (instead of a staff member) to conduct an evaluation in your agency? What are some criteria you might use to select an outside evaluator?

5. Assume you are an evaluator who has been asked to assist in preparing pretest and posttest instruments for an evaluation of a premarital workshop for couples. The evaluation is intended to measure the extent to which the participants improved in their communication with each other in several areas, including their sexual needs. You are asked to come to a board meeting to explain what the evaluation is all about. During the board meeting, an officer of the board states that he would like to add a "newly effective method of natural child birth" as a topic to add to the premarital workshops. He points out that he knows of a study that found that the divorce rate was significantly lower for a group of couples practicing this new form of natural birth control. He doesn't give the board members a specific reference for this study. Up to this point, no material had been offered in previous workshops on specific forms of birth control or family planning. As the evaluator you are concerned that this seems like it may be an effort to emphasize one form of birth control over other

forms based on the religious preference of this board member. As the evaluator you are not a member of the board and do not attend board meetings on a regular basis. What would you do?

References

American Evaluation Association. (2007). The principles of the American Evaluation Association. Fairhaven, MA: American Evaluation Association. (Available from http://www.eval.org).

Anderson, J., & Carter, R. (Eds.). (2003). *Diversity perspectives for social work practice.* Boston: Allyn & Bacon.

Council on Social Work Education. (2002a). CSWE educational policy 3.0: Foundation program objectives. Alexandria, VA: Author.

Council on Social Work Education. (2002b). Educational policy and accreditation standards (sections renumbered December 2001). Alexandria, VA: Author.

Dudley, J. R. (1986). *Program evaluation of Logan Community Development Assistance Project and Logan Community Development Corporation* (Philadelphia). Unpublished manuscript.

Dudley, J. R. (2005). *Research methods for social work: Becoming consumers and producers of research.* Boston: Allyn & Bacon.

Fitzpatrick, J. L., Sanders, J. R., & Worthen, B. R. (2004). *Program evaluation: Alternative approaches and practical guidelines.* Boston: Pearson.

Linhorst, D., Hamilton, G., Young, E., & Eckert, A. (2002). Opportunities and barriers to empowering people with severe mental illness through participation in treatment planning. *Social Work, 47*(4), 425–434.

Mak, M. H. J. (2002). Accepting the timing of one's death: An experience of Chinese hospice patients. *Omega, 45*(3), 245–260.

Marlow, C. (2005). *Research methods for generalist social work* (4th ed.). Stamford, CT: Thomson Learning.

National Association of Social Workers. (1999). Code of ethics of the National Association of Social Workers (approved by the 1996 NASW Delegate Assembly and revised by the 1999 NASW Delegate Assembly). Washington, DC: Author.

North, C., & Smith, E. (1994). Comparison of white and non-white homeless men and women, *Social Work, 39*(6), 637–649.

O'Neill, J. (1999). Advocacy takes a new tack. *NASW News, 44*(8), 4.

Reese, D., Ahern, R., Nair, S., O'Faire, J., & Warren, C. (1999). Hospice access and use by African Americans: Addressing cultural and institutional barriers through participatory action research. *Social Work, 44*(6), 549–559.

Chapter 4

Commonly Used Evaluation Models

Which evaluation models are readily practiced in the everyday world of social agencies?

Anyone wanting to conduct an evaluation in today's world has many models from which to choose. One overall consideration, of course, is to decide whether you want to conduct a program or a practice evaluation, an important distinction. A further way to differentiate evaluations is to consider variations in methodology, especially whether you wish to use quantitative, qualitative, or mixed methods. There are many other ways to distinguish evaluations, and both experienced and novice evaluators are encouraged to become familiar with them. They are referred to as *models* in this chapter because they are practical approaches that are readily evident in numerous settings in which social workers and other human service workers are employed. These models are different from the perspectives and approaches described in chapter 2, which are largely theoretical.

The purpose of the chapter is to acquaint readers with most of the evaluation models commonly used in social agencies. After reading this chapter, you should be able to identify them in your agency, attach names to them, and have a general understanding of their respective purposes. Most of these types of evaluations are commonly practiced in social agencies, hospitals, health departments, schools, and residential and institutional programs across the country, and most are elaborated on in later chapters when we get further into the implementation of an evaluation. Let's first look at common models of program evaluation followed by models of practice evaluation.

Common Models of Program Evaluation

The program evaluation models presented here vary considerably in terms of the extent that they are research oriented and use systematic and rigorous research methods. Some of the models are naturally viewed as research models. Outcome studies are a good example: their designs have to be rigorous to be able to accurately determine whether an intervention has a positive impact on clients' outcomes. Other models such as quality assurance studies may be designed to be less rigorous. However, the research rigor that is evident in any of these models depends largely on the evaluators and their commitment to the methodology.

The models to be presented include needs assessments, program monitoring, client satisfaction studies, outcome studies, efficiency and cost-benefit analysis studies, licensing of programs serving clients, licensing of professionals, auditing and other accounting investigations, accreditation of social programs, quality assurance studies, court decisions, and newspaper and other media reports.

Needs Assessments

Needs assessments are a type of evaluation that usually occurs prior to implementing a program. These assessments are used to determine whether there is enough documentation of the need for a new or expanded program or to justify the initiation of a program. Needs assessments often use questionnaires disseminated to the potential users of proposed programs. Other methods of data collection include informant interviewing, focus groups, public forums, and use of existing data from such documents as the Current Population Surveys, conducted periodically by the U.S. Census. Needs assessments are more fully described in chapter 6.

Example of a Needs Assessment

Two social workers (Muehlbauer & Runnberg, 2006) conducted a basic needs assessment of immigrants and refugees who were students of an English as a second language program in Duluth, Minnesota. They conducted face-to-face interviews with twenty-three students using both forced response and open-ended questions. The students were from several countries in Asia (China, Laos, Thailand, Vietnam), Poland, Bosnia, Ecuador, Russia, Germany, and Somalia. Among the questions that the authors asked were the reasons they were living in the Duluth area, the amount of time they had spent in the United States and in Duluth, their employment status, and the extent to which they spoke English. They were also asked whether they had health and dental insurance. In addition, they were asked simple questions about their mental status (e.g., "Do you often feel sad or cry easily?") and their worries, joys, and dreams. The results revealed a variety of needs, ranging from medical and dental care to qualitative comments about joys and worries.

Program Monitoring

A wide variety of evaluations are used to monitor how an existing program is functioning. Program-monitoring evaluations are also referred to as evaluations of program processes. They may be initiated voluntarily by an agency sponsoring the program or required by funding or regulatory agencies. These evaluations ask such questions as the following:

- Is the program reaching its intended target population?
- Is the program being implemented as it was proposed?
- Do current staff members evidence equal employment and affirmative action policies?
- How do employees spend their time?
- Are clients satisfied with the program?
- Are agency facilities safe and accessible (e.g., are elevators to upper floors available for clients in wheelchairs)?

Program monitoring typically uses many different types of data-collection strategies, such as questionnaires given out to clients or staff members, individual and group interviewing of staff and clients, observations of programs and specific interactions between staff members and clients, reviews of existing documents such as client files and personnel documents, and use of consulting experts.

Client Satisfaction Studies

The purpose of client satisfaction studies is to find out how the clients are feeling and perceiving the services that they are receiving. These evaluations usually elicit the views of a fairly large number of clients, perhaps all those receiving the services of a program or all who have completed a program. These studies use either questionnaires or interview strategies to ask clients a series of questions about the various dimensions of a program.

The results of client satisfaction studies can provide helpful insights and other ideas about improving a program or even clearing up clients' misperceptions of programs. The results also offer numerous opportunities for service providers to engage in informal conversations with clients on topics for which they have different views. These conversations can be conducted without violating confidentiality if they are simply introduced as general topics deriving from the responses to client satisfaction evaluations.

How Much Do Clients and Staff Agree about Client Satisfaction?

A client satisfaction interview was conducted with people with a dual diagnosis of mental illness and mental retardation. There were twenty-one forced-response questions, such as "Do you like living here?" "Do staff listen to you or ignore you?" and "Do the staff treat you like a child or an adult?" (Dudley, 2002). The same questions were asked of the staff member who knew each client best, but staff were asked to guess the clients' answers to each question. The results revealed agreement 60 percent or more of the time on seventeen of the twenty-one questions. However, there were some discrepancies, such as a question on whether the clients wanted to continue to live at their current residence (more clients said they wanted to leave than staff guessed) and whether they felt afraid rather than safe (more clients felt afraid than staff guessed).

The clients' responses to satisfaction questions are undoubtedly subjective and may be biased as a result of their status as recipients of services. Clients may not be able to be objective about those providing them services, and they could easily blame providers for problems that could be more their own. Regardless of the confidentiality promised by the evaluator, clients may also report being more positive about services than they actually are. This can happen for numerous reasons, such as a fear of jeopardizing client status, continued access to services, or desire for the approval of staff members. The accuracy of their responses also depends on whether they have adequate knowledge about what is being asked and whether they have the same understanding of what is being asked as the interviewer does. Other possibilities for error are that they may have little recall of the time frame of the questions or the specific wording used in a question.

Outcome Evaluations

Outcome evaluations are conducted to determine whether the recipients of a program are reaching the goals set for them when they began the program. These outcomes can take many forms and are typically socially desirable goals intended to help them. Outcome evaluations mostly use quasi-experimental and experimental group designs to control for, to varying degrees, other factors that could influence clients' progress on their goals. A program can usually take no more than partial responsibility for any progress that clients make. Chapter 9 is largely devoted to outcome evaluations and the various types of quasi-experimental and experimental research designs available for outcome evaluations. The results-oriented model described in chapter 2 can be considered a theoretical version of outcome evaluations.

Efficiency and Cost-Benefit Analysis Studies

Efficiency evaluations are conducted to find out whether the resources allocated to a program are being used as efficiently as possible. These studies examine the ratio of inputs to outputs, and measure the amount of a specific output (e.g., number of clients served, number of clients completing a program) against the costs. In this example, the higher the number of clients served at a fixed cost, the better. These studies usually want to get the maximum amount of money spent to help clients. A major limitation of efficiency studies is that they do not assume that program goals are being accomplished; evaluating outcomes are not part of their purpose.

In contrast, cost-benefit analysis studies are designed to determine whether programs are reaching their goals in a cost-effective way. In other words, are the incurred costs reasonable? Cost-benefit studies look at the ratio of inputs to outcomes. These studies typically aim to find out how much a program costs and whether the program is less costly than another program that has been found to be equally effective. Often cost-benefit analyses are conducted by comparing two or more programs using, for example, different approaches or different combinations of staff members and other resources. The program that meets its goals with the least amount of cost is usually the most desirable one. Examples of questions asked in cost-benefit studies that compare one program to another are the following:

- Is the per capita cost of an institutional program more or less than a community program for people with mental illness or developmental disabilities?
- Are outpatient rehabilitation programs for offenders serving time for victimless crimes less expensive per capita than are similar programs for such offenders in federal prison?
- Are the public health costs of preventing cigarette smoking among teenagers more cost effective than the public health-care cost of treating cigarette smokers for lung cancer?

Licensing of Programs

Licensing of the programs serving clients is an important form of evaluation. Licensing is usually concerned with basic health and safety standards and related concerns. Licensing is particularly relevant for residential programs, such as group homes for adolescents, people with developmental disabilities, or older adults. Also licensing is likely to be required for health-care agencies and agencies that provide meals to clients. Licensing may occur annually or more often, and it may be conducted to detect unsanitary conditions in food preparation, the adequacy of safety in bathrooms, and safety in use of floors and stairs. Licensing activities are also conducted to find out whether there are such things as fire doors, sprinkler systems, alarms, extinguishers, and adequate fire exits.

Either local or state governmental agencies usually assume responsibility for licensing programs, and the policies defining the parameters of licensing regulations are usually enacted as laws passed by legislative bodies and further developed into regulations by licensing agencies. Usually, licensing evaluations require that only minimal, not maximum, standards be met.

Licensing of Professionals

Licensing of professionals in social work and other helping professional areas is another type of evaluation. This type of licensing is becoming increasingly evident as human services become more complex and professionalized, and as expectations about client outcomes are raised to higher levels. Licensing laws exist to protect the use of a professional title, like clinical social worker, psychologist, or family therapist, so that the public can be assured that qualified people provide them with services.

State governments license professional titles, including the title of professional social worker. Many states use the acronym LCSW, which stands for licensed clinical social worker, as a standard social work title. Other titles are also often used and are viewed more as certifications than licenses. These certificates are not usually required titles for hiring; nevertheless, they provide a status that can distinguish the holder from those with fewer or different credentials. Such certification titles include certified bachelor of social work, certified master of social work, and social work manager. Although state licensing of social workers is a recent development, primarily having occurred in the past two decades, all fifty states now have some form of professional licensing for social workers.

To be professionally licensed, a person is usually required to have an advanced degree in the professional area of licensing. Additional professional employment, such as two years of post-degree practice under the supervision of a licensed supervisor, and passing an exam on the knowledge and skill areas of the profession are also usually required.

Auditing and Other Accounting Investigations

Auditing of an agency's financial affairs and other accounting measures are another form of program evaluation. In this case, the evaluation involves an independent review of the financial policies, procedures, and records of an agency to make sure that they are accurate and meet existing legal codes and procedures. Auditing is important to ensure that tax codes are followed and to detect and prevent misuse of funds by agency personnel and others. Trained accountants and tax experts who represent private firms independent of the agency being audited usually conduct audits. Obviously, audits are carried out by accountants, who have very different training from social workers. Nevertheless, social workers in administrative positions should know the basics of auditing and other accounting procedures, their varied purposes, and the appropriate procedures to follow in hiring qualified auditors and overseeing their work.

Accreditation of Social and Educational Programs

Program accreditation is another important form of evaluation. Agencies that accredit programs are concerned with programs meeting specific standards rather than the qualifications of individual professionals. Accreditation is a form of quality control that program sponsors recognize and seek out to ensure that a program meets professional standards. Because the standards of a professional accrediting organization and the policies of their member agencies are likely to differ, it is almost inevitable that the accrediting body and the agencies being accredited experience some tension and possible conflict over priorities. For example, while the member agencies are likely to base many priorities on their access to funding and the demands of their board members, accreditation groups may stress value-oriented areas, such as promoting client dignity and greater client independence. Accreditation groups are likely to expect programs to maintain relatively low ratios between the number of direct-care staff members and the recipients of services, while a member agency may feel less compelled to follow such ratios, particularly if it has a shortage of funds or wants more independence to freely transfer resources from one program to another.

What makes accreditation so unusual is that it is run by nonprofit professional organizations rather than governmental agencies. Accrediting agencies essentially propagate specific professional standards or requirements that university and agency members are expected to follow. At times, member agencies may perceive that the accreditation standards interfere with their internal decision making; they may also complain about the relatively high fees required for accreditation. Yet accreditation processes are a remarkable example of a decades-long cooperative partnership among professionally sponsored accreditation agencies, accredited member agencies, and governmental agencies that allow an independent group to enforce professional standards. Accreditation organizations are very familiar to agencies that employ social workers (table 4.1).

TABLE 4.1   Accreditation Organizations and Their Member Agencies

Accrediting organization	Web site	Member agencies
Child Welfare League	www.cwl.org	Child protection agencies, adoptions, foster care
Council on Social Work Education	www.cswe.org	BSW & MSW programs
Family Service Association of America	www.fsa.org	Family service agencies
Joint Commission on the Accreditation of Health Organizations	www.jcaho.org	Hospitals, home health
Commission on Accreditation of Rehabilitation Facilities	www.carf.org	Developmental disabilities facilities and community agencies

Accreditation is usually a voluntary process, but programs are strongly persuaded to obtain it for status and program legitimacy. Social work education accreditation, for example, is essential for both BSW and MSW degree programs that expect to succeed in admitting a critical mass of students to their programs and to gain support from their university sponsor. Furthermore, when graduates of a nonaccredited program look for jobs as professional social workers, it will not be long before they receive questions about their program's legitimacy. The benefits of graduating from an accredited program include eligibility to apply for a state social work license, ability to receive third-party payments as reimbursement for work with clients, and ability to enjoy many of the benefits of membership in NASW and other professional associations.

Quality Assurance

Quality assurance is a rather distinct collection of evaluation activities implemented in many agencies to monitor how well their programs work. The quality of the program's functioning is the obvious intent of such evaluations. Quality assurance (QA) is also sometimes referred to as quality improvement (QI) or quality control. The QA activities are implemented to gather information about the processes of programs and to determine whether they function the way they are supposed to. Such activities have their earliest origins in health-care settings and are likely to be implemented most easily in these settings. However, with some minor modifications, QA activities are also relevant to evaluation of programs in other social welfare settings, such as child welfare and aging.

Example of Quality Assurance or Improvement

Youth Homes is an agency that provides specialized foster care, residential group homes, and family-strengthening services for abused, neglected, and other at-risk children. The agency works closely with the local Department of Social Services and Office of Justice. Youth Homes has a full-time staff member, an experienced social worker with an MSW degree, assigned to oversee its QA services. The staff member works with three staff committees to conduct reviews. The Clinical Care Committee meets every eight weeks to review a random sample of client cases and another sample of high-risk cases to determine whether four types of documentation are evident in each case file and whether recommendations have been implemented. The Client Rights Committee meets quarterly and reviews client incident reports (e.g., accidents, administrative errors), client grievances, feedback from the suggestions box, results of client focus groups, and results of a client satisfaction survey (administered annually) to investigate whether the rights of the clients have been violated. The Staffing and Facilities Committee meets quarterly to review staff turnover reports, staff training reports, employee satisfaction survey results, annual staff exit interviews, and a variety of facility issues (e.g., new facility needs; assessment of vehicles; maintenance needs; fire, safety, health, and accident reports). The QA social worker convenes the committees, reviews and coordinates the committees' corrective action requests, and prepares evaluation reports quarterly and annually. The annual report is then incorporated into an annual plan that provides projected agency goals and plans for the next year (B. Lackey, quality improvement coordinator with Youth Homes, Charlotte, NC, personal communication, January 2005).

Quality assurance activities can be most easily distinguished from other program-monitoring approaches by the specific methods and techniques that are used. These methods and techniques include peer-conducted reviews, heavy reliance on client records, observation of small samples of the services, ensuring that minimal standards are met, and immediate incorporation of useful results into program improvements. These special characteristics are elaborated on next.

Peer Reviews.   First, the methods of QA involve peer reviews rather than the more typical administrative reviews. A QA approach empowers staff members to conduct their own evaluations instead of relying on administrators to conduct the reviews. Peer review teams usually include representatives of the different specializations and disciplines of the agency's staff. It should be noted that peer assessments will likely have a natural tendency to be biased in favor of the staff members' attitudes, needs, and practices over administrative perspectives. To bring some balance to this tendency and to maintain as much objectivity as possible, peer-review teams often use special methods, such as representation from all staff groups and reports to administrative staff.

Many administrators actually prefer QA activities because they are delegated to the staff members involved most directly in a program. Many administrators like this approach because it places staff members in charge of evaluating their own programs, which can instill in them a mind-set of self-evaluation. Also, delegation of QA activities can free up administrative time and energy for other important matters. From an ethical perspective, QA promotes the social work value of self-determination, as it empowers staff members to continually evaluate themselves and how they can improve.

Use of Client Records.   The QA approach typically relies on appraisals of staff revealed in client records rather than direct observation of services. Such a data source makes it much easier to conduct a review in a short period of time because records already exist and are easily accessible, whereas direct observations take considerably more time and could inconvenience or interfere with the delivery of services to clients. Also, a focus on record keeping reveals a secondary characteristic of QA; it monitors the quality of the record-keeping system, which in itself is an important means of accountability.

Reviewing Small Samples of Services.   Another methodological aspect of a QA approach is that observes only a small percentage of a program's activities and serves only as a spot check on how the program is functioning. Typically a small sample of program recipients is selected, and sometimes a sampling of only a few components of a program. In contrast, many other program evaluation approaches tend to examine all components of a program and virtually the entire client population that they access. Quality assurance typically uses random sampling to avoid selection bias, and the evaluators usually do not notify the direct service staff of when the evaluation will occur and which clients will be involved until the evaluation actually happens. Theoretically, this approach ensures that virtually every client and component of service can be included in an evaluation, thereby precluding any attempt on the part of direct service staff to select specific records to review or to prevent the review of other records.

Minimal Standards.   Another characteristic of QA is its limited goal of meeting minimal standards. On the one hand, a staff review team could easily decide that it is not important to meet exceptionally high standards. Yet lower expectations from external sources could also give a QA team more freedom and flexibility to strive for higher standards on their own with the application of self-imposed standards. A disadvantage of emphasizing minimal standards is that a QA team may not be able to focus on the more dysfunctional aspects of a program.

Immediately Implemented Results.   A final characteristic of QA is that if its findings suggest the need for program improvements, the changes can be implemented immediately. This benefit has obvious advantages over an approach that expects a study to be completed before any results are considered for implementation. In the case of QA, an administrator can take immediate steps to correct a program component or add a new procedure when an omission is discovered in program operation.

Court or Judicial Decisions

Judicial decisions are often an overlooked form of program evaluation even though they are most likely to focus on policies, not programs. Our judicial system at the local, state, and federal levels is a form of checks and balances on the executive and legislative branches of government. Class action suits in particular are pursued when all other attempts to seek justice for a group of people may have failed. A class action suit brings together a large number of people who have similar circumstances and conditions and have been treated unjustly according to an existing law. Such a lawsuit, if successful, can lead to the propagation of new or corrective policies that must be implemented as long as the suit is in existence. In this case, a special master and staff are set up to oversee implementation of the lawsuit and report to the ruling judge. The judge temporarily removes from legal responsibility the governmental agency that has been found negligent and replaces it with the judge and a special master who oversees the implementation of court-mandated corrective measures and monitors their implementation.

Although the initial focus of a class action suit is on government policies, an evaluation often is implemented to determine whether new or modified programs address the needs and problems of the class of people who are the plaintiffs. An example is a lawsuit conducted in North Carolina for more than ten years on behalf of more than 1,200 people with a dual diagnosis of mental illness and mental retardation. These class members had all been misplaced in state hospitals because there was no other reasonable alternative available (Dudley, Calhoun, & Ahlgrim-Delzell, 2002). However, by admitting them to state hospitals for a decade or more, the federal district court order specified that the plaintiff class members had their constitutional rights violated in several basic areas, including safety, protection from harm, treatment under safe conditions, freedom from undue restraint, minimally adequate habilitation or treatment, and treatment necessary to remedy any injuries caused by the class members' stay in the hospitals. A longitudinal evaluation was established to monitor how the implementation of the court order affected the class members, and it primarily focused on existing and new programs that were expected to remedy the violations incurred.

Newspaper and Other Media Reports

Television and newspaper journalistic accounts often focus on the inadequate and sometimes-scandalous conditions of social programs that purport to serve a neglected group of people. Reporters' accounts may not be considered evaluation per se, but they are typically investigations that are thorough, are based on the specific conditions of the people who are investigated, and provide valuable information to the public and those who are expected to protect them. Sometimes these reports are case studies that vividly portray one person's conditions as excerpts.

Could the State Have Saved Lynnette?

Another patient dies in mental health care. . . . The girl in the hospital bed looked nothing like Lynnette. Purple bruises covered her face, arms, chest and legs. Her mouth was swollen. Blood dripped from her nose. She had a rug burn on her shoulder. She was unconscious, and a ventilator helped her breathe. Donald Morris threw himself across her bed and cried. Ileine Morris whispered, "Mommy's here. Mommy's here." Twenty-four-year-old Lynnette Martin, who was mentally ill and mildly retarded, had suffered a head injury about eight hours earlier in a Moore County home operated by a company called Preferred Alternatives. Police believe she and her caregiver may have struggled, and Lynnette hit her head on the floor. Her caregiver waited about seven hours before calling an ambulance, police say. On December 19, Lynnette died after seven weeks in a coma. She is one of the most recent mental health patients to die under questionable circumstances while in the care of group homes, psychiatric hospitals, and other mental health facilities.

Morrises and a growing group of supporters are launching a push to change North Carolina's mental health laws, particularly for a group of 2,500 of the state's most vulnerable patients. They are adults like Lynnette, known as *Thomas S.* clients, who have both developmental disabilities and mental illness. (Cenziper, 2000)

Newspaper and television series have covered numerous stories of massive program dysfunction and have often provided the first report that educates the public on such outrages. One could say that these reports are one-sided, in favor of the people who are alleged to be exploited, but otherwise they seem to be objective in reporting what actually happens in local communities throughout the country. They can be viewed as program evaluations in the broadest sense of the term, and they are an important community tool for exposing many types of inadequate existing policies and programs provided to the public. They have been instrumental in exposing such problems as inadequate housing, the hiring of untrained workers, misuse of medications, inadequate staff supervision, safety concerns, clients' exposure to inappropriate hardships and harm, and the overlooking of groups of people who need access to a program's services.

Common Models of Practice Evaluation

Just as there are common and well-known models for evaluating programs, there are also models for evaluating professional practice that are popular across agency settings. They fall under four broad categories: (1) assessing client needs, (2) monitoring the quality of practice, (3) client satisfaction, and (4) client outcomes.

Assessing Clients' Needs

Based on the problem-solving approach, an assessment of clients' problems logically precedes the taking of any steps to help them. Assessing clients' problems and related circumstances is a common practice that is needed to determine what the next steps should be, that is, the interventions that will effectively help them. Familiar assessment tools include family genograms, ecomaps, a variety of biopsychosocial assessment tools, and assessments of client strengths and weaknesses. Family genograms provide a visual display of a family across two or more generations and offer insights into and understanding of the patterns evident in families. Ecomaps are a visual tool that identify the person-in-environment constellation of a client, including relationships with friends and family members, agencies and schools, jobs, and other social supports. Biopsychosocial assessment tools are available in most agencies and identify questions and topical areas to be explored in all three areas of a client's life: biological, psychological, and social. Sometimes these tools include assessment questions about the spiritual, mental, and cultural dimensions of a client as well. Assessments of client strengths and weaknesses, especially assessment questions about a client's strengths, are an area that is often overlooked in assessments. Cowger, Anderson, and Snively (2006), for example, have constructed an elaborate qualitative assessment tool of client strengths for use with clients.

Monitoring Practice

Process Recordings.   Social work practitioners often use various means to monitor their practice. In many cases, these monitoring efforts may not even be considered evaluations. Process recordings are one well-known practice. Supervisors and practice teachers often ask new practitioners or students to complete a process recording of a sampling of their client contacts. These recordings are then carefully reviewed in a supervisory session to explore how the social worker responded to the client's comments and conducted the session overall. Often these recordings help reveal missed opportunities to respond to a subtle message of the client or that a worker may have ignored the client's affective responses. In these instances, the supervisor can help the worker explore how to address such client behaviors differently in future interviews. Such supervisory discussions have been known to help new workers consider alternative responses and to be more disciplined in future interviews.

Direct Observations.   Direct observations of practice through a two-way mirror or videotaping have helped supervisors and workers critique practice to make improvements. Audiotaped interviews should not be overlooked, as much can be learned from listening to how one sounds and to what one says in an interview.

Case Summaries, Journals, and Logs.   Other devices such as case summaries and personal journals or logs have been known to help monitor practice. A case summary of one individual or group session, or a summary of work with a client over a period of time along with questions and plans for future interviews, can be very helpful to review. Having clients keep a log of some aspect of their behavior that they wish to change (e.g., circumstances when they are depressed, desire to use alcohol or to partake in negative self-talk) and discussing the results with their social worker is another form of monitoring practice.

Case Management.   Case management is a formal employment title often held by a social worker (e.g., Frankel & Gelman, 1998). In this position, the employee often monitors the individual practice of other human service workers and the programs that are provided to a client. Case managers typically find services for their clients, negotiate or facilitate contracts with the agencies offering services, monitor them to ensure that they actually deliver the contracted services, and advocate when necessary on behalf of clients. Case managers continually monitor the range of services that are provided to their clients to ensure their quality and continued appropriateness.

Client Satisfaction

Client satisfaction not only is important to introduce in monitoring programs but also has important value for practice. Client satisfaction is usually conducted at the time when a client is terminating services. However, inquiring about client satisfaction while services are being delivered adds the possibility that changes can occur in practice interventions for future sessions. It is wise for social workers to periodically hold informal client satisfaction discussions with their clients. The workers can ask clients whether they are satisfied with the services that they are receiving. When clients are not fully satisfied, they can be asked how the services could be provided differently or in a more helpful way. Also, such inquiries often help empower the client and increase the bond between a worker and client. Typical client satisfaction questions that can periodically be asked of a client include the following:

- What am I doing that is helpful to you? How is it helpful?
- What do you like about what I am doing to help you?
- What would you like for me to do that I am not doing that could be helpful?
- What am I doing that is not helpful to you?
- How am I helping you reach your goals?

Client Outcomes

Practitioners are expected to adequately document that their interventions are effective in improving outcomes for clients, that is, in meeting their clients' goals. Basic questions that all practitioners need to frequently ask themselves are the following:

- Are my interventions helping clients reach their goals?
- Are my interventions responsible for bringing about positive or constructive changes in my clients' lives?
- How are my interventions helping?
- In what ways could my interventions be more effective in helping my clients reach their goals?

Several evaluation tools are available to help practitioners evaluate whether their clients are reaching their goals. These tools include single-system designs, which plot the changes that a client makes in an observed behavior over time and observe whether the interventions are responsible for changes in behavior when they occur. Single-system designs focus on the impact of one or more worker-introduced interventions on a client system. A goal attainment scale (GAS) is another helpful tool that can be used to evaluate the extent to which the worker's interventions affect the clients' goals in a favorable way. It is an incremental scale that can be used to measure degree of progress. A target problem scale (TPS) is another outcome scale that can be used particularly when client goals are difficult to identify. A TPS is helpful, for example, if clients remain focused on their problems and are not prepared to pursue goals beyond the problems. More information is provided about all three of these evaluation tools in chapter 9.

Models and the Three-Stage Approach

The three-stage approach introduced in chapter 2 is an important organizational framework. Using this framework, the models commonly used to evaluate programs and practice described in this chapter can be further classified on the basis of whether they focus on the planning, implementation, or outcome stage. It seems notable, as indicated in table 4.2, that most of the types of evaluation models introduced in this chapter are primarily process evaluations conducted during the implementation stage. These models primarily focus on how well program or practice interventions function and evolve to help clients. These types of evaluations are more abundant and var-

Table 4.2   Examples of Common Evaluation Models

Planning stage	Implementation stage	Output and outcome stage
	Program evaluations	
• Needs assessment	• Program monitoring	• Outcome study
	• Efficiency evaluations	• Cost-benefit analysis
	• Client satisfaction studies	study
	• Licensing programs	
	• Licensing professionals	
	• Auditing investigations	
	• Accreditation of social and educational programs	
	• Quality assurance	
	• Court or judicial decisions	
	• Newspaper and media reports	
	Practice evaluations	
• Needs assessment	• Tools for monitoring practice (e.g., process recordings, observations, case summaries, journals, case management)	• Single-system designs
		• Goal Attainment Scale
		• Target Problem Scale
	• Client satisfaction	

ied than models evident in the planning and outcome stages, largely because there are so many interacting elements during the implementation stage.

Now that you have a grasp of several commonly used evaluation models and how they can be classified using the three-stage approach, we turn to the next section on topics important to the planning stage.

Key Terms

Accreditation of social/educational programs
Auditing investigations
Client satisfaction studies
Cost-benefit analysis study
Court or judicial decisions
Efficiency evaluations
Goal attainment scales
Licensing professionals
Licensing programs
Needs assessment
Newspaper and media reports
Outcome study
Program and practice monitoring
Quality assurance
Single-system designs
Target problem scales

Discussion Questions and Assignments

1. Select a program evaluation approach from one of the types described in the chapter that gives emphasis to research methods. It could be, for example, a needs assessment, a program-monitoring study, a client satisfaction study, an outcome study, or a cost-benefit analysis. Try to find an actual evaluation that uses this approach conducted at your agency or another agency with which you are familiar. If such a study is unavailable, look for an example of this approach in a professional journal. Carefully review the evaluation, look closely at how it was conducted, and report to your class on what you learned.

2. Several other types of evaluations tending to emphasize research methods less are also described in this chapter. They include quality assurance, licensing, and court decisions. Find out if your agency has conducted any of these evaluations in the past two to three years. Find out what the agency learned from the study and how the findings were used to improve the program.

3. Select one of the accreditation agencies listed in table 4.1. Visit the agency's Web site and find out what specific kinds of agencies are members. Also identify two standards that the accreditation organization requires of member agencies. List one compelling reason to

require these standards and one reason why some member agencies may find it difficult to implement these standards.

References

Cenziper, D. (2000, February 12). Could the state have saved Lynnette? *The Charlotte Observer*, 1A.

Cowger, C. D., Anderson, K. M., & Snively, C. A. (2006). Assessing strengths: The political context of individual, family, and community empowerment. In D. Saleebey, *The strengths perspective in social work practice* (pp. 93–115). Boston: Pearson.

Dudley, J. (2002). When staff and consumers disagree about consumer satisfaction. In J. Dudley, M. Calhoun, & L. Ahlgrim-Delzell (Eds.), *Lessons learned from a lawsuit: Creating services for people with mental illness and mental retardation* (pp. 117–122). Kingston, NY: National Association for the Dually Diagnosed Press.

Dudley, J., Calhoun, M., & Ahlgrim-Delzell, L. (Eds.). (2002). *Lessons learned from a lawsuit: Creating services for people with mental illness and mental retardation.* Kingston, NY: National Association for the Dually Diagnosed Press.

Frankel, A. J., & Gelman, S. R. (1998). *Case management: An introduction to concepts and skills.* Chicago: Lyceum Books.

Muehlbauer, N. A., & Runnberg, M. (2006). A needs assessment of immigrants and refugees attending the English as a second language program at an adult learning center. Duluth, MN: College of St. Scholastica.

Zimmerman, M. A. (2000). Empowerment theory: Psychological, organizational, and community levels of analysis. In J. Rappaport & E. Seldman (Eds.), *Handbook of community psychology* (pp. 43–63). New York: Plenum.

Part III

The Planning or Input Stage

Chapter 5

Focusing an Evaluation

How do you focus an evaluation?

How does an evaluator decide how to focus an evaluation? This is an important question that has several ramifications and no simple answer. As was discussed in previous chapters, social programs and practice areas tend to be complex and multifaceted. Furthermore, they cannot be fully understood in a vacuum. The agency sponsoring the program and its social and political context also must be taken into account.

A general approach for conducting an evaluation involving seven general steps was introduced in chapter 1. The first two steps are important to explore before moving ahead to focus an evaluation. These steps include identifying the problem to be evaluated and exploring ways to involve the stakeholders. This chapter elaborates on these steps and recommends a set of questions to ask initially to gain a fuller understanding of the stakeholders, clients, and the larger agency context. Once these questions are explored and have been answered, a set of specific guidelines assist an evaluator in articulating a focus for an evaluation.

Important Initial Questions

Some initial questions should be directed to all of the stakeholders, including the following:

- What are their perceptions of the program/practice area generally?
- What do they perceive to be its goals?
- To what extent do they understand the program/practice area, how it is supposed to be implemented, and how it actually is implemented?
- What do they believe are the problems and issues that are most important to address in an evaluation?
- Why are these issues important to them?
- What would each of them hope to accomplish by conducting an evaluation?
- How would they like to use the results of such an evaluation?

Let's assume that there is more than one stakeholder. As was discussed in chapter 1, stakeholders of a social program can include the administrators of the agency sponsoring the program, relevant funding and regulatory agencies, agency staff members, clients, family members of clients, members of the geographic community surrounding the agency, and others.

If we ask each of these stakeholders many of the preceding questions, we are likely to hear a multitude of perspectives and concerns. For example, an agency administrator may want to determine why there is so much staff turnover, a funding agency may want to know whether the program recipients are reaching their designated goals, and staff members may want to explore whether their caseloads are too large. In this instance, all of the stakeholders' responses would need to be reviewed individually and in conjunction with one another. Concerns of stakeholders may be not only very different from one another but also, in some cases, in conflict with one another. In such cases, decisions would need to be made about which concerns are given priority and how conflicts are addressed.

The Input of Clients during the Planning Phase

Ultimately, a more in-depth set of questions needs to be asked of a special group of stakeholders: clients and their families. These questions can offer insights into some of the central reasons for conducting an evaluation, such as the following:

- How can clients benefit from an evaluation of the program?
- How can an evaluation contribute to clients' well-being?
- How will the results of an evaluation be used to more fully promote the clients' quality of life?

Most evaluations are not likely to involve the program recipients in planning, even though the evaluation may focus directly on them. In some ways this is logical, as clients may wonder whether the personnel of the agency know what they are doing if they have to ask for client input. Also, many client populations have cognitive limitations, psychiatric and substance abuse diagnoses, and other challenging attributes that may prevent them from offering substantially useful input. Other clients have involuntary status with the agency; they do not choose to be there. Such clients may have difficulty thinking about how they can help the providers because of their adversarial relationships with them. In addition to all of these points, one could argue that the demands on clients' time need to be protected and reserved for work on their own problems.

Nevertheless, consulting clients, former clients, prospective clients, and other program recipients in the planning of an evaluation can be especially positive and useful for a program. Indeed, social work ethics expect such involvement. Ultimately, a program or practice area exists because of clients, who likely know the most about their personal problems and the help they need. They may also have views and suggestions that are pertinent to the methodology to be selected for the evaluation. For example, they may be able to advise an evaluator on whether clients would be more responsive to observations, interviews, or questionnaires.

The participatory action approach (PAR), introduced in chapter 2, assumes that the people studied or evaluated can be involved in implementing any or all stages of an evaluation. Such involvement largely depends on the perspective of the evaluators and other stakeholders. In the case of planning an evaluation, clients, for example, could be consulted to help in the following areas:

- They can be asked how important the program/practice concerns already identified are to them.
- They can become involved in several ways, such as being interviewed on a relevant topic, sitting on an advisory committee, assisting a collaborative team of stakeholders, or informal consulting.
- They can be encouraged to react to the views expressed by other stakeholders.

The Social and Political Context of the Agency Sponsor

Once the concerns of all stakeholders are identified, clearly understood, and prioritized, further questions will need to be asked about the agency context of the program. As was discussed in chapter 1, several contextual factors are likely relevant and need to be taken into account in preparing an evaluation plan. For example, how do decisions get made in the agency and who will participate in the initial and ongoing decisions and advisory processes involving the evaluation? Will the executive director be the sole decider or will several key staff members and possibly an advisory group be primary decision makers? Also, if staff members are expected to participate in an evaluation (e.g., by filling out forms, by preparing clients for participation), such demands on their time and a possible fatigue factor should be explored.

An Exercise: Example of Decision Making as a Factor

In an earlier example in chapter 1, a graduate student planned an evaluation of the morale of staff members with her supervisor. The supervisor seemed quite interested in such a study because she was concerned with occasional complaints of staff, a tendency among some to resist following administrative policies, and more staff turnover than usual in recent years. The student proceeded to construct a questionnaire for staff members to fill out that asked them to comment on the extent to which several work-related issues were a concern. These concerns included salaries, medical and pension benefits, caseloads, supervision, staff meetings, opportunities for staff training and educational advances, and relationships with administrators. When the questionnaire was completed, returned to the student, and tallied, the results revealed that supervisory and administrative relationship issues were most frequently cited as a problem for most staff. Other concerns were also mentioned but much less frequently. When the student shared the results with her supervisor, who then shared them with her supervisor, concerns emerged about the results, and the student discovered that the study was never fully understood or formally approved by the administration. She was instructed to write up her report for her social work course assignment but to do nothing more with the results. She was forbidden to share the results in any form with the staff members, who had anticipated hearing about them. Unfortunately, she had not adequately explored the focus of the evaluation initially with key administrative stakeholders, before conducting the study. What do you think the student should have done at this point? If staff members asked her to share the findings with them, what should she have said that would be both ethical and consistent with the administrator's decision? How could this conflict of interest possibly be prevented at the time of the study's initial planning and negotiation? What do staff members, administrators, clients, and the student potentially lose from this experience?

The degree to which the agency sponsor understands what evaluations entail, in general, and the degree to which it values and respects what an evaluation can provide are important issues to explore initially. Evaluators will be more likely to succeed in conducting their evaluations if they are respected and understood. Another contextual issue to explore is to determine the essential material resources required for the evaluation. For example, evaluators will need to be paid if they are not employed by the agency, and considerable release time will need to be provided if the evaluators are staff members of the agency overseeing the evaluation. Also, a budget is inevitable to pay for such things as electronic equipment and statistical software, supplies like postage and paper, the purchase of scales, costs of typing a report, and extra phone use.

Crafting Good Study Questions for an Evaluation

Before embarking on a specific program or practice investigation, a general focus is needed to guide the evaluator so that he or she knows what is to be investigated. General study questions provide that focus. General study questions are broad in nature and open ended. They serve two purposes. First, they provide parameters for an evaluation, limiting the topic of investigation. Second, they provide enough specificity to know what is to be explored in a specific sense. In other words, they are not too broad to be unrealistic and not too specific to be too restrictive.

These general research questions are not to be confused with the specific questions that may be asked of participants or the specific behaviors to be observed in a study. A general study question is likely too broad if the number of specific questions it generates seems endless. Similarly, a general study question is likely too narrow if it generates only one or two specific questions. Each general study question when further delineated should generate a manageable number of specific questions to ask participants.

In brief, the best study questions to ask in an evaluation have several notable characteristics:

1. **Importance:** They identify a program concern that is important to address.
2. **Not too broad or specific:** Each general study question is broad enough to generate several specific questions to be asked (or behaviors to be observed) of the people being studied.
3. **Feasible:** Each question is focused enough to address issues that can be answered within the time period and with the available resources.
4. **Based on the literature:** Previous studies and agency experiences that have focused on this or similar topics have been considered.
5. **Client feedback:** Some clients and family members of clients who are personally affected by the program have been consulted.
6. **Clarity:** The study questions are well written, clear, and succinct.

The next section introduces guidelines to help shape or define these study questions.

Guidelines for Focusing an Evaluation

A set of four guidelines can be followed to a focus the evaluation. These four guidelines are partially based on the work of others, especially that of Stecher and Davis (1987).

1. Identify the stage of the program/practice area's development in which the evaluation is being emphasized (planning, implementation, or outcome). Identifying the program/practice stage that reflects the evaluation concern is the first guideline. As an evaluator begins to focus an evaluation, the stage of interest is easy to identify. As was discussed in chapter 2, programs have developmental stages, and evaluations address important issues at all of these stages, including a planning or input stage, when the ideas and vision for a new program/practice area emerge and are developed and detailed in a proposal; the implementation stage, by far the longest; and the outcome stage, when the program's impact on client outcomes is the major focus. As noted previously, these program stages may not always occur in this order, and they sometimes overlap.

2. Identify the program elements. The second guideline is to identify the program/practice elements that are the primary interest and focus of an evaluation. A program or practice element is a distinct entity of a program or practice that is critical to its functioning. Figure 5.1 provides a closer look at the most common program elements at the various program stages. In addition, you might be able to identify elements that are not in the figure. As figure 5.1 shows, each element or combination of elements could become the focus of an evaluation.

For example, if input elements are the evaluation focus during the conceptual and planning stages, they could include target goals or purposes of a program, prospective client populations to be recruited, characteristics and professional training of staff members to be hired, and a proposed operational budget for the program. The focus of the program's implementation stage is program process elements, which may include theoretical underpinnings of the program or practice approach, the served client population, staff members and volunteers working in the program, available staff training and educational opportunities, available electronic technologies, and the record-keeping system. During the output/outcome stage, output elements and outcome elements are different. Output elements include statistics such as number of clients served and number of contact hours that staff members spend with clients. Outcome elements are the outcomes that measure clients' progress in reaching their goals.

3. Formulate evaluation questions. Once the stage and program element(s) are identified, study questions can be formulated about the element(s) of interest. Such questions are best identified through a brainstorming process that involves as many stakeholders as possible. At this stage, do not worry if the questions chosen seem realistic or not. Because this is a brainstorming step, a fairly open-ended, creative process can occur that yields several evaluation questions. Let's look at some examples of possible evaluation questions during each of the three program stages.

In the planning stage, prospective clients are a central element that requires more in-depth examination. Any number of questions could be asked about prospective clients, such as the following:

- What characteristics provide a pertinent client profile (e.g., age, ethnic group, socioeconomic status, evidence of particular problems, clinical diagnosis, particular medical condition)?
- Where could we find and recruit such prospective clients?
- Have we consulted them to find out more about their needs and views about the proposed program? Have we consulted a representative sample of such people?
- If there are more clients than the proposed program can serve, what characteristics and qualities of the client population will receive priority?
- What are some obstacles to reaching prospective clients who have, for example, a clinical diagnosis?

FIGURE 5.1   Examples of Program or Practice Elements at Different Stages of the Intervention's Development

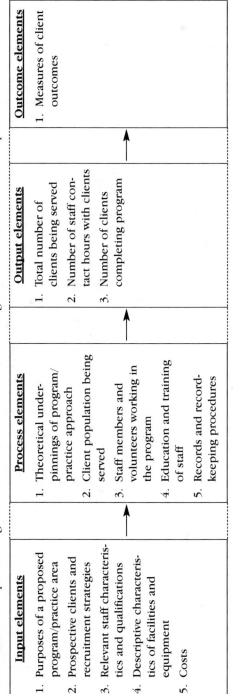

Input elements	Process elements	Output elements	Outcome elements
1. Purposes of a proposed program/practice area	1. Theoretical underpinnings of program/practice approach	1. Total number of clients being served	1. Measures of client outcomes
2. Prospective clients and recruitment strategies	2. Client population being served	2. Number of staff contact hours with clients	
3. Relevant staff characteristics and qualifications	3. Staff members and volunteers working in the program	3. Number of clients completing program	
4. Descriptive characteristics of facilities and equipment	4. Education and training of staff		
5. Costs	5. Records and record-keeping procedures		

Given the needs of the prospective client group, it is important to explore other sets of elements as well, such as the types of direct-care staff that need to be hired; qualifications of staff members who can provide the proposed services, and the recruiting and hiring of people with these credentials; and staff applicants' educational level, specialized degree or discipline, prior skills and experience, and various demographic characteristics. As figure 5.1 suggests, other elements of the planning stage could be the focus of an evaluation, including the facilities needed to house it, the technologies required to run it, and the costs described in a budget.

The implementation stage requires consideration of another set of elements, those that make up a program/practice area and move it forward. Such elements include the purpose, goals, and objectives of a program; the clients who are being served, their needs, problems, and diagnoses; current staff members; funding sources; an operating budget; necessary facilities; and technologies in use.

Each of these elements could pose any number of evaluation questions. For example, several questions could be posed about existing staff members:

- Are professional staff members using best practices?
- Are the racial and ethnic characteristics of staff consistent with the affirmative action standards of the agency and the government? If not, how can we recruit and retain minority staff members?
- Are staff trained to effectively help clients with psychological, psychiatric, and other mental problems (e.g., helping people with developmental disabilities socially integrate in the community)?
- How do case managers use their time? How much time, on average, do they devote to direct contact with clients? To evaluation activities? To advocacy? To paperwork?
- Why is there such a high turnover rate of occupational therapists in the program?

Output elements are manifestations of such things as resources that have been used or the extent to which clients have participated in the program. For example, resource outputs could be such things as the number of staff or volunteer contact hours with clients, the costs of running the program, and the wear and tear on physical resources. Client outputs could be the number of clients who have attended at least some program sessions, the number who have successfully completed the program, and the number who have dropped out.

Many evaluation questions could be raised about each output element. Let's take the subgroup of clients completing the program as an example:

- What are the demographic (e.g., gender, socioeconomic group, ethnicity, age) characteristics of clients who completed the program?

- How long did it take for clients to complete the program? Which clients needed more time than others? How much professional staff time was needed to help them on average?
- What are the characteristics of those who dropped out of the program early? At what stages did they most frequently drop out? What factors explain why they dropped out?

Outcome elements are a special type of output element that reflects the impact of the program/practice area on the clients after they completed it. These elements are usually client focused and reflect a measure of progress or lack of progress in achieving their goals. Output and outcome elements are sometimes difficult to distinguish. For example, successful completion of a job-training program is more of an output element because it is not an actual indication of client progress in itself, whereas finding a job as a result of training is more of an outcome element. Similarly, completing rigorous drug rehabilitation counseling is a practice output but discontinued drug use is the ultimate desired outcome. When you think about it, completion of a counseling program is not an adequate justification for a program to continue, but making progress toward discontinuing drug use is.

Exercise on Outcome Elements

Formulation of outcome elements tends to require more effort and creativity than the formulation of output elements. The following questions pose examples of this. Try to answer each question:

- What would be an *effective* measure of improved marital relations in a family agency beyond completing weekly sessions for three months?
- Beyond the initial physical placement, how can we know whether a foster-care agency was *successful* in placing children with disabilities in family home care?

Ultimately, evaluation questions focusing on outcome elements ask whether the clients who have completed a program function considerably better than they did when they first began receiving services. Statistical measures are often used to determine not only whether clients have made progress but also whether that progress is statistically significant. If evaluators decide that clinical significance is more important than statistical significance, the question is, Did clients improve their outcome scores from pretest to posttest to meet the clinical criteria of success? In some agencies, it is important to determine both outputs and outcomes for staff members. For example, an agency may want to know what new skills a staff member learned from attending a particular training session or workshop. This can be an important question especially if the skills are critical for providing services effectively to clients. Note that the learning of such skills could be either an output element or an outcome element. They are output elements in the context of the program that serves clients but they are outcome elements if the training workshop is the sole focus of an evaluation.

4. Identify supportive and resistant forces that need to be considered and addressed before conducting the evaluation. The previous guideline is largely meant to be a creative, brainstorming step that does not allow feasibility issues to interfere with decisions. However, feasibility becomes an important consideration with this guideline. In addition, the contextual issues of the program and agency become more important. There are two basic questions to ask about the larger context of the program: (1) what resources are available to support the evaluation? and (2) what factors do we need to consider that could cause resistance or interference in conducting the evaluation?

Identify the Potential Resources

Identifying resources to support the evaluation is often critical. Most evaluations will be feasible only if they have resources available to support them. In some settings, these resource factors may be referred to as strengths of the agency context. It is important to consciously and deliberately identify potential resources because supportive factors are often present but unrecognized. In the case that the resources are required, they can be more easily engaged if you know about them and have considered them from the beginning.

Possible examples of resources or strengths that support an evaluation can be any number of things. The subsequent partial list can help evaluators and stakeholders begin to consider such resources:

- Strong interest in conducting an evaluation among some or all stakeholders
- Prior agency experience in completing useful evaluations, especially successful ones
- Financial support for an evaluation
- Awareness among stakeholders of the problem (or concern) inherent in a program that is the focus of the evaluation
- An openness among stakeholders to examine a problem in greater depth rather than just on the surface
- Some understanding, expertise, and respect for evaluations among stakeholders
- Expressed interest in the evaluation by clients and their families

- Staff interest in helping with the evaluation
- Openness to an evaluator as a helpful resource and ally of the program/practice area

Examine Factors Resistant to Conducting a Program Evaluation

Although it is important to examine the factors that can support an evaluation, resistant factors are also extremely important to consider, as they may determine the success or failure of the evaluation. They can also be decisive in determining whether to conduct the evaluation (e.g., the evaluation of staff morale described earlier in the chapter).

Once resistant factors are identified, it is critical to explore their impact on an evaluation and address them if warranted. In some cases, this involves discussions with resistant or misinformed stakeholders to listen to and respond to their views. In other instances, this may involve seeking an outside evaluator with more expertise or finding a qualified practitioner in the agency who can conduct the evaluation on a limited budget.

Examples of resistant factors, like resources, include any number of things. The following list can help evaluators and stakeholders begin to identify them:

- Are there time limitations that may preclude conducting an evaluation?
- Are the costs of conducting an evaluation so high that it is not affordable to do so?
- Is the payoff risky in terms of what the findings might suggest?
- Is the type of evaluation that we want so subjective that it may not be feasible or even acceptable to some stakeholders?
- Could the results of the evaluation suggest a need for a change that the agency is not prepared to consider?
- Are there limits to what we can change about the program, given the funding agency's requirements or limited resources?
- Are the special interests of various stakeholders and others likely to lead to counterproductive results or divisiveness?
- Does the agency lack the expertise to conduct such a study?
- If there is no need to justify such an evaluation to the funding agency, why rock the boat?
- Will there be problems in gaining access to client data?
- Do stakeholders and/or the collaborative team have the required creativity and flexibility to implement the evaluation?

Focusing an Evaluation: A Practical Tool

Stecher and Davis (1987) offer a practical way to begin focusing an evaluation on issues important to the agency. Their exercise begins by identifying the program or practice elements that are of concern, followed by writing a general study question, identifying potential resources to support the evaluation, identifying resistant factors, and finally considering specific evaluation procedures. This exercise is intended as a creative way to quickly focus an evaluation on one or more concerns.

Table 5.1 can be used to explore two or three program or practice concerns of importance to an agency. Feel free to use it for that purpose. You may be surprised how quickly you can find a focus for your evaluation. After identifying two or three program or practice elements for a possible focus, work across the chart from left to right for each element. In the second column, identify one or more general study questions to explore for the element. For example, if a practice element is the high rate of client cancellations and no-shows for appointments with social workers, a general study question could be, Why are there so many client cancellations and no-shows in this practice area? This is a good study question because it can lead to several specific questions:

- What percentage of the clients show up for the initially scheduled interview with the social worker? What reasons do clients give, if any, when they do not show up?
- Are the same clients missing appointments over time?
- Are these clients rescheduling canceled appointments?
- What are the characteristics of clients who are canceling or not showing up for appointments?
- Do people from particular ethnic, age, or gender groups cancel more often than members of other groups?
- Are the clients' illnesses preventing them from showing up for appointments?
- Do clients have adequate transportation to get to appointments?
- What is the average time that a client has to wait to see a social worker after an intake interview?

Next, in the third column of table 5.1, identify potential available resources that are likely to be valuable in supporting a study that addresses

TABLE 5.1   Exercise on How to Focus an Evaluation Plan

Program or practice elements	General study question	Resources	Resistant factors	Evaluation procedures
1)	1)	1)	1)	1)
2)	2)	2)	2)	2)
3)	3)	3)	3)	3)

each identified study question. Then do the same, but with constraints or resistant factors that could potentially work against such an evaluation. A final step in the far-right column is to begin considering overall evaluation procedures, such as a one-group pretest and posttest design, a needs assessment interview of prospective clients, or observations of worker-client relationships through a two-way mirror.

Examples of Questions Formulated by Students

This section offers several examples of how students in an MSW program used this exercise to develop a focus for the evaluations they conducted as part of a course assignment. Note that many of these general study questions focus on practice more than programs; they are also often quite specific.

Examples of Study Questions Focusing on Clients' Issues

Encouraging client diversity

- Why are there so few non–African American clients served in this program? Why are other racial groups not using agency services?
- To what extent is the Latino community being served?
- Is there sufficient and open communication between school social workers and Spanish-speaking parents? What are the potential communication problems between them?

Clients not actively participating in treatment

- Does a lack of day-care services prevent some parents from attending a program? Why isn't day care for clients' children available?
- When clients do not speak in group therapy, what are the likely reasons? Are they shy, resistant to change, not understanding the topics of discussion, or are there other reasons?
- Are eligible teens aware of this group service? Why are some not aware?
- Is the existing group designed to meet members' immediate needs?
- Who is and who is not benefiting from group therapy?

Meeting goals and objectives

- Are clients reaching their initially identified goals?
- Is the goal of getting newly pregnant women into prenatal care being reached?
- Why are some clients completing the program successfully and others are not?

Satisfaction with a program

- Are Latino clients satisfied with the pregnancy-testing program?
- What do clients find most helpful about the social worker's services? What could the social worker do to be more helpful?

Examples of Study Questions Focusing on Staff Members and Technology Issues

Staff hesitations or negligence in pursuing particular interventions

- Do staff members make appropriate referrals? What do they do when clients initially choose not to follow through with a referral?
- Are intake staff members adequately trained to conduct comprehensive intake interviews?
- Are in-service training programs successful in preparing staff to do their jobs?
- Are staff members using evidence-based approaches? How can we find this out?
- Are staff members completing their client records in a timely way after each client contact?

Hiring and staff turnover concerns

- Are staff satisfied with their positions? What are they dissatisfied about?
- Why is there a high staff turnover among long-term-care workers?
- Is there a shortage of qualified staff available to fill existing employment openings?

Technology

- Are the family-skills videos appropriate and useful for existing clients?
- Are clients using the family-skills videos at home? If not, what are the reasons for not using them (e.g., have appropriate equipment [VCR or DVD] to run the videos)?
- What are clients learning from viewing these videos?
- How satisfied are they with these videos?

The final step in the focusing exercise in table 5.1 involves identifying possible evaluation procedures. This topic is covered in more depth in later chapters. However, identifying evaluation procedures is an important consideration in the focusing exercise because the evaluation questions eventually selected must be answerable. Put another way, a successful evaluation requires feasible evaluation procedures. Evaluation questions can address major concerns of a program that everyone wants to investigate, but there is no point in proceeding with an investigation without a realistic plan.

Example of Formulating a Feasible General Study Question

A substance abuse agency wanted to find out whether its clinical program was successful in bringing sobriety to its clients. This could be the ultimate type of question that any agency wants to ask: can the agency claim that the program is responsible for changing the lives of its clients related to the goals of the program? However, this is not a feasible question to answer unless the agency can do all of the following:

- Develop a valid measure of the outcome variable: sobriety
- Conduct an experimental design and randomly assign participants to a treatment or control group
- Find the funds and other resources to conduct such an evaluation
- Stay committed to the evaluation from beginning to end
- Conduct a follow-up evaluation to find out whether clients maintained sobriety over a reasonably long period of time

A more feasible evaluation question could be, Are most clients making statistically significant improvements in their specific goals by the time they complete the program?

The next chapter considers another important topic of the planning stage, a needs assessment. Conducting a needs assessment is probably the most effective way to plan for a new program or practice area.

Key Terms
Formulating evaluation questions
General study questions
Program elements
Resistant factor working against an evaluation
Resources supporting an evaluation
Stages of program development

Discussion Questions and Assignments
1. Select a program element from the input stage, implementation stage, or outcome stage listed in figure 5.1 and identify three general study questions about the element.

2. Develop a focus for an evaluation in your agency. Attempt to arrive at a focus for three different program concerns using table 5.1. Then choose one focus that you would recommend be pursued. Consult your supervisor as you explore each step so that your focus will be useful to the agency.

3. In the exercise described in Question 2, identify one supportive force and one resistant force to conducting the evaluation you have proposed. How could the supportive force assist you in implementing your proposed evaluation? What steps could you take to address or counteract the resistant factor?

4. Two questions are posed in "Exercise on Outcome Elements." Select one and create a measurable outcome element.

References

Stecher, B. M., & Davis, W. A. (1987). *How to focus an evaluation*. Thousand Oaks, CA: Sage Publications.

Chapter 6

The Planning Stage and Needs Assessments

Why become informed about prospective clients before designing a new intervention?

The need for a new program or practice area should be sufficiently documented before valuable resources are committed to its development. The planning stage is the primary period when this documentation can happen. During this stage, various stakeholders can identify, document, advocate, and debate the need for a new program or practice area. In other words, well-conceived, well-conceptualized programs and practice areas are typically preceded by an important planning period that involves a variety of helpful inputs.

This chapter describes what can be done to document the need for a proposed program or practice area before it is implemented. Figure 6.1 provides an overview of many of the activities. As figure 6.1 indicates, only a few activities may be directly classified as evaluations (e.g., needs assessments,

FIGURE 6.1   Spectrum of Activities during the Planning Stage

Planning Stage
Types of evaluations
- Needs assessments for programs
- Crafting program/practice goals and objectives
- Designing a program/practice approach
- Needs assessments in practice areas

Other types of activities involved in planning
- Literature review to understand theoretical underpinnings of approach
- Literature review to find empirical evidence of program effectiveness
- Proposal writing
- Identifying funds
- Identifying and recruiting clients
- Hiring/training staff
- Finding facilities
- Purchasing equipment and technology
- Determining decision-making and accountability mechanisms

crafting goals and objectives, designing a program). Others have an obvious indirect bearing, including reviewing the literature to find out more about a proposed approach, writing a proposal, hiring staff members, and carrying out fund-raising or development activities.

Although rigorous planning makes sense during this period before implementation, such preparation is often ignored or underplayed, and there are many excuses. The agency provider may be rushed into getting a program under way prematurely because of deadlines imposed by a funding agency, an agency board, or another party. Or perhaps a needs assessment seems unnecessary because there is plenty of anecdotal data available in support of a program. Another excuse is that there is no expectation to systematically document the need. Finally, program administrators sometimes are not well versed in the necessary planning work for a new program. Thus, this chapter provides guidelines for planning a new program.

Introducing the Logic Model

The logic model is a tool to theoretically analyze a program. The logic model helps highlight how the stages and elements of a program can be logically linked to an organic whole. With this model, it is important to examine the sequence of steps in a program's development, beginning with the problems of prospective clients and culminating in anticipated client outcomes, which helps stakeholders link the stages together. In brief, the tasks especially pertinent to the logic model at each stage of program development are the following:

Planning or input stage

- Identify the problems and unmet needs of prospective clients and link them to underlying causes.
- Craft goals and measurable objectives as guideposts or signs that the problems have been resolved and unmet needs filled.
- Design a program to address client problems or unmet needs and their underlying causes.

Implementation stage

- As the program is implemented, monitor whether it actually does what it is designed to do.

Output and outcome stage

- Measure whether and the extent to which clients' goals and measurable objectives are reached. These outcomes are typically measured for the short, intermediate, and long runs.

The example that follows outlines some steps taken by one group in implementing the logic model in the design and implementation of a parenting education program for teenage mothers. In this example the outcomes are established at three different points in time: initial, intermediate, and long run, reflecting what is expected at the completion of the program and at two later times. Unfortunately, the problems, unmet needs, and underlying causes are not explicitly stated during the input steps and become apparent only in the outcome stage.

Example of a Description Using the Logic Model of a Parenting Education Program for Teenage Mothers

Input steps

- Agency and high school identify pregnant teens to participate in program.
- Agency provides appropriate teaching materials, staff, etc.

Program activities implemented

- Program provides parenting classes on prenatal care, infant nutrition, safety, proper care, feeding, and so on, twice a week for one hour to teen mothers with a child from three months prior to birth to one year after delivery of child.

Output steps

- Pregnant teen mothers attend all sessions of the program.

Initial outcomes

- Teens are knowledgeable about prenatal care and nutrition.
- Teens are knowledgeable about proper care and feeding.

Intermediate outcomes

- Teens follow proper nutrition and safety guidelines.
- Teens deliver healthy babies.
- Teens provide proper care and feeding.

Long-term outcomes

- Babies achieve appropriate twelve-month milestones for physical, motor, verbal, and social development (Ross, Lipsey, & Freeman, 2004).

Introducing the logic model into the program-planning process has the potential to create fundamental changes in how a proposed program is shaped and implemented, especially when the effort is initiated in an early stage, such as during conceptualization of a program. Aspects of the logic model are increasingly being built into funding agencies' requirements for most grant proposals. Grant proposals are expected to document such things as the links among clients' problems, causes, and the program approach proposed to help them. This chapter and those that follow describe some of the issues that are raised and addressed when the logic model is incorporated into the planning process, such as the following:

- Identifying the link between problems and specific needs
- Determining how problems and needs relate to underlying causes
- Identifying the goals of the program from the problems, needs, and underlying causes
- Crafting measurable objectives for these goals
- Logically linking the goals and objectives to a program approach that can be effectively implemented so that clients achieve them
- Anticipating that the introduction of the program approach will result in clients progressing satisfactorily toward the goals and measurable objectives initially identified and crafted

Example of the Use of the Logic Model in Designing a Program

A group of students were asked to design a program that would effectively help clients overcome substance abuse problems. They used the logic model to complete this exercise. They began by identifying some suspected causes of substance abuse, including heredity, peer influence, low self-esteem, social isolation, and inadequate coping skills. Next they decided to design a program to address only the suspected causes that revolved around interpersonal issues, including peer influence, social isolation, low self-esteem, and inadequate coping skills. They decided to offer psycho-educational groups to teach clients the skills needed to manage these and other personal and interpersonal issues. They decided to cover specific topics such as how to find positive peer influences and avoid negative peer influences, how to find and participate in support groups, and some self-esteem building exercises. They anticipated that once participants had completed the psycho-educational group sessions they would be able to identify the factors that reduced their self-esteem, to identify specific ways to build more positive self-esteem, and to learn three or four new coping skills. By completion of the program, participants would also have made two or more visits to a support group in the community to help them stop using substances.

The Link between Problems and Needs

The logic model is introduced during the program-planning stage to stress the vital need for evident connections among clients' problems and needs, the underlying causes, and the link to the goals and objectives of the program or practice area, the selection of the approach, and the expected outcomes for clients. Figure 6.2 shows these relationships.

FIGURE 6.2   Clients' Problems, Needs, and Causes

Client Problems → Client Needs → Causes of Problems →

Implementation of Intervention → Outputs →

Client Outcomes (short-term → intermediate term → long-term)

A note about the link between needs and problems is helpful here. The reference to a needs assessment may imply that problems are not pertinent. For example, why isn't this process referred to as a problem assessment? Although clients' problems and needs are similar, there are some important differences. Some prefer using the term *needs* over *problems* when referring to the nature of the help clients receive because it puts a more positive face on the focus and less on client deficits. *Needs* may also imply something that is manageable and capable of being changed, whereas a larger social problem may seem more insurmountable and unsolvable, at least in the immediate future. *Needs* also refers to some aspects of a problem that can be immediately addressed, while that may not be possible for other aspects of the problem.

DePoy and Gilson (2003) view needs as a systematic, evidence-based phenomenon linked to all or part of the problem. They suggest that identification of the need-related aspects of a problem helps specify the conditions and actions necessary to address the focus of the problem. For the purposes of this text, a revised version of DePoy and Gilson's definition of needs is used. Needs are considered only part of an overall problem that is identified by a client and selected because there is evidence that it can be overcome, alleviated, or ameliorated by an intervention (see table 6.1).

Note that the problems in the examples of table 6.1 are usually stated in broad terms that may fit many different client circumstances. In contrast, the needs linked to each problem are more specific and intended to fit some clients with these particular circumstances and not others. For example, truancy is a problem that could result from any number of needs going unmet. In table 6.1, truant students face two types of needs: trying to cope with challenging family conflicts and needing more supervised time before and after

TABLE 6.1   Examples of Connections between a Problem and a Need

Problem	Specific need
1. Inadequate housing	1. Housing needs plumbing repairs
2. Unemployed	2. Needing a job
3. Marital estrangement	3. Healthy marital communication
4. Truancy from school	4. Buffer from family conflicts and having something to do after school
5. Social isolation	5. Healthy social contact with peers

school because parents are employed outside of the home during the day. In other instances, truancy results from a lack of preparedness for academic courses, a lack of interest in school, a substance abuse problem, interpersonal difficulties pertaining to acceptance at school, difficulty adapting as a recent immigrant, and so on.

The Link between Problems and Needs, and the Underlying Causes

So a need is an aspect of a larger problem identified by a client and perceived to be amenable to change. Meeting a set of needs, then, is the intended focus of a proposed program. However, before rushing too quickly into the design of such a program, another important question is, What are the underlying causes of the problem that prevent the need from being met? This is a critical question for stakeholders to explore if a proposed program or practice area is to be designed to directly confront underlying causes. Underlying causes partially reflect barriers and other resistant factors that prevent needs from being met. Therefore, identified needs are likely to be met only if the underlying causes are understood and confronted.

Let's return to the example of the five sets of problems and specific needs described in table 6.1. Once we identify the underlying causes, problems, and needs as described in table 6.2, we discover that we have a more

TABLE 6.2   Examples of the Connections among a Problem, Need, and the Underlying Causes

Problem	Need	Underlying causes
1. Inadequate housing	1. Housing needs plumbing repairs	1. Deteriorated housing conditions, limited funds for repairs, and no repair skills or repair resources available
2. Unemployed	2. Needing a job	2. Lacks training in a skilled job area and lacks hope and motivation
3. Marital estrangement	3. Healthy marital communication	3. Lacks communication skills, no models for healthy marital relationships, and no incentives to stay married
4. Truancy from school	4. Protection from family conflicts and having something to do after school lacking	4. Problems involving parental relationship and parental guidance
5. Social isolation	5. Healthy social contact	5. Lacks social skills and no groups or organizations available to offer positive social contacts

complete understanding of what a program has to be designed to do to be effective.

Let's look more closely at the first example in table 6.2 of inadequate housing as the problem and plumbing repairs as the specific need to be met. We might next ask why the plumbing (and other aspects of housing) has not been addressed. After all, most plumbing repairs seem fairly straightforward and relatively easy to make. Yet the example suggests that the group of clients with this housing problem have modest incomes, no funds available for major repairs, and no plumbing repair skills or resources available even if funds were found.

You may still wonder why it is so important to identify and distinguish problems, needs, and underlying causes. This will become more evident in later chapters when the focus is on developing an intervention that will succeed in meeting unmet needs. For now it is important to remember that an effective new program or practice approach must be linked to a clear sense of what the problem and needs are and how they can be solved. Let's look first at how needs assessments are important for developing programs.

Input Stage and Planning the Proposed Program

The input stage of program development is when planning becomes the major focus. Several important tasks are completed in this stage, including identifying the prospective client population that is to be the focus of a new program and the problems of the clients that the proposed program is to address. Here is where the complex tasks of exploring the problem in more depth occur. The clients' problem, the specific needs that are part of the problem, and the underlying causes are all a focus of this task. Once the client population has been identified in general terms and the target problem has been examined in more depth, a decision needs to be made as to how to assess, in a systematic way, the clients' problems and needs. This is where a needs assessment becomes front and center.

Before delving into the mechanics of a needs assessment, it is important to emphasize that this is both a subjective and a political process. Meenaghan, Kilty, and McNutt (2004) identify some key overall social and political factors that can influence the implementation of a needs assessment. They recommend that evaluators and stakeholders be fully aware of the people and groups involved in each of the following activities:

- Who chooses what problems are to be examined?
- Who identifies what information is collected and why?
- Who analyzes and interprets the information that is collected?
- Who controls access to dissemination of the information collected?

These activities are critical to the shape that a needs assessment will take, to how the data will be analyzed, to the results that will be emphasized and ignored, to who will have access to the results, and to how the results will be disseminated. These points illustrate how the evaluation process is always a political process as well as a research undertaking, as mentioned in chapter 1. The specific stakeholders, in particular, can be crucial in influencing this process. Thus, it is important to identify all relevant parties who have a stake in the results and to get them involved as early as possible. It also means that the stakeholders should be as fully involved as possible in every step. The participant action approach along with the empowerment approach, described in chapter 2, are good models to follow in this regard.

Why Conduct a Needs Assessment?

Why conduct a needs assessment? A broad, systematic research effort like a needs assessment can be highly beneficial in addressing many community-wide needs and problems. Most important, such an assessment can provide valuable information for understanding a particular social problem that is troubling a local community. The alternatives—depending on hearsay or a few case examples as evidence, or having hunches about a problem—are not enough documentation to take the problem seriously (Marlow, 2005).

Needs assessments are particularly useful when considering a new policy or program initiative or when considering changes to or discontinuation of an existing program. Also, if outside funding sources (e.g., federal, state, or local government; private foundations; corporate support) are needed to support a program, the documentation from a needs assessment takes on even greater importance.

A needs assessment can answer several important questions. Consider the example of parenting children in a low-income neighborhood. Several questions could be asked about their parenting in this neighborhood:

- To what extent and how are the (biological, step, surrogate) parents actively involved in raising their children?
- To what extent and how are the parents economically able to provide for their children?
- What problems do mothers and fathers face in their roles as parents?
- What trends are evident in teen pregnancy, unmarried parenting, single parenting, and divorce? Are these family patterns increasing or decreasing?
- To what extent do services exist in the community to help parents with their parental roles?
- What are the demographic characteristics of the mothers and fathers who use existing services? What are the characteristics of those who do not use existing services?
- What barriers exist to access existing services?
- What service gaps are evident?
- What new policy initiatives could benefit these parents?

Some Purposes of Needs Assessments

You may ask, "What good will a needs assessment do, anyway?" Of course, there are no guarantees, but many positive benefits can come from a needs assessment of a particular group of people. Further, the more stakeholders and potential stakeholders that are involved and committed to such an assessment and informed by it, the more likely it is that a genuine communitywide concern for a client group will emerge.

Although a needs assessment is particularly important in documenting the need for a new program, it has other important purposes:

- Determining the adequacy of existing programs
- Determining the adequacy of existing informal resources
- Assessing client accessibility
- Obtaining data for crafting goals and measurable objectives for a new program

New Programs

One purpose of a needs assessment is to explore in more depth whether a new program is needed. A key question in this exploration is whether there are enough prospective clients to warrant such an initiative. Specific questions could be asked about the activities or programs that the respondents would be interested in using, possible priorities for some activities over others, how important the activities are to clients, and the times when they would be most likely desired and used. Another set of questions can explore possible barriers that prevent some people from accessing any of the activities. Potential barriers could emerge related to decisions about particular times a program is offered; the location, costs, and need to charge any fees; and possible psychological issues related to such things as how welcomed clients would feel.

Adequacy of Existing Programs

A needs assessment can also be very useful in determining the extent to which programs are already available to meet the needs of a particular group. This line of questioning naturally precedes attempts to document the need for a new program, even though this may not be taken seriously because of competition among agencies. Assessing the existence of other programs similar in nature to a proposed program is desirable to determine whether the need is already being met. Such a task is important not only to avoid program duplication but also to explore and create complementary and collaborative relationships with relevant existing agencies and programs.

An assessment of programs that already exist begins with finding them. Next, the programs could be visited and evaluated in terms of their relevance to the needs of the particular group targeted for the proposed new program. The assessments should also explore the ability of existing programs to serve additional clients, particularly the targeted group that is the concern of the initiators of the needs assessment.

The sources of information for a needs assessment of existing programs may include the administrators and service-delivery staff members of the agencies that provide such services. Assessment tools can help obtain information on such topics as demographic characteristics of the people who use services, characteristics of those who tend not to use them, explorations of the nature of their services, and any indicators that the programs are effective. The barriers that keep some groups from accessing services could be explored and service gaps documented. In addition, the assessment process could explore the agencies' views on new program initiatives that would be beneficial to particular groups in the community.

Adequacy of Existing Informal Resources

Although it is important to assess whether existing agency programs are available to address a pressing need, it can be equally important to assess the adequacy of existing informal resources. Informal resources may include extended family; other family members not in the household; neighborhood clubs, centers, and civic groups; advocacy groups; churches, synagogues, mosques, and other religious groups; libraries, museums, and theatrical resources; and so on. Often informal resources are the first line of defense and the easiest resources for clients to approach.

Client Accessibility

There are many potential barriers that will inevitably discourage some people from using the services of a program, such as an unfriendly receptionist, a delay in returning a call, a misunderstanding of the purpose of a program, unawareness of the program, or a perceived insensitivity to a particular group's culture. Access issues are important to consider in the planning stage of program development. Serious consideration must be given to the various groups that are targeted as recipients and to the factors that could prevent any of them from using the program's services.

Chapter 8 describes several factors that could be sources of confusion or resistance that keep potential program recipients from using services. The most effective way to identify these access issues is to ask potential recipients to share their views on accessibility. Such questions can be included as a component of a needs-assessment questionnaire or as interviews with recipients. Stakeholders who are concerned about the recipients can also be enlisted to share their views. Also, access issues can be relevant to consider when selecting a particular program approach or deciding on what kinds of staff members to hire.

Crafting Goals and Objectives

An additional purpose of a needs assessment can be to gather data pertinent to the goals of a proposed program. Goals of proposed programs tend to be crafted from the providers' perspectives. To address this bias, a needs assessment could be used to obtain specific data from the perspectives of potential recipients. Most of the questions would be open-ended explorations. Questions can be designed to obtain information related to the proposed goals and objectives of the program by exploring the following:

- What do clients perceive as realistic goals for themselves?
- What do they perceive to be some measurable objectives? In other words, how might things be different once they reach their goals?
- How motivated are they to seek these goals?
- How important are the goals to others in their immediate circle of social support?

Example of Needs-Assessment Questions on Family Planning Asked of Potential Recipients

- Do you have an interest in planning the size of your family?
- Would you consider using any existing birth control methods that are available?
- Would you have an interest in discussing your family-planning needs and questions with a professional counselor if one were available?
- What are some questions about birth control that you would want to discuss with a counselor?
- Would you be open to possibly obtaining a birth-control method such as an IUD if a program was available to fit one for you?
- Do you currently have easy access to the birth-control methods you want to use?
- Would you be comfortable using a family-planning program if it existed?
- What would be your hesitations in using such a program, if any?

Methods of Conducting Needs Assessments

A needs assessment is an organized, systematic effort to assess the need for something, in this case the need for a new program or practice area. Conducting a needs assessment of some or all of the prospective recipients of a program is often wisest, because they are some of the people who will choose whether to use the program. The more that the program takes into account their specific needs, the more likely it is that they will find it relevant and use it. The specific methods for conducting a needs assessment can take many forms, including using existing data, constructing and administering a questionnaire, conducting interviews, conducting focus groups, arranging public forums, observing, or any combination of these.

Documenting Needs with Existing Data

Sometime existing data is available to provide all or some of the documentation of the need for a new program. If so, this may be the place to start. Thus, the first recommended step in documenting the need for a new program is to explore whether relevant data already exists. This will be the least expensive way to conduct a needs assessment.

Steps for Reviewing Existing Data

DePoy and Gilson (2003) recommend a rigorous set of steps to effectively and efficiently review existing data for a needs assessment.

1. Determine the purpose of the review.
2. Set some search parameters.
3. Access relevant databases.
4. Obtain relevant information from the databases.
5. Organize the selected information.
6. Critically evaluate the information.
7. Prepare a report of the selected information.

Let's take a closer look at the numerous sources from which relevant existing data can be obtained (see steps 3 and 4 in DePoy & Gilson's list). There are often several relevant choices: local studies, governmental studies, studies of research firms and academic units, secondary research, data available from social agencies, and mapping resources. Let's take a closer look at what each of these sources can offer.

Local Studies.   Local studies can be an excellent source of data because they may include the actual client populations considered for the proposed new program. Local studies also may have more credibility with some stakeholders, especially when sponsored by colleagues in the geographic area. Local agencies may include the local United Way office, a local governmental agency, or the local newspaper. All of these organizations are known to conduct such studies. A simple way to begin an investigation of local studies is to do a Google search of the name of your community, county government, university, or local agency, followed by the words *needs assessment*. For example, a United Way agency in North Carolina conducted a needs assessment that focused on eliminating disparities in access to and use of available social agencies.

Example of United Way Needs Assessment

In July 2003, a United Way agency (United Way of Central Carolinas, 2003) conducted a needs assessment that focused on how to make the elimination of disparities a priority, so that "everyone [could] get the services they need without bias or fragmentation." This meant that services would be provided in a way that enables access to all who need them, with priority to those who have the greatest need and those for whom services could promote significant and lasting improvements in their lives. The study involved focus groups with various community and agency constituencies. Common themes that emerged from analyzing the data coalesced around six factors that contribute to inequities in access and outcomes and ten values that are central to addressing disparities.

Six Themes

1. Complexity of service delivery systems
2. Ineffective service provider–client relationships and engagement (e.g., lack of cultural competence in service provision, unclear expectations, lack of trust)
3. Communication issues (e.g., language barriers, illiteracy)
4. Transportation barriers
5. Economic constraints (e.g., limited program capacity, lack of insurance or other means of affordability)
6. Limited education and awareness (e.g., of needs, services, and systems)

Ten Values

1. Client centered
2. Decentralized and available in communities where people need them
3. Collaborative
4. Holistic
5. Agency board members and staff reflect characteristics of people who need service
6. Accepting and nonjudgmental
7. Culturally sensitive and culturally competent
8. Based on a relationship of trust between service provider and person receiving service
9. Fair
10. Including an emphasis on lifelong learning

Governmental Studies at the National and State Levels. Governmental agencies at the national and state levels conduct studies of relevance to social service agencies. Two good sources are the U.S. Census (www.census.gov)

and the National Center for Health Statistics (www.cdc.gov/nchs). The U.S. Census conducts not only a census of the entire U.S. population every ten years but also numerous smaller studies, known as Current Population Surveys, with nationally representative samples in between years. The surveys are conducted on numerous topics, have a good reputation for accuracy and reliability, and often are pertinent in documenting the needs of many subgroups in a population (e.g., elderly, families, children).

Studies of Nonprofit Research Firms, Academic Units, and Professional Journals. Many research firms and academic groups are also known to conduct and disseminate large-scale studies. Reports on some of these studies can be found on the Internet. Such firms often have large representative samples that can be generalized to even larger populations. A good example is Child Trends (www.childtrends.org), a nonprofit, nonpartisan research organization dedicated to improving the lives of children by conducting research and providing science-based information to improve the decisions, programs, and policies that affect children. Child Trends produces books, research briefs, and full research reports on such topics as child poverty, child welfare, health, marriage and family structure, teen sex and pregnancy, parenting, and family dynamics. They widely disseminate their reports, which are often free.

University-conducted studies can also be useful and are often reported on university Web sites and in professional journals. Several professional journals focus specifically on program and practice evaluations, including the following:

- *Evaluation: The International Journal of Theory, Research and Practice*
- *Evaluation Review: A Journal of Applied Social Research*
- *Evaluation and the Health Professions*
- *New Directions for Evaluation*
- *Evaluation and Program Planning: An International Journal*
- *American Journal of Evaluation*
- *Practical Assessment, Research and Evaluation*
- *Canadian Journal of Program Evaluation*

Evaluation reports can also be found in many other professional journals, such as *Social Work, Child Welfare,* and *Families in Society.*

Example of a Needs Assessment in a Professional Journal

Weinman, Buzi, and Smith (2005) focused on the risk factors, service needs, and mental health issues of 143 young fathers (aged sixteen to thirty-three) when they entered a fatherhood program. They found that almost 70 percent were unemployed, 42 percent had been in jail, and 39 percent were school dropouts. The most frequent mental health issues that the fathers identified included sadness and depression, nervousness and tension, helplessness, and aggression. Although the fathers identified these and other risk factors, they did not often request services to address them; the most frequently requested services were related to jobs and training. Because the results of this study were mostly problem focused, the authors recommended that future assessments use a strengths perspective.

Secondary Research.   Another option to consider when relying on other studies is secondary research or data from a previous study. This option is pertinent only if a data set from a previous study exists and is available. Many research firms offer their data sets to interested parties for secondary analysis, and usually for a reasonable fee.

Example of a Study Using Secondary Analysis

John O'Donnell (1999) conducted a secondary analysis of data from an earlier federally funded research and demonstration project on casework practice in kinship foster care. Kinship foster care refers to the placement of children in the home of a relative approved by the agency as a foster parent. The data was collected in the prior study from caseworkers in two private child-welfare agencies. O'Donnell reported on a subset of the original data set that focused on the involvement of African American fathers. His findings documented the lack of fathers' involvement in the caseworkers' assessment and planning of foster-care services for their children. Although useful secondary data was available about several of these fathers, the data had limitations because it emphasized their problems, not their strengths. Further, the data did not explore some issues of importance to O'Donnell, such as why more fathers of children in paternal kinship homes participated in casework services than fathers of children in maternal kinship homes.

Agency Data.   Virtually every social agency, school, and institutional setting collects an enormous amount of data on their clients. Often these data have great potential as resources for a needs assessment. For example, the client records of these organizations can be valuable in providing information about the demographic and diagnostic characteristics of clients, numbers of clients with specific problems, different types of interventions that have been used to help them, the amount of time that clients have received services, and in some cases outcome data for current and former clients.

Example of Using Agency Data

A study by Faithfull, Cook, & Lucas (2005) investigated the need of patients with malignant brain tumors and their caregivers in a cancer and palliative care program for support services. The evaluators were interested in finding out which community support services clients were using. Data were drawn retrospectively from case notes and clinical records for a population of 1,254 patients referred to the palliative care program over one year. Data collected from the records included demographic characteristics, extent of palliative care service use, other health and social service use, symptoms experienced, and time from diagnosis to referral and death. This evaluation identified some important clinical needs and questions for this particular client group related to palliative care. A critical question recommended for investigation in a later study was what services the caregivers needed. A limitation of the study was that it was not known how accurate the case notes and records were.

In another instance, a study was conducted of runaway and homeless lesbian, gay, bisexual, transgender, and questioning youths in New York City (Nolan, 2006). The agency wanted to find out what happened to the youths after they left a transitional living program by using case files about them. The files included information on the youths discharged from the program over a five-year period. Information was taken from the files on demographic characteristics, pre- and post-housing status, pre- and post-educational status, foster-care history, abuse history, length of stay in the transitional living program, and reason for discharge. The case files had an abundance of helpful data. For example, in the area of abuse history, the study found that half the youth had reported experiencing physical abuse, and one-third had reported being sexually abused, mostly by family members, boyfriends, and family friends. Half had reported experiencing verbal or emotional abuse, including homophobic and transgender-phobic remarks.

Mapping Resources.   Another recently developed approach uses computer and electronic files. Mapping visually locates specific groups or clusters of people or problems in a particular geographic area and helps users recognize where there are concentrations of problems. The concentrations can then be explored in terms of how they are associated with other characteristics, such as income level or ethnicity. For example, the U.S. Census tool American Factfinder (AFF) can be used to select specific Census data and map it across a geographic area of interest, such as a city or county. The tool, which allows for creating, viewing, printing, and downloading maps, is available online at www.factfinder.census.gov. The Reference Maps tool can be used to view boundaries of Census geographies, such as counties, cities and towns, urban areas, congressional districts, Census tracts, and Census blocks. The Thematic Maps tool can be used to view geographic patterns in Census data. Thematic maps are available for the 2000 Census, the 1990 Census, the Economic Census, and the Population Estimates program. The tutorial "Creating and Using Maps" is available for guidance.

Thematic maps may be particularly helpful when you want to compare statistical data of specific groups, such as population or median income, displayed in a map format. You can change the view of the thematic map by clicking on the area of the map you want to view in more detail or by selecting a new geography, theme, or data set. The Quick Tips command assists in navigating or customizing your map.

Example of Mapping as a Form of Assessment

A specific mapping program, referred to as a geographic information system (GIS) can help an evaluator gather more information about the characteristics of a local community, city, or county. The GIS can create maps for such things as the location of all senior centers, the degree to which neighborhoods are healthy, poverty levels in a community, locations of Medicaid users, crime rates, and particular agencies. More information can be found about the GIS program and its various features in the work of Hillier (2007).

Administer a Questionnaire

A questionnaire is a frequently chosen method to obtain relevant data for a needs assessment. A questionnaire can be an excellent way to inquire about the needs of a particular target group on a specific topic, such as family planning, housing improvements, or social activities for seniors. The questionnaire could be mailed to the intended audience, hand-delivered door-to-door, or handed out at a meeting or community gathering. An advantage of a questionnaire is that it can be distributed to a fairly large group of people without much effort. However, the questionnaire must be constructed so that it is completely self-explanatory and simple enough to fill out, as an interviewer will not be present to clarify anything.

Example of a Parks and Recreation Needs Assessment

Using a questionnaire mailed to every resident of the neighborhood, Line (2007) used a community needs assessment to explore neighbors' interest in several activity areas considered by an expanding community center. First, respondents selected from a list of activities the ones that they believed their family members would likely participate in, including baseball, T-ball, volleyball, tennis, after-school programs, nature and bike trails, tutoring, senior social clubs, educational seminars, and concerts. Next, respondents were asked about their interests in specific classes, such as karate, CPR and first aid, self-defense, arts and crafts, gardening, cooking, and safety. Then they were asked what methods they would prefer to receive information about upcoming park and recreation events. Options included monthly newsletters, flyers, public service announcements, e-mail, announcements in local newspapers, and information posted at the community center. Several questions followed about the best times for their availability, such as the best times for children's activities (e.g., mornings, midday, afternoons, evenings, weekdays or weekends). In addition, respondents were asked how they felt about existing activities at the center. On a scale of 1 (very unsatisfied) to 5 (very satisfied), questions included how much they felt that various existing activities met their needs and how satisfied they were with the community center generally. Finally, they were asked about their readiness to participate in new activities if they were provided (e.g., "Would you come to the center to preregister for these classes, and how much could you afford to pay for such classes?"). A final question asked if respondents wanted to be contacted about a particular program interest and, if so, to list the program and their name and phone number.

A disadvantage of questionnaires is that they almost always use quantitative methods and ask forced-response questions, because respondents are not likely to answer more than one or two open-ended questions. Another disadvantage is that questionnaires usually have low response rates. This problem could be addressed by administering the questionnaire to people attending a social event and encouraging them to fill it out at the event, which can work especially well if either the evaluator or the organization sponsoring the event are known and trusted by the people asked to participate.

Examples of Questions Used in a Domestic Violence Needs Assessment for the Victims

---

Stewart (2005) administered the following questionnaire:

1. How important is it for you to have information about domestic violence? (Circle 1 response.)
   Not important   Somewhat important   Very important

2. How important is it for you to have a safe place to stay if there is an emergency? (Circle 1 response.)
   Not important   Somewhat important   Very important

3. How important is it for you to attend an educational/support group? (Circle 1 response.)
   Not important   Somewhat important   Very important

4. How important is it for you to have help when you go to court? (Circle 1 response.)

   Not important   Somewhat important   Very important

5. How important is it for you to have individual counseling? (Circle 1 response.)

   Not important   Somewhat important   Very important

The example from Stewart (2005) uses a forced-response question format and identifies a few of the questions used by an MSW student to assess the needs of victims of domestic violence. Although the questions are effective for quickly finding out the degree to which respondents need each program area, qualitative questions could be added to gain insight into how the specific needs manifest and how respondents would *use* such a set of services if available.

Another way to structure a needs assessment in an agency that serves victims of domestic violence is to focus on victims' knowledge of what constitutes domestic violence and how it should be addressed. Examples of some of the types of question that could be asked are the following (Women's Commission, 2005):

Multiple-choice questions

Domestic violence affects
   (a) Only children who observe the violence in their home
   (b) All children living in homes with domestic violence
   (c) Only teenagers
   (d) Only young children
   (e) Does not affect children
   [Correct answer is b]

True/false questions

Domestic violence only occurs in low-income families.
   (a) True
   (b) False
   [Correct answer is false]

A batterer is never nice to his/her partner.
   (a) True
   (b) False
   [Correct answer is false]

Questionnaires with informants could also be implemented, particularly if there are experts with special knowledge on a topic and who are well acquainted with the needs of the community. Informants can share their own and others' perspectives. Informants might be professionals or volunteers in counseling or advocacy programs, or teachers, administrators, and others who have frequent contact with a population of interest. Their expertise would be based largely on their familiarity with the population.

Example of Informant Interviews

Charla Williams (2006), an MSW student, conducted a needs-assessment inquiry of staff members of a crisis intervention unit of a family agency that provides shelter, case management, counseling and advocacy services to victims of domestic violence or sexual assaults. The purpose was to find out from informants what additional programs they felt were needed for those experiencing domestic violence. The results of the questionnaire ranked support groups and transitional housing as the most important missing programs. The study also revealed that the family agency sponsoring the crisis intervention should advertise its services more, as many agencies were not familiar with it.

Conduct Interviews

Interviews are also a good choice for conducting needs assessments. An interview could be conducted with the target population, similar to using a questionnaire. Because an interview takes more time to administer than a questionnaire and requires training of the interviewer, interviews likely focus on a smaller group of respondents. Yet an advantage of interviews is that they can probe more deeply to elicit the views, attitudes, and needs of interviewees, which results in valuable qualitative data.

Informant interviews are a particular type of interviewing approach to consider, particularly if there are experts with special knowledge and who are well acquainted with the needs of the community. The informants can share not only their own perspectives but also those of others who may be more difficult to reach. Informants could be civic leaders, gang leaders or former leaders, representatives of advocacy groups, teachers with extensive experience in the community, volunteers and staff members of community agencies, and others.

Eliminating Health and Social Disparities: Some Interview Questions to Ask Agencies

- What role do you think your agency can play in community-based efforts to eliminate health and human service disparities?
- What does it take for agencies to be effective in eliminating disparities in the community?

- What other resources exist in the community aimed to eliminate disparities? How can these resources be strengthened?
- What goals do you think need to be measured in determining
  whether the community is making progress in increasing access to services and reducing health and social disparities?

Case studies and other in-depth interviews with a few people are another way to conduct a needs assessment. Case descriptions can be very useful in determining the need for a program by providing a fuller understanding of someone's circumstances and experiences or something of interest.
By illuminating the complexities of the social circumstances faced by one or
a few prospective clients or client families, for example, case studies can provide insights that may be relevant to understanding their struggles and resilience as well as how to help them.

The professional literature provides many examples of case studies that
have focused on a few individuals or on a larger social system such as a cultural group, gang, or social system such as a mental institution or prison.
These studies have often been enormously helpful in providing new insights
into the lives of a particular group not previously understood or known in
society and in discovering new ways to help effectively address unmet needs.

Goffman's book *Asylums* is a case study of a mental hospital in the
1950s. In this case, his study was a catalyst for beginning the deinstitutionalization movement of the 1960s, which led to the creation of a whole new
system of community-based residential and vocational programs for people
with mental illness and mental retardation intended to replace programs
that had been provided in institutional settings.

Example of a Case Study

Erving Goffman (1961) conducted a two-year participant-observation study of a large state mental institution in a book titled *Asylum*. In *Asylum*, Goffman vividly depicts what life was like in this institution and how the patients were regimented into a rigid,
imposed schedule. The case description was most effective in conveying how the institution was harmful and counterproductive to
patients. The book was timely and served as a strong catalyst for the
deinstitutionalization movement initiated a few years later.

A case description of an undocumented family of immigrants from Mexico could also provide valuable insights about the numerous difficulties they
face. Using an in-depth interview approach with one family, an interviewer
could obtain information about the difficulties that recently arrived families

face in the United States and programs that could be developed to help. Likely problems that could be more fully understood through a case study approach include how to receive adequate medical care, find adequate housing, enroll children in day care and public schools, find transportation, get help if exploited on the job, and obtain legal assistance.

In-depth interviews with a sample of staff members and volunteers of local agencies that provide similar programs or help similar clients are another way to proceed with a needs assessment. Often social workers and others on the front line have a wealth of information from their daily contact with clients. Tapping into this wealth of information is another valuable data source for a needs assessment.

The number and variety of possibilities for conducting a needs assessment with either a questionnaire or an interview method are almost endless.

Examples of Other Needs Assessments

1. Residents of an older-adult assisted-living center were assessed on the basis of the importance of their spiritual beliefs and practices (Franco, 2004). A major intent of the study was to explore the need for additional programs to address residents' spiritual needs. Ten residents were interviewed with such questions as, Do you belong to an organized religious group? What spiritual practices do you use? How important is prayer or meditation to you? What do you think happens after death? How can the center provide more assistance to you in response to your spiritual needs?

2. In exploring the need for a new program for Latino children who had witnessed domestic violence, Wolochwianski (2005) administered a questionnaire for mothers who had been victims of domestic violence about their children. The simple questionnaire asked whether they had any children, their ages and sex, and whether they would be interested in their children receiving services for witnessing domestic violence. Further, mothers were asked about convenient locations, transportation, whether children could receive services while the mother was receiving counseling, and the best times for such services.

3. Caliento (2004), whose field placement was in a foster-care agency, assessed the need for a specific program for teen mothers in foster care. She asked the professionals serving the teens to fill out a structured questionnaire using a five-point Likert scale (strongly agree to strongly disagree). She asked them to rate the mothers on the basis of their needs for

parenting-skills training, one-on-one in-home support, their ability to parent, education for preventing further pregnancies, child-care services for the baby, and several existing programs offered by the agency.

Conduct Focus Groups

Focus groups are a special form of group interview in which participants are invited to discuss a particular topic, for example, the needs of African Americans for hospice care. Focus groups can be used to find out the views of several people on an issue of importance to a needs assessment. Members of focus groups are usually selected because they have personal knowledge about or expertise in a particular topic. The leader of a focus group facilitates a group discussion by asking members several general questions on the topic.

Example of a Needs Assessment Using Focus Groups

The United Way of Central Carolinas (2003) conducted a needs assessment focusing on eliminating disparities in social services. To "put its arms around" the complexity of the disparities issue, the group solicited input from the broader community. It convened thirteen "learning conversations" with community members and service providers to better understand disparities and to identify strategies in practice to eliminate them. They also facilitated four problem analysis sessions with community stakeholders to answer three basic questions: What are the precursors to disparities? What are the consequences of not addressing them? and Where can we, as a community, most appropriately intervene?

Arrange Community and Other Public Forums

Community forums are similar to focus groups in that a fairly open selection process is used to bring people together to discuss a topic of interest to all of them, such as new or improved housing or fighting crime. This open selection process can be a special invitation to selected members of the community or a more open invitation to the entire community with a public announcement informing people of the upcoming community forum and its purpose. Participants are likely to belong to the same community or neighborhood, and the topic is likely to focus on an issue that has broad implications that affect large numbers of people.

Example of a Community Forum on the Growing Mortgage Foreclosure Rate

The local newspaper wrote a series of articles on the growing rate of foreclosure among homeowners, particularly in lower-income neighborhoods. After that, a housing assistance agency decided to pursue this need further in one of these neighborhoods. It held a community forum to openly discuss the problem and to determine the extent to which it was a concern of residents. Along with a presentation of the results of the newspaper series and an open discussion of the problem, agency personnel handed out a confidential questionnaire on foreclosures for affected residents to fill out about themselves or close friends. Some of the questions asked were the following:

- What kinds of loans did you/they purchase?
- What were the interest rates and other charges in the mortgages?
- Did you/they feel that the rates were unusually high or unfair?
- How much down payment was required?
- What circumstances led to the foreclosures for individual families?
- What kinds of help do they want?

Make Observations

Observations are another approach for assessing the need for a program. Social workers regularly depend on their observational skills in practice, such as when visiting clients in their homes. The nonverbal communication of clients, in particular, is often considered as important as their verbal communication. Observational evaluations use all of the senses, particularly sight and hearing, to collect data about a program and/or the needs it intends to address. Observations focus on what can be seen or heard, especially the behaviors of people. Behavior includes any number of things, such as a verbal comment or nonverbal expression, a conversation between two or more people, body movements, and physical contact between people.

Windshield surveys are one form of observation in which an individual new to a neighborhood drives through it to gain information (Shuster & Goeppinger, 1996). A windshield survey is usually structured such that the observers know what they are looking for. Usually these observations focus on the physical aspects of a neighborhood, such as types of housing, physical conditions of housing, street conditions, commercial entities, people who are out and their activities, and other observable characteristics.

Some Guidelines for a Windshield Tour of an Agency's Neighborhood

Kelly Koney (consultant to Council for Children's Rights, Charlotte, NC, personal communication, 2002) provides the following guidelines for a windshield tour:

1. Keep your observations objective.
2. Observe what can influence how a client uses the agency's services.

   - Is there a nearby bus stop?
   - Is there an easily accessible parking lot?
   - How safe is it to walk around?
   - Is this an affluent neighborhood that may intimidate some lower-income people?

3. Is the agency located in a residential neighborhood? Are there mostly houses, apartments, or businesses? What are the conditions of the buildings, streets, sidewalks?
4. What types of people are out? What are they doing? What are their facial expressions toward you and others?

An important variation in observation studies is whether the evaluator participates in the activities or event being observed. Sometimes participant-observation is used, which is unstructured observation involving the evaluator as a participant. A participant-observer role helps the evaluator become more of an insider who observes people and their social context without drawing excessive attention to his or her presence. Participant observers are likely to use fairly unstructured interviewing methods and unstructured observations in their data collection (e.g., Patton, 1987).

Example of a Needs Assessment Using Participant Observation

An MSW student (Jordan, 2005) wanted to evaluate the extent to which collaboration occurred in decision making of teams of collaborative agencies meeting at a child advocacy center. She used the participant observation method to collect data on the leadership styles of team leaders and the activities evident in the team meetings. She chose to observe a random sample of client cases discussed by the teams at each meeting. Leadership style was defined and measured as of four fairly distinct types: telling, selling, participating, and delegating (Hersey & Blanchard, 1977). Participating and delegating styles reflected a more collaborative leadership style.

Jordan's thesis was that the leadership styles were related to such activities as number of information disclosures, number of team agreements toward action steps, and number of team recommendations.

An example of how one evaluator took on the participant-observation
role in a needs assessment of the stigma problems of people with mental retardation was partially revealed in several activities that he participated in
with these participants once they informed him of their comfort with his
presence (Dudley, 1983). The activities provided firsthand exposure to some
stigma problems in social situations and facilitated more open sharing of reports of stigma problems:

- Dancing with the people being studied
- Eating with them at restaurants
- Riding public transportation with them
- Joining them for visits at their home
- Sitting with them at their workstation at a sheltered workshop
- Double-dating
- Talking with them or listening to their conversations at various social
  occasions

An important caveat for the participant is to minimize or avoid any interference with the behaviors being observed. This requires a balance between being able to participate enough to become an insider but not too
much so as to create unnecessary reactivity. A drawback to participant-observation is that it takes a much greater amount of time to build rapport and
to gain acceptance from those being observed before fully concentrating on
data collection. This initial period is a time in which such things as informed
consent issues and the evaluator's role can be clarified and supported. This
method also usually takes additional time during the data collection period
to obtain a saturation of types of behaviors that reflect the many possible
variations that could be key to a special area of need. In the example on
stigma, it is evident that observations occurred during a variety of activities
to obtain a saturation of various types of stigma expressed with a wide range
of familiar people and strangers in several different social situations.

Using a Combination of Approaches

Many needs assessments use multiple methods of data collection to
capture a picture of a community from several different perspectives and
formats. Considering the variety of approaches described previously, a comprehensive needs assessment could, for example, involve obtaining demographic data from the U.S. Census or from a local health department, administering a questionnaire to the population of interest or informant
interviews with key neighborhood leaders, observing discussions at neigh-

borhood meetings, and carrying out informal interviews with professionals from social agencies in the area.

Example of a Multimethod Needs Assessment

Hymans (2000) reported on a multimethod study in which BSW and nursing students joined together to complete a comprehensive communitywide assessment of a local neighborhood as part of a macro practice course. The goals of the project included understanding community assessment, assessing how a community functions, developing a broader understanding of social work practice, and providing a service to a community. The students used several data collection methods, including interviews with key informants, observations of neighborhood meetings, gathering existing demographic data, reviewing official documents, using mapping tools, conversations with political and religious leaders, and networking with professionals in the area.

Practice Areas and Needs Assessments

Although needs assessments are commonly used to plan new programs, they are much less frequently considered in planning new or expanded practice approaches. Yet needs assessments at the practice level can have some of the same purposes as programs. For example, needs assessments can help in planning new practice areas or approaches by providing information on clients' needs, their perceptions of their needs and prior experiences in addressing them, and their thoughts on how helpful a proposed practice approach appears to be.

Needs-assessment information can also be helpful in investigating any accessibility barriers for a new practice approach. A most effective way to learn more about accessibility barriers is to explore this issue with prospective clients. Psychological and cultural accessibility may be the largest accessibility areas to confront. In this regard, a needs assessment can uncover whether a new practice approach comprises goals, techniques, and lines of questioning that are sensitive to and compatible with particular cultural beliefs of some groups. For example, a practice approach intended to help clients gain new insights into their problems may not be as practical or even relevant to some groups as a training approach that stresses learning new skills.

Similarly, a needs assessment can be a vehicle for learning more about how to craft goals and objectives for a new or expanded practice area. Goals crafted from the provider's perspective may need to be cross-checked by the perspectives of potential recipients. Asking recipients questions about proposed goals and objectives of a practice approach such as the following may help:

1. What do you perceive as realistic goals for yourself?
2. What might be some measurable indicators that your goals are being reached?
3. How important are these goals to you and others in your circles of social support?

Assessments conducted in practice areas, like those conducted for new programs, have several methodological options at their disposal. They can be qualitative or quantitative. Qualitative methods can include in-depth interviews with clients, minimally structured observations, and brief questionnaires with open-ended questions. Pertinent qualitative data for a needs assessment can also be drawn from existing client records and client journals. Family genograms and ecomaps can also be used as assessment tools and can provide visual descriptions of family relationships and complicated connections to external social systems.

Quantitative needs assessments are also frequently used in developing practice areas. Standardized scales are one form of assessment. These scales are used to assess a wide range of needs and issues, such as self-esteem, depression, addictions, family well-being, and other complex and multidimensional variables. Several sources of standardized scales are available in social work and related fields (e.g., Fischer & Corcoran, 1994; Ginsberg, 2001; Jordan & Franklin, 2003; Royse, Thyer, Padgett, & Logan, 2006). These scales should have strong validity and reliability. Questionnaires and interviews developed by experienced practitioners are other quantitative tools that can be used.

Example of a Standardized Scale Used in Assessments of Practice

One agency used an anger evaluation scale as a needs-assessment tool in developing a new group approach. This scale helped adolescent clients focus on discussing goals and objectives in this problem area of their behavior (Patrick & Rich, 2004). The individual items of the scale were used to facilitate discussions with clients about the many ramifications and variations in expressions of dysfunctional anger. They also used the scale as a baseline measure of the clients' dysfunctional anger and as an ongoing measure of their anger at different points in their work together. The anger evaluation scale consisted of ten statements on anger using a five-point Likert scale (strongly agree to strongly disagree). Examples of scale items are the following:

- I often get angrier than necessary.
- I usually stay angry for hours.
- As a result of my anger, I use threatening language or gestures.
- I use alcohol or drugs to calm my rage.

Steps in Conducting a Needs Assessment

A needs assessment should not be planned and executed in a vacuum for its results to be well received by all stakeholders. Several steps are important to consider that focus primarily on involving stakeholders from the beginning and incorporating them into each step to the extent possible. Keep in mind the participatory action approach, described in chapter 2, as one guide. Other resources provide additional information on these steps (e.g., Meenaghan, Kilty, & McNutt, 2004).

1. **Create a broad-based committee or team to sponsor the assessment.** Attempt to include all actual and potential stakeholders. Make sure that they represent the varying views of their constituencies, including different views and experiences on how the program or practice area should look.
2. **Have an extensive discussion with the committee on the general intent of a proposed program or practice area.** General intent can include identifying target groups of clients that you wish to help, general goals for helping them and their families, and initial assumptions about the causes of their problems and possible solutions.

Example of Data Gathering from Different Types of Fathers

A coalition of several local agencies prepared to conduct an assessment of the needs of uninvolved and minimally active fathers and existing services to fathers in the county. Fortunately, a nearby foundation was willing to provide a small grant to complete the study. A strategic-planning firm was enlisted to assist. The coalition proposed to conduct a needs assessment of four subgroups of fathers using multiple methods: fathers living with their very young children, nonresidential fathers who pay child support, nonresidential teen fathers, and fathers with children with special needs. Fathers of special needs children were selected because of the coalition's previous commitment to such children. The other three groups represented fathers perceived to have special needs that could be realistically met by the coalition's effort. Five methods were identified: (1) a series of focus groups with representatives of the four targeted subgroups of fathers, (2) one-on-one interviews with fathers, (3) key informant interviews with pertinent professionals, (4) an assessment of existing agency services to fathers, and (5) further examination of existing U.S. Census data on fathers in their county.

3. **Explore funding support for your project** and incorporate the ideas of potential funding agencies in your continued articulation of the problem and goals of your project. Also, begin articulating a pro-

posal for obtaining funds. Possible funding supports could be identified earlier in the process in a more general way.
4. **Decide on the methods that you will use** to conduct your own
   needs assessment. This is often a firsthand, in-depth study of the
   community. Possible methods to consider are focus groups, informant interviews, interviews of a sample of prospective recipients, and
   interviews with existing agency resources and services. Decide
   whether you need either a professional firm or an individual consultant to help develop your research methodologies.
5. **Conduct your needs assessment** and compile an easy-to-read report of your findings for your stakeholder committee.
6. **Involve all stakeholders in your committee in articulating a proposal for a new program or practice area.** Develop the proposal
   by supplementing and revising any earlier versions of your problem
   definition and goals on the basis of your needs-assessment results.
   Then develop a set of general strategies and specific program/prac-
   tice components that you could implement to achieve your goals.
7. **Be sure to consider program/practice interventions at various
   levels** in your general strategies. These could include individual and
   family services to prospective recipients, group services, community
   education efforts, advocacy, and new agency policies initiatives that
   would directly or indirectly support your new program.

The preceding steps are designed especially for a needs assessment of
an at-risk group in a city or county. This general outline has been used to
conduct a needs assessment with one at-risk group and could be used with
other at-risk populations as well, such as teenage mothers with their first
baby, recent immigrants from Mexico or Central America, cancer survivors,
homeless people without access to adequate housing, and elderly, socially
isolated lesbian women.

Steps in a Needs Assessment of Caregivers

An evaluation group conducting a needs assessment of family
caregivers of older adults defined its own steps for conducting a
needs assessment (Kietzman, Scharlach, & Dal Santo, 2004).

1. Describe the current population of caregivers by compiling a
   descriptive profile.
2. Determine the existing and unmet needs of caregivers by obtaining input from professionals, consumers, and advocates.
3. Inventory existing caregiver resources and services by identifying all programs and services already serving caregivers.
4. Identify service gaps including existing barriers to equitable
   access to caregiver resources and services by assessing what
   the gaps and barriers are.

5. Prioritize the identified service needs of caregivers by synthesizing information gathered and ranking the needs.
6. Design a plan for the delivery of caregiver services that reduces identified barriers to access, supplements existing services, and creates new services where none exist, in the most effective and efficient manner possible by implementing a decision-making process that results in a plan of action.

As an exercise, compare the steps of Kietzman, Scharlach, and Dal Santo (2004) to the seven steps proposed just before them in this chapter. Who might be some of the stakeholders in Kietzman and colleagues' project? How do you think their stakeholders could become more involved in conducting their needs assessment? What would be some of the advantages and disadvantages of adding the PAR steps to their needs assessment?

The next chapter considers a third important topic of the planning stage, crafting goals and measurable objectives. It is important to carefully craft goals and objectives before implementing a new program or practice area.

Key Terms
Community forums
Conducting interviews
Constructing questionnaires
Data available in social agencies
Focus groups
Governmental studies
Local studies
Logic model
Mapping
Needs assessments
Observations
Participant-observation
Purposes of a needs assessment
Secondary research
Steps in conducting a needs assessment
Studies in professional journals and on the Internet
Studies of nonprofit organizations
Using existing data

Discussion Questions and Assignments
1. Use the logic model to design a program for older adults who have lost their spouses and are socially isolated, have some chronic medical problems affecting their mobility, and live in multicultural neighborhoods. Begin by finding a needs assessment article or report that identifies some of the needs for this population. Then brainstorm

with classmates or other colleagues to identify some ways to meet these interpersonal and mobility needs. Describe a proposed program that addresses many of the needs so that the adults can maintain their independence and natural supports in their neighborhoods.

2. This is a project for two or more students to complete. Focus on assessing the needs of families in a community context. Conduct an informal, multifaceted needs assessment of families in the community and the resources that already exist to help them. This assignment is partially intended to help you integrate work at several different system levels, especially family and community assessments. Specific suggestions for carrying out this assignment are as follows:

- Attempt to talk with a variety of parents and other adult family members in the community, asking them what they think are the critical needs and problems that families and family members face. Ask for their opinions on how these needs can be met. What types of resources and services are needed, and how can social workers help them overcome the problems they identify? Be sure to explain to them your purpose and your intention to keep all information that they share confidential.

- Consider observing what is happening with the family members (e.g., parents, grandparents, children, teenagers, babies) that you see. What are they doing, what does their affect seem to communicate, what strengths do they appear to have, and what problems and needs seem evident through your observations?

- If you have difficulty talking with parents and other adult family members because they are unwilling or hesitant, identify and talk with advocates of families in the community, such as community leaders, volunteers, teachers, agency personnel, and other informal leaders.

- Look at the findings of any recently conducted local studies that might reveal something about the needs of families. Consider newspaper articles and community hearings. Explore citywide and countywide studies and the U.S. Census if they offer data that pertain to your particular community.

- Think about and share other ways to learn about the needs of families in the community. Thinking outside of the box is often overlooked in doing an assessment like this.

- After assessing the needs of families, identify and locate social agencies, community centers, churches, schools, day-care centers, businesses, and other organizations in the community and find out how they are attempting to help families or individual family members.

3. Using data from the U.S. Census, investigate the needs of children younger than five years of age in your community. This can be done online at www.census.gov. Select one report and describe what you learn about their needs.

4. Conduct a windshield tour of the neighborhood surrounding your agency or another neighborhood in which a large concentration of your clients live. Use the suggestions in this chapter to help you conduct the assessment. Then share what you learned with the class or agency colleagues.

5. Conduct a needs assessment using the American Factfinder mapping tool available at the U.S. Census Web site (www.factfinder.census.gov). Use the Thematic Maps tool to view some of the geographic patterns in the Census data. Select a city or county of interest to you, identify a data set of the Census, and create a map that visually displays data for the city or county.

6. Work in small groups of three to five to complete this project (which can be carried out in conjunction with a policy course and is a variation of an exercise that appeared on the Baccalaureate Social Work Program Directors Listserv).

   - Select a community and identify a policy question that highlights an apparent unaddressed need (e.g., Do children need somewhere to go after school? Do teens need something to keep them off the street? Is a domestic violence hotline needed in the community?) You may want to seek assistance in identifying your policy issue from local agencies or funding agencies.
   - Once you have identified a policy question, conduct a needs assessment of the local community that provides data to tentatively confirm or refute your initial policy question. One of the questions of your needs assessment can be the policy question that you identified. Other questions can be used to document the suspected need(s) that you have identified.
   - Write a policy change proposal that can address the need that you have begun to document. Your proposal should include the following:

     (a) What is the unmet policy reform that is needed?
     (b) How did you discover and document it?
     (c) What do you propose to do to meet this need?
     (d) How can it lead to advocacy for social justice issues?
     (e) Where will you get funding?
     (f) How will you secure other resources (e.g., space, materials)?
     (g) Who will be your staff and volunteers? How will they be paid?
     (h) How will they be recruited and trained?

(i)   What will be your budget?
(j)   What are the limitations or obstacles to implementing your plan? How might these obstacles be overcome?

- A reaction paper of one or two pages can also be requested from each group member reflecting on such questions as, What was difficult? What was fun? What did you learn about the field of policy reform and community-based social work?

References

Caliento, K. (2004). Needs assessment for adolescent parents in foster care: Program development. Unpublished manuscript, University of North Carolina at Charlotte.

DePoy, E., & Gilson, S. F. (2003). *Evaluation practice: Thinking and action principles for social work practice*. Pacific Grove, CA: Brooks/Cole–Thomson Learning.

Dudley, J. (1983). *Living with stigma: The plight of the people who we label mentally retarded*. Springfield, IL: Charles Thomas.

Faithfull, S., Cook, K., & Lucas, C. (2005). Palliative care of patients with a primary malignant brain tumor: Case review of service use and support provided. *Palliative Medicine, 19*, 545–550.

Fischer, J., & Corcoran, K. (1994). *Measures for clinical practice: A sourcebook*. New York: Free Press.

Franco, S. (2004). Spirituality among residents at Presbyterian Wesley Care Center. Unpublished manuscript, University of North Carolina at Charlotte.

Ginsberg, L. (2001). *Social work evaluation: Principles and methods*. Boston: Allyn & Bacon.

Goffman, E. (1961). *Asylums: Essays on the social situation of mental patients and other inmates*. Garden City, NY: Anchor Books.

Hersey, P., & Blanchard, K. H. (1977). *The management of organizational behavior*. Upper Saddle River, NJ: Prentice Hall.

Hillier, A. (2007). Why social work needs mapping. *Journal of Social Work Education, 43*(2), 205–221.

Hymans, D. J. (2000). Teaching BSW students community practice using an interdisciplinary neighborhood needs assessment project. *Journal of Baccalaureate Social Work, 5*(2), 81–92.

Jordan, A. M. (2005). Development of a multidisciplinary team assessment tool for a child advocacy center. Unpublished manuscript, University of North Carolina at Charlotte.

Jordan, C., & Franklin, C. (Eds.). (2003). *Clinical assessment for social workers: Quantitative and qualitative methods* (2nd ed.). Chicago: Lyceum Books.

Kietzman, K. G., Scharlach, A. E., & Dal Santo, T. S. (2004). Local needs assessment and planning efforts for family caregivers: Findings and recommendations. *Journal of Gerontological Social Work, 42*(3/4), 39–60.

Line, S. (2007). *Harrisburg parks and recreation*. Harrisburg, NC: Harrisburg Parks and Recreation.

Marlow, C. R. (2005). *Research methods for generalist social work*. Belmont, CA: Thomson.

Meenaghan, T. M., Kilty, K. M., & McNutt, J. G. (2004). *Social policy analysis and practice*. Chicago: Lyceum Books.

Nolan, T. C. (2006). Outcomes for a transitional living program serving LGBTQ youth in New York City. *Child Welfare*, *85*(2), 385–405.

O'Donnell, J. (1999). Involvement of African American fathers in kinship foster care services. *Social Work*, *44*(5), 428–441.

Patrick, J., & Rich, C. (2004). Anger management taught to adolescents with an experiential object relations approach. *Child and Adolescent Social Journal*, *21*(1), 85–100.

Patton, M. (1987). *How to use evaluative methods in evaluation*. Newbury Park, CA: Sage Publications.

Ross, P. H., Lipsey, M. W., & Freeman, H. E. (2004). *Evaluation: A systematic approach* (7th ed.). Thousands Oaks, CA: Sage Publications.

Royse, D., Thyer, B., Padgett, D., & Logan, T. (2006). *Program evaluation: An introduction* (4th ed.). Belmont CA: Brooks/Cole.

Shuster, G. F., & Goeppinger, J. (1996). Community as client: Using the nursing process to promote health. In M. Stanhope & J. Lancaster (Eds.), *Community health nursing: Promoting health of aggregates, families and individuals* (pp. 289–314). St. Louis: Mosby.

Stewart, B. (2005). Domestic violence needs assessment. Unpublished manuscript, University of North Carolina at Charlotte.

United Way of Central Carolinas. (2003, July). Community works: Eliminating disparities initiative. Retrieved March 5, 2007, from http://www.uwcentralcarolinas.org/resources/?fuseaction=uwresources.

Weinman, M. L., Buzi, R. S., & Smith, R. B. (2005). Addressing risk behaviors, service needs, and mental health issues in programs for young fathers. *Families in Society*, *86*(2), 261–266.

Williams, C. (2006). A crisis intervention needs assessment. Unpublished manuscript, University of North Carolina at Charlotte.

Wolochwianski, J. (2005). A needs assessment for a new program for Hispanic child witnesses of domestic violence in Mecklenburg County. Unpublished manuscript, University of North Carolina at Charlotte.

Women's Commission. (2005). Adult domestic violence pretest/posttest. Charlotte, NC: Author.

Chapter 7

Crafting Goals and Objectives

The paramount question is, What is the intervention intended to accomplish?

Frequently, planning a new program involves preparing a grant proposal for funding, and the proposal can be an important exercise in describing what the program is supposed to look like. The program description includes many components of an evaluation infrastructure, including the following clearly articulated elements:

- Program goals and objectives
- Services and technologies for helping clients reach goals
- A budget
- An evaluation plan to determine whether the program is effective

An evaluation plan, the last component mentioned, is typically required in most grant proposals. Unfortunately, such a plan is often largely incidental to the program construction process of many proposals. What often happens is that it tends to be an add-on prepared by someone in tune with research methods who is not directly involved in the construction of the program; the primary motivation for preparing the evaluation plan is to satisfy the funding agency.

In any event, evaluation considerations are extremely important to think about and plan for while a program is in the development stage. The logic model helps explain why. As described in chapter 6, the logic model recommends that the input, implementation, output, and outcome elements be logically connected. These stages and their respective elements need to be carefully thought out in relation to one another, and this all needs to begin in the planning stage. This chapter examines two critical components of program and practice interventions: goals and objectives. Goals and measurable objectives are formulated during the planning or input stage, when a program or practice area is under construction. Goals and objectives provide a central anchor or reference point for conducting most evaluations.

The goals and objectives of a new program or practice area need focused attention. Some pertinent questions are the following:

- What are the goals of the program?
- Are measurable objectives crafted for each of these goals?
- Are the goals and objectives logically linked to clients' problems, unmet needs, and underlying causes?
- Is there a logical link between the goals and objectives and how the program is implemented to reach these goals?

Helping an Agency Develop a New Program with an Evaluation Infrastructure

A graduate student devises a set of questions to guide her while helping her agency integrate an evaluation component into a new proposed program:

1. What is the problem that you want to solve or tackle? What do you believe are the causes of this problem?
2. Who are the people experiencing this problem whom you want to help?
3. What are your overall goals for solving this problem? How long will it take to reach each goal?
4. What intervention strategy do you plan to use to meet your goals? Describe your intervention plan. How will it contribute to meeting goals?
5. Identify the specific indicators (measurable objectives) that will tell you that you have reached your goals. List as many as possible.
6. What resources do you have that will help you to conduct an evaluation?
7. What constraints may hinder you in conducting an evaluation?

Goals for Program and Practice Interventions

Every program and practice intervention should have a set of goals that provide direction and an end result to pursue for clients. Basic questions about goals are the following: Where is this program/practice area going? What do we want to accomplish? How feasible is it to have success in achieving this goal? What approaches are known to work in helping clients reach these goals?

Although having goals is something that every agency intervention should have, most staff members and some agency administrators may not be well versed in them. This can result in the interventions spinning their wheels, going in unproductive directions, and/or wasting valuable resources. In other instances, agency interventions may have goals, but goals that are too vague to provide any direction or benchmarks for measuring progress. Examples of some vague goals that are used in helping clients are the following:

- Becoming more independent
- Resolving conflicts in a parent-child relationship
- Becoming an empowered family
- Being discharged from the hospital
- Increasing positive social behaviors
- Reducing antisocial behaviors

- Improving performance in school
- Successfully working in a competitive job
- Keeping youth safe
- Alleviating crises
- Reuniting a client with her or his family

Example of a Frequently Ignored Program Goal

During the past several decades, sheltered workshops have been considered an essential type of vocational program in the array of program offerings available for people with mental retardation. This has been the case in both community-based and institutional systems. A major goal for most sheltered workshops is to prepare people for the competitive workforce. Sheltered workshops are protected work sites for people with disabilities that employ them in assembling consumer goods like the airplane headsets used for watching movies or small hardware items like small bolts sealed in a plastic bag and sold in hardware stores. Yet these programs are often, in reality, driven by two implicit goals that are in direct tension with the major goal. The implicit goals are to find contracts of any kind to occupy the clients in the workshops and to provide a safe environment for them during the daytime hours. Because the implicit goals are important, sheltered workshops seldom succeed in accomplishing the major goal of preparing participants for competitive employment (e.g., Dudley & Schatz, 1985).

Characteristics of Goals

Measurable goals are critical to any successful program or individual practice intervention. They are important because they provide an intervention with a direction to pursue and an outcome to reach. Without goals, an intervention could be an aimless effort that does not seem to go anywhere important. Goals have many other characteristics that are important to understand as well. Goals are needed at all system levels. Goals are oriented to a time period. They are expected to be relevant to the intervention to which they are linked, and they should be responsive to the needs of the clients whom they serve. They can have one dimension or be considered in combination with other related goals. Some focus on program implementation while others focus on the outcomes of clients.

All System Levels

Social work has the potential to operate at all system levels, including the individual, family, group, community, organization, and policy. Primary and secondary prevention are preferred to tertiary prevention, because problems that can be avoided or headed off at an early stage will bring less harm and cost less to achieve. Yet most programs and practice interventions that governmental agencies are willing to fund focus on tertiary issues or treatment. Treatment interventions usually provide help once a problem is fully evident and has obvious adverse effects on clients' lives. Unfortunately, government agencies tend to be unwilling to invest in funding or sponsoring interventions until clients reach this tertiary stage. Nevertheless, goals can be formulated at all system levels, even though goals at macro levels such as community and policy need to be given greater consideration in most social work circumstances.

Time Oriented

Goals are oriented to a time period, for the short run, middle run, or long run. Short-term goals can be helpful as stepping-stones to midrange goals, and midrange goals are intended to lead to long-term ones. Although short-term goals are important, long-term goals are ultimately most important because they reflect the outcomes expected of successfully functioning people. For example, a short-term goal for a client with an addiction problem may be to no longer desire drugs while attending a drug treatment program, a midrange goal may be to live drug free in a halfway house for six months, and the long-term goal may be total withdrawal from drug use and drug culture. Similarly, a short-term goal for an ex-offender may be to stay out of trouble and regularly report on his or her activities to a probation officer during the probation period, while the long-term goal is to discontinue committing crimes altogether. Later in the book, we will discuss how agency evaluations tend to give primary emphasis to short-term goals and overlook the midrange and long-term ones.

Linked to the Intervention

The goals of an intervention should be a logical outgrowth of the intervention. After having a reasonably thorough description of the intervention, one should have a good grasp of what it intends to accomplish. The goals of the program should logically and realistically reflect this. For example, if a program involves counseling, its goals are likely to reflect some form of psychological and/or interpersonal improvement in the client, whereas a program designed to refer clients to other agencies is likely to have goals related to connecting clients with the referral agencies and using their services.

Responsive to the Clients' Needs

Social workers always advocate for clients in some form or another. We want our interventions to make a difference in our clients' lives and prefer to involve them to the greatest extent possible in the decisions that will help that to happen. While program and practice interventions need to be responsive to client needs, so does an evaluation. A bold way to increase client participation is to involve them in the evaluation as it progresses. The participatory action approach (PAR), described in chapter 2, is designed to do this.

Interrelated with Other Goals

Programs and practice interventions can have one central goal or several interrelated ones. It often depends on what the problem is, the expectations of the agency provider, and the resources available. Interrelated goals are important because some goals cannot be effectively addressed without considering their interdependence with other goals. For example, a welfare reform program may emphasize one goal: clients' obtaining of jobs. Or the program could be more comprehensive, giving fairly equal emphasis to two or three interrelated goals, such as obtaining a decent-paying job, securing day care for the client's children, and securing a safe home for the family. A program that has a set of interrelated goals often tends to be more effective in helping clients than one with a single goal.

Focused on Either Programs or Client Outcomes

Goals can focus on any number of things, including clients, staff members, and other program activities. Posavac and Carey (1997) identify three types of goals: setting up a program, implementing a program, and determining whether the program's services meet recipients' goals. All three types of goals are interdependent. Outcome goals for clients are the ultimate reason for having a program. In addition, outcome goals depend on a program that is fully implemented and that runs well, which results from implementation goals. Similarly, program implementation goals cannot be justified unless they benefit a group of clients who need them, which refers to planning goals.

Example of Types of Goals (Posavac & Carey, 1997)

Planning goals: Goals that are involved in setting up a program (e.g., locating a satellite facility site for the program, hiring a team of five clinical supervisors).

Intermediate goals: Goals involved in executing or carrying out the program (e.g., admitting twenty-five qualified clients, providing weekly supervision of each direct-care worker).

Outcome goals: Goals for clients to achieve as they complete the program (e.g., learn communication skills that help express anger verbally).

Limitations of Goals

Some goals for interventions have limitations that should be noted. These limitations overlap in some ways. They are not always easy to measure, they can be too theoretical or global, and they can be unobservable. Also, some goals are only discovered after a program has been implemented.

Not Easy to Measure

Many goals do not easily convert into measurable forms without losing some of their properties or meaning. A severe case of anxiety, for example, is a complex psychiatric condition to diagnose and measure. This is particularly the case when overcoming anxiety becomes a goal of a clinical program. In this instance, we often want to know not just whether the client has an anxiety disorder but also the severity of the anxiety and what constitutes improvement or decline. In practice, changes in a severe anxiety disorder can be most easily detected by a clinical social worker who uses qualitative questions individualized to a particular client's sources of anxiety and other circumstances. Obtaining a standardized quantitative measure of improvement in an anxiety disorder appears to be more challenging. However, existing standardized scales with established properties of validity and reliability may be another way to measure whether such a goal has been reached, even though the scales may miss some subtle but important properties of this psychiatric condition.

Other goals may be fairly easy to convert into measurable forms but difficult to measure practically. In this case, methodologies are sometimes lacking for obtaining valid data, such as when reliance depends on a client's self-reporting. Many types of behaviors that are considered personal and private can be intentionally distorted. Clients typically underreport alcohol and drug consumption. Reporting of abuse by perpetrators and victims is also challenging to measure, as is accurate disclosure of safe sexual practices like condom use and number of sexual partners.

Too Theoretical

Many program and practice interventions are constructed from an abstract model that begins with theoretical notions of goals. Such theoretical goals are difficult to measure empirically. For example, many mentoring programs for young African American teenage males offer a surrogate father for a parent who is missing or unavailable in the biological family. These programs typically choose outcome goals for the teenagers such as developing a healthy male identity, preparing to become an active father, and contributing to the well-being of the African American community. Although several overt indicators of the theoretical notions may come to mind, measuring them as they were intended in their theoretical form becomes more challenging.

Too Global

Other goals of interventions begin as global outcomes that are expected in the larger community or society, such as reducing the number of homicides or drug trafficking. One small program may be able to address these larger social problems in very limited terms, but many other causal factors beyond the reach of the program are difficult to influence. In other words, a global goal may be very difficult to link to one small program focused on a small number of people and their immediate social circumstances.

An example of a global goal for a community program is reducing the number of divorces in a community of seventy-five thousand people. The community group First Things First, in Gastonia, North Carolina, established a premarital group-counseling program for couples sponsored by local churches, synagogues, and mosques. The hope is that the program will have an impact, however small, on the divorce rate. However, they need help in considering less global goals, such as participants staying together, particularly during the challenging years of early marriage. Reducing the number of divorces in their community, while relevant and noble, is something that the group had to admit was much bigger than anything it could tackle on its own. The group came to realize that the divorce rate has multiple causes, many of which were beyond its influence and ability to change.

Unobservable

Many goals that are important for programs to influence are internal aspects of human functioning, including people's attitudes toward themselves and others, their feelings, and their cognitive mental processes. Take racial attitudes, for example. A program may be set up to improve its members' attitudes toward one another in a culturally diverse community. Such a community could have, for example, African American, Latino, and white members who have lived there for several years, along with recent immigrants from Mexico, Central America, and/or Iran. In this case, positive racial and ethnic attitudes could be a crucial ingredient in helping such a community function well. Racial attitudes have been measured numerous times in the past, primarily using surveys. Yet we know that such surveys have many limitations: they often do not elicit totally honest reporting of attitudes, particularly deep-seated attitudes that are difficult for a person to express when faced with self-perceived racial conflicts or threats. A challenge for such programs is to find more accurate, in-depth ways to uncover these deeply seated and distorted thought processes and how they can change over time.

Unintended Goals

Without question, it is essential to identify the goals of a program during the planning stage. This often takes place as part of a larger effort to describe the purpose of a program and the expected outcomes. Nevertheless, unanticipated or unintended goals can also emerge once a program is implemented and may become as important as the initial goals. When this occurs, which can be often, it is recommended that the new goals, if relevant, be added to the existing ones but not replace them. In this case, measurable objectives should be quickly crafted for them and evaluation data collected as part of an overall evaluation plan.

Identifying unintended goals during program implementation is helpful. Program providers can then address them by adding a new program component or giving new emphasis to collaboration and referrals to other agencies. For example, adding a special referral component to a program is important if an unanticipated client problem is identified that is related to the existing goals but that falls outside of the program's focus and resources.

Unanticipated goals can easily emerge as staff members become more familiar with their clients and their needs. For example, conversations with some teen parents in a family-planning program revealed that some teen mothers viewed pregnancy as a prize if the father was popular or a well-known athlete (Dudley, 2007). Such a discovery could drive the program to expand its attention to this faulty viewpoint and to the importance of the father's responsibilities; it could also drive the program to target such popular guys for outreach as well.

Crafting Measurable Objectives

As indicated at the beginning of the chapter, every intervention should have a set of goals to provide it with direction and an end result. A second principle naturally follows this one: goals should be accompanied by specific measures or indicators that can inform whether they are being reached. These specific indicators are measurable objectives. The educator Mager (1997) describes a concise and entertaining way to learn how to develop measurable objectives within educational settings; his writings are primarily concerned with measuring students' performance in the classroom. With some modifications, Mager's conceptual material has been applied to evaluations in the human services.

Defining Measurable Objectives

Measurable objectives are statements that identify indicators of whether a goal is reached by one client or a set of clients. Let's first look at measurable objectives for clients at the practice level. Typically, each goal has several measurable objectives, as each objective may reflect only one small aspect of the broader goal. A social worker developing measurable objectives should begin by selecting a specific time in the future (e.g., two weeks, six months) and imagining what would be expected of a client at that time and how it will be manifested in measurable objective terms. For example, the social worker might determine that the goal is to improve a client's parenting skills. In this case, the goal can be that the client will have improved parenting skills with a particular child six months from now. Next the social worker and client can think of several indicators of improved parenting skills six months in the future. They may come up with such items as verbally (not physically) express anger toward the child nine out of ten times, or set a time limit when permitting the child to go out to play.

A Goal and Measurable Objectives for Mr. Lopez

Goal: Mr. Lopez, a frail elderly adult, will remain as independent as possible in a minimally supervised living facility in his community.

Measurable objectives in eight months: Mr. Lopez will

- Wash his own clothes once a week
- Attend all of his meals in the dining hall
- After reminders, take his required medications in the morning, at noon, and before retiring
- Attend one or more social events offered by the facility each week
- Attend the religious services of his church in the community at least twice a month if a volunteer is available to drive him to the church

As you can see in the example of Mr. Lopez, the goal to remain as independent as possible is rather vague and impossible to accurately measure as stated. In this case, Mr. Lopez is living in a minimally supervised living facility and must remain fairly independent to avoid placement in a living facility for more dependent older adults. Remaining independent would mean different things to different people, so this goal needs specificity that is most relevant to Mr. Lopez's functioning at the facility. As the five measurable objectives indicate, independence for Mr. Lopez refers mostly to taking care of his clothes, eating in a dining hall, taking his medications, having some social contact, and participating in the religious life of his church.

Larger Goals

Goals can focus on larger systems as well. Two goals that focus on the impact of community-level interventions are described next. The first focuses on cleaning up a neighborhood and the other attempts to promote better cross-cultural relationships. Each goal has three measurable objectives.

Goal: Neighborhood volunteers will improve the appearance of a neighborhood.

1. Neighborhood volunteers will clean at least twelve empty lots.
2. Neighborhood volunteers will remove at least twenty-five abandoned cars from the neighborhood within six months.
3. Ten neighborhood volunteers will sweep targeted areas of the neighborhood on one Saturday morning in February.

Goal: Southeast Asian and African American neighbors will improve their relationships in the Logan neighborhood.

1. The Logan neighborhood will increase the number of requests for the Human Relations Council to become involved in resolving neighborhood conflicts in February over January.
2. The Logan neighborhood will decrease the number of police calls resulting from neighborhood conflicts in February so that they are less than January.
3. After electing co-leaders (one African American and the other Southeast Asian) for a neighborhood block, the Logan neighborhood will sponsor (gather) neighbors for one block party on a Saturday that involves at least 25 percent attendance from each racial group.

Writing measurable objectives is known as "crafting." Crafting suggests that this task is as much an art as a science. Essentially, there is not one perfect way to craft objectives. Each set of measurable objectives crafted for a goal can be uniquely applied to a particular client or group of clients. Several different outcomes may be considered and the wording can vary widely. Ideally, objectives are formulated after extensive discussion between the social worker and the client about what the client wants to achieve and what seems realistic. The worker is primarily a guide in helping clients articulate what makes sense to them and, at times, suggesting various ways to state the objective.

Example of Measurable Client Objectives in a Palliative Care Facility

Needham and Newbury (2004) conducted a study in a hospice agency of explicit goals (or measurable objectives) crafted by the patients, caregivers, and staff members as part of a clinical audit. Over six months, 79 percent of the patients set goals, along with 63 percent of the caregivers and 98 percent of the admissions staff. Examples of patient goals include being able to eat properly, being able to get out of bed, being able to be well, not having to take drugs. Of the ninety-seven patients who set goals, one-third were completed directly by the patients and two-thirds required assistance from staff members.

Objectives for Clients, Not Staff Members

Sometimes an agency uses the term *measurable objective* to measure outcomes for service providers, such as, "The social worker will provide a psycho-educational group service for ten sessions to clients," or "The social worker will help the client find a job." These are examples of measurable objectives that focus on staff interventions, not client outcomes. These objectives are appropriate ones, but they are not client outcomes.

Goals are often confused with the processes or the means of reaching goals. In this case, students sometimes mistakenly identify the activities of staff members as the measurable objectives for a client's goal. In the preceding example of Mr. Lopez, measurable objectives could be mistakenly identified as teaching Mr. Lopez how to use the washing machine and dryer or contacting a church volunteer to pick him up for church. In other words, both goals and measurable objectives typically focus on the client, not on the activities of staff members. In brief, measurable objectives are indicators of the changes sought for clients.

Three Properties: Performance, Conditions, and Criteria

Measurable objectives have three properties (Mager, 1997): performance, conditions, and criteria. A performance is always necessary to have in an objective, while conditions and criteria are often helpful but not required. Usually, conditions and criteria provide details that are helpful in understanding the objective.

Three Properties in a Measurable Objective

Performance: what a person is expected to do

Conditions: prior circumstances or conditions needed before performance can be expected

Criteria: standards of acceptable performance reflected in such things as speed, accuracy, or quality

---

Performance. A performance is an action that a client is expected to take. The performance is required in every measurable objective because it describes the outcome that is sought. It should be an overt, observable action word, rather than an abstract or covert word.

For practice, try to identify the words in the following list that are observable or overt:

- Write
- Count
- Understand
- Ask
- Accept
- Attend

You were correct if you selected *write, count, ask,* and *attend* because each is an overt "action" word that you can observe. Any of these words could be selected as the performance in a measurable objective because they can be observed as happening or not. In contrast, the word *understand* is not overt or readily measurable. How do we know when our client understands something? Usually we have to ask a question and the answer can reveal understanding. So we could replace the word *understand* with *correctly answer* as the performance. In this case, we would be able to either hear or observe on a questionnaire whether the client gives the correct answer. *Accept* is another abstract word that social workers often use, and while it is an important term for social work, it can be easily misunderstood because it can mean different things to different people. Can you come up with another word that is like *accept* but overt or observable?

Some Suggested Performance Words to Use in Measurable Objectives

Choose	Find	Quote
Distinguish	Identify	Repeat
List	Recite	Spell
Read	Speak	Give
Restate	Tell	Match
Separate	Summarize	Select
Sort	Name	State
Write	Eat	Use
Attend	Ask	Call

Sometimes, a performance needs an overt indicator, a word or phrase that is added after a performance to help make it more observable. For example, "comply with instructions" is the performance in the measurable objective "The child will comply with instructions given by her mother." This performance may not be clear to some people, so an overt indicator can help. In this example, adding the overt indicator "follow them" helps. The objective can now read, "The child will comply with instructions (follow them) given by her mother."

"Provide documentation" is another example of a performance needing an overt indicator in the objective "The client will provide documentation of his citizenship (show his social security card) to receive food stamps." In this case, "show his social security card" is the overt indicator that indicates the documentation that he will provide.

Condition.   A condition is the second important factor to consider in crafting measurable objectives. A condition refers to a prior observable circumstance that takes place before a performance can occur. Conditions often begin with words such as *if, after, as, during, when, while, with,* or *unless.* For example, a measurable objective for a student enrolled in an evaluation course could be, "After identifying an agency's program goal, a student will write three objectives that will measure whether the goal has been reached." In this example, the condition that needs to occur before a performance is expected is "after identifying an agency's program goal." Now let's go further with this objective. What is the performance? You are correct if you decide the performance is "write." When you think about it, it makes sense that a goal has to be identified before you can write objectives for it. You could also say that the performance is "write three objectives." However, the word *three* is actually a criterion for the performance. So you could more correctly say that the performance is "write" or "write objectives."

Sometimes conditions are located in a measurable objective statement after rather than before the performance. For example, in the measurable objective "The client will say 'please' when asking for anything to be passed to him while eating dinner," can you identify the condition in this case? The performance?

You are correct if you identified the condition as "when asking for anything to be passed to him." Another condition is "while eating dinner." Both conditions make sense with this objective, as it would not make sense for the client to say "please" without asking for something to be passed or if he is not eating.

Criteria.   The third property often included in a measurable objective is criteria. Like conditions, criteria are not required in an objective but usually can add helpful details to define the objective. A criterion is a standard of acceptable performance, and is sometimes referred to as a quality that is expected in the performance. For example, an objective may be crafted for a client such as, "The client will attend Alcoholics Anonymous meetings." A criterion can be added to this objective to give it more detail and clarity: "The client will attend AA meetings weekly for twelve months." In this example, the criterion "weekly for twelve months" is added to the expanded version of the objective.

Criteria can describe any of the following qualities of the performance:

- Duration (e.g., six months)
- Frequency (e.g., five job interviews)
- Repetition (e.g., eight of ten times)
- Degree of accuracy or progress (e.g., 70 percent or more correct answers)
- Speed (e.g., complete the assignment in ten minutes)

Example of Performance, Condition, and Criteria

The subsequent goal for clients has three measurable objectives and was crafted for several clients receiving services in a mental health outpatient program. Can you identify the performance, condition, and criteria in each measurable objective? (The answers are in appendix C.)

Goal: Clients will increase compliance with medication appointments.

Objective A: If clients wish to remember the dates and times of medication appointments, they will write the time of their next appointment on a calendar.
Objective B: If transportation is needed to appointments, clients will call to arrange for it at least two days prior to the appointment.
Objective C: If clients are ill or otherwise cannot come to their medication appointment, they will call and reschedule their appointment more than twenty-four hours before the missed appointment.

Although the chapter has thoroughly covered how to craft goals and measurable objectives, it has not considered how to involve stakeholders. Martin and Kettner (1996) offer a simple three-step approach to include stakeholders:

Step 1: A focus group representing the stakeholders is convened and informed about the most recent, widely accepted research and conceptual frameworks, theories, evaluations, and practice experiences pertinent to a proposed program. In addition, the social problem to be addressed by the program and assumptions about this social problem are made explicit and discussed.

Step 2: The focus group is asked to identify, discuss, and consider as many goals and measurable objectives for the proposed program as it can.

Step 3: The group arrives at a consensus on the best goals and measurable objectives.

Summary of Principles

In brief, measurable objectives are statements that usually have four elements: conditions, subject, performance, and criteria. The subject and performance are necessary in every objective, while conditions and criteria are not required but are usually preferred. The subject is the client in most cases. The performance is the action verb describing what the client will be expected to do at the point in time when the goal is reached. Conditions, such as interventions by the social worker, are necessary to implement before the performance or action verb can occur. The criteria provide a standard of acceptable performance and could take the form of one of the standards introduced earlier (e.g., duration, frequency, degree of accuracy).

Several principles about goals and measurable objectives have been discussed that are important in crafting a measurable objective:

- Goals and objectives should be useful and have meaning to both the client and the agency.
- Objectives, like goals, are outcomes, not means.
- Crafting objectives is partially an art; there is no one perfect way to craft them.
- An overt indicator is a word or phrase added to the statement in parentheses after a performance to help make it more observable.
- Conditions typically are located in a measurable objective statement before the performance, though they can be located after the performance.
- Criteria are often needed in addition to the performance to indicate the level of quality of the performance expected.
- Criteria refer to a special quality of the performance (e.g., duration, accuracy, speed).

Exercise Regarding a Short-Term Goal and Its Measurable Objectives

Identify the performance, conditions, and criteria in each of the following measurable objectives crafted for victims/survivors of domestic violence (Fenske, 2006) (answers are in appendix C):

Goal: Clients will decrease their depressive symptoms.

Measurable Objective A: When feeling depressed, clients journal their feelings, thoughts, and behavior 80 percent of the time.

Measurable Objective B: At the outset of depressive feelings, clients demonstrate (carry out) one positive coping skill one out of three times.

Additional suggestions can help craft a measurable objective statement:

- List only one objective in each statement or sentence.
- Clients are usually the subject of statement, unless the focus is on staff members.
- Think of the performance as only the action word and not the words that follow it.
- Leave out of the measurable objective the intervention used by the staff member to reach the goal; it only tends to clutter it.
- A condition can sometimes be confused with either criteria or the subject. Therefore, it is a good idea to list the condition prior to the subject and performance.

Exercise

What's wrong with each of the following measurable objectives? (The answers are in appendix C.)

1. Clients will meet with their counselor and take their meds.
2. The social worker will meet with the client for five counseling sessions to help the client express his or her anger verbally.
3. The father will spend nurturing time with his three-year-old son.

Differences between Program and Practice Objectives

Often it is difficult to distinguish measurable objectives of program and practice. As indicated previously, a measurable objective statement typically has the following elements in this order: conditions, subject, performance, and criteria. Typically, both program and practice objectives will have all these elements. Then how are they different? Practice objectives are usually more detailed and unique to a particular client, whereas program objectives are stated in more general terms to reflect the circumstances of all or some clients who are recipients of services.

The subjects of programs are all or some clients in the program and may be referred to simply as "the clients"; the subject of a practice objective would be one particular client or client system who could even be named in the objective. Performance words could also be more specific for practice objectives because they can focus in on a specific action that possibly only one client would be expected to perform by a particular time. Likewise, conditions and criteria can be tailored more to the needs of one client in practice than to a group of clients in a program.

For example, an individual client with a substance abuse problem might identify a specific behavior such as "state something positive about myself in front of my family" or "go out to see a movie if I stay drug free for a week," but this specificity may not be possible in an objective of a program. A program objective for a group of clients with similar circumstances will likely be more general, such as "attend a fun activity outside the home once a week" without identifying further specifics.

Goals Promoted by the Council on Quality Leadership in Supports for People with Disabilities

The Council (1997), an accreditation organization, emphasizes the importance of personal goals for people who have developmental disabilities by taking the position that these people should define their own outcomes from their perspective and experiences. The Council emphasizes that there are no standard definitions of personal outcomes, as no two people will define them in the same manner. Instead, personal outcomes reinforce differences and diversity. The authors go on to say that helping clients develop their own personal goals provides three types of opportunities. First, it offers a way of getting further acquainted with the client; second, it provides a focus for organizing resources and coordinating supports to facilitate goals; third, the goals are the actual outcomes to be used to determine whether the client ultimately achieved what the agency intended.

The accreditation organization the Council emphasizes the importance of personal goals that are truly those of the clients, even if the clients have severe cognitive disabilities. This is a good example to close on not only because it places significant emphasis on personal goals for this organization but also because it expresses the value that clients should be empowered to craft their own goals.

The next chapter describes evaluations during the second stage, the implementation stage. A range of types of evaluations can be conducted during the implementation of the program, the longest and most varied stage for evaluation activities.

Key Terms
Characteristics of goals
Conditions
Crafting objectives
Criteria
Goals
Limitations of goals
Measurable objectives
Overt indicator
Performance
Program versus practice objectives

Discussion Questions and Assignments

Answers are found in appendix C.

1. What is needed to improve these measurable objectives?

   - The clients will be monitored by the appropriate staff while at the group home at all times.
   - After ten to twelve therapy sessions, the client will engage in negative self-talk 10 percent of the time.
   - When arriving for her appointment, the client will wait less than fifteen minutes to see the doctor 90 percent of the time.
   - During the school year, my client will turn in a progress report completed by teachers every week.
   - While at X agency, the mother will spend nurturing time reading to her child 100 percent of the time.

2. Identify a policy-level goal. Then craft three measurable objectives for the goal.

3. Identify the performance, conditions, and criteria in measurable objectives A and B:

   Goal: Clients with a mental retardation label will strengthen their socialization skills.

   Measurable Objective A: When introduced to a new person, the client will shake hands nine out of ten times.

   Measurable Objective B: After breakfast, the client will make his bed before leaving for work.

4. Identify the performance, conditions, and criteria in measurable objectives A, B, and C (Guy, 2006):

   Goal: Mental health clients will achieve optimum mental health.

   Measurable Objective A: If prescribed, clients will take (swallow) the correct amounts of medication daily for six months.

   Measurable Objective B: After ten to twelve sessions, clients will state four out of five techniques to control anxiety taught in sessions.

   Measurable Objective C: When experiencing thoughts of self-harm, clients will ask for help from their identified support system within twenty-four hours.

5. Identify the performance, conditions, and criteria in measurable objectives A, B, and C (Guy, 2006):

   Goal: John Doe will have stronger interpersonal skills.

   Measurable Objective A: John will say, "Good morning" to six out of ten coworkers when arriving at work each morning.

   Measurable Objective B: After six sessions, John will talk for ten minutes to one or two coworkers each week.

   Measurable Objective C: When talking to others, John will look at the person's face 75 percent of the time.

6. Identify the performance, conditions, and criteria in measurable objectives A, B, and C (Hawkins, 2006):

Goal: Clients will develop assertiveness skills in a group on assertiveness.

Measurable Objective A: After three group sessions, the clients will circle assertive comments and cross out aggressive comments on a worksheet and be correct eight out of ten times.

Measurable Objective B: After five group sessions, the clients will write two ways they were assertive.

Measurable Objective C: At the conclusion of treatment, clients will tell the social worker two things they liked and two things they did not like about group therapy without raising their voices.

7. Create a fictitious client with a problem and role-play a social worker and the client exchanging ideas about what to do. After the problem has been identified and thoroughly assessed, have the social worker help the client identify a goal and two measurable objectives in the client's own words. The worker's role is to ask questions that will help the client identify his or her goal and measurable objectives in his or her own words (e.g., What will it look like when you have reached your goal? How will you know that the goal has been reached? What will you be able to do or what will you be able to see when you have reached your goal?).

References

Council on Quality and Leadership in Supports for People with Disabilities. (1997). *Personal outcome measures*. Towson, MD: Author.

Dudley, J. (2007). Procreative consciousness and procreative responsibility of teenage parents. Unpublished data, University of North Carolina at Charlotte.

Dudley, J., & Schatz, M. (1985). The missing link in evaluating sheltered workshop programs: The clients' input. *Mental Retardation, 23*(5), 235–240.

Fenske, M. (2006). Crafting measurable objectives. Unpublished paper for a program evaluation course, University of North Carolina at Charlotte.

Guy, P. (2006). Crafting measurable objectives. Unpublished paper for a program evaluation course, University of North Carolina at Charlotte.

Hawkins, K. (2006). Crafting measurable objectives. Unpublished paper for a program evaluation course, University of North Carolina at Charlotte.

Mager, R. (1997). *Preparing instructional objectives* (2nd ed.). Atlanta: Center for Effective Performance, 1997.

Martin, L. L., & Kettner, P. M. (1996). *Measuring the performance of human service programs*. Thousand Oaks, CA: Sage Publications.

Needham, P. R., & Newbury, J. (2004). Goal setting as a measure of outcome in palliative care. *Palliative Medicine, 18*, 444–451.

Posavac, E. J., & Carey, R. G. (1997). *Program evaluation: Methods and case studies* (5th ed.). Upper Saddle River, NJ: Prentice Hall.

Part IV

The Implementation Stage

Chapter 8

Implementation Stage: Improving How Programs and Practice Work

How is the intervention supposed to be implemented?
How is it actually implemented?

Documenting and monitoring how an intervention is implemented are vital areas of evaluation and essential for program integrity. During the implementation stage, many questions are asked and answered that revolve around the theme of how well the program or practice approach is working. Figure 8.1 provides an overview of many of the activities that are important to the implementation stage. As figure 8.1 indicates, some of the activities

FIGURE 8.1   Spectrum of Activities Involved in the Implementation Stage

Implementation Stage
(Examining Processes)

Types of evaluations

- Program consistency with the logic model
- Program meets its intention
- Quality improvement
- Program accessibility
- Client satisfaction
- Staff views/attitudes and performance
- Documenting how program works
- Monitoring practice
- Practice accessibility

Other types of activities involved in process evaluation

- Refining measurable objectives
- Refining program designs
- Experimenting with variations in program interventions
- Evaluating staff performance
- Improving decision-making processes

are types of evaluations; others are also pertinent to this stage and often affect or are affected by evaluations.

As discussed in the last two chapters, the logic model provides a helpful organizing framework for understanding evaluations. Introducing the logic model at the stage of implementing an intervention provides a framework for considering many ways to improve an intervention, to correct its course if needed, and to maintain its quality. The logic model helps focus on the sequence of steps that link the implementation of the program back to the clients' unmet needs and forward to the clients' anticipated outcomes or accomplishments. In this regard, interventions should address the needs of program recipients and the underlying causes of their needs. Furthermore, the implementation of an intervention should result in the clients achieving their anticipated outcomes.

Increasingly, funding agencies are endorsing and adopting the reasoning behind the logic model in requirements for most grant proposals. Grant writers are expected to document such things as the links between clients' problems and the program approach they propose to implement. In brief, a convincing explanation needs to be mounted to the funding agency for how a proposed program can help clients resolve the problems of concern.

The Links among Problems, Needs, Causes, and Interventions

During the input or planning stage, major attention is focused on the problems and needs of prospective clients. As stated in chapter 6, a need is an aspect of a larger problem identified by a client that is perceived to be amenable to change. Meeting a set of needs is the intended focus of a proposed program. Another issue is also important to explore: what are the underlying causes that prevent the need from being met? This is a critical question because the proposed program is expected to address the underlying causes for such a problem or need. An example of the logical link between the causes of a problem and the approach used by a program to address it is briefly illustrated in table 8.1 for the problem of child abuse.

As table 8.1 suggests, several known causes of child abuse have been identified in studies, including abuse being passed down from generation to generation, inadequate parenting skills such as disciplining a child, stresses

TABLE 8.1   Link between Causes of a Problem and the Logical Intervention

Identified cause of child abuse	Logical program intervention
A. Intergenerational cause (abusing parent was abused as a child)	A. Facilitation of insight into intergenerational link through therapy
B. Lack of parenting knowledge and skill	B. Training in parenting skills
C. Economic stress from a low-income job	C. Increase in income through new job training and/or job change
D. Stress from social isolation	D. Peer support group of parents

from not having enough economic resources, and isolation from important social supports. Each cause suggests a different program response.

The child abuse example is somewhat simplistic because it infers that a complex problem like child abuse has a single cause, which is usually not the case. Yet the example makes an important point. An intervention should be logically linked to the underlying causes of a problem. Each of the causes of child abuse begs for a response that will address it. As the example suggests, child abuse perpetrated by parents who were abused as children will not be reversed if it does not include some type of insight therapy or reeducation as part of the intervention. Similarly, parenting-skills training is absolutely essential if parents abuse their children when disciplining them without knowledge of alternative disciplinary techniques. The link is also evident in addressing an inadequate income by preparing parents for a higher-paying job; if social isolation is an underlying cause of abuse, offering healthy social contacts is a logical response.

Variety of Ways to Evaluate Program Processes

The implementation stage of an intervention is an opportune time to conduct a variety of evaluations that focus on the program's implementation. These evaluations can raise numerous important, if not essential, questions about the integrity of a program. For example, are all the required components of a program implemented as planned? What program components seem to work and which ones do not? Has a team of qualified and competent staff members and volunteers been hired to provide the designated services? Are the key parties (administrators, staff, volunteers, and clients) communicating adequately? Many of the types of process evaluations covered in the chapter are identified in table 8.2, along with the general evalu-

TABLE 8.2 Types of Program Process Evaluations and the Question Posed

Types of process evaluations	General question asked
1) Linking the client problems and the program approach	1) Can the program's approach be used to successfully resolve the clients' problems and the causes?
2) Implementing the program as intended	2) Is the program being implemented as intended or proposed?
3) Program quality	3) Is the program's quality level acceptable to stakeholders?
4) Program accessibility	4) How accessible is the program to all the important intended client groups?
5) Client satisfaction	5) How satisfied are clients with interventions?
6) Staff studies	6) What are the views, attitudes, and practices of staff and volunteers related to program implementation?

ation question that each of them raises. Although this is not intended to be an exhaustive list of evaluations of program processes, it offers numerous examples of what is important.

Linking Client Problems with the Program Approach

Some important implementation questions are raised as a result of the logic model. Does the program's approach seem to be directly linked to clients' problems, and, more to the point, is there evidence that the approach can provide solutions to these problems?

According to Pawson and Tilley (1997) an evaluation of the links between the causes of a problem and the program approach answers three key questions:

1. What are the mechanisms for change triggered by a program?
2. How do these mechanisms counteract the existing social processes?
3. What is the evidence that these mechanisms actually are effective?

For example, what are the mechanisms of an Alcoholic Anonymous (AA) support group that can overcome the addictive tendency of substance abusers to continue to drink? Is it, as the philosophy of AA suggests, the spiritual ideology and message of the twelve steps? Is it the support that comes from others going through the same struggles? Is it a combination of their spiritual ideology and support of other recovering alcoholics? Or is it something else? Evidence of what makes AA work for so many people can be found in the answers to these questions from an evaluation of a representative sample of some of the hundreds of thousands of AA programs that meet regularly across the country.

Evaluation studies also have to answer the question about the social and cultural conditions necessary for change to occur among program recipients. In other words, how are the sociocultural factors recognized and addressed within a program? A new mentoring program for young African American men who did not have an adequate father figure for bonding provides an example. Several sociocultural questions could be asked of an agency sponsoring such a program. For example, to what extent and how does this program recognize the sociocultural factor? Are older African American men available to serve as mentors? Are the mentors capable of providing some of the missing pieces in well-being that these teenagers need? Do the mentors have any training or other preparation in male bonding based on an evidence-based curriculum?

One evaluation identified the essential elements of a program for preventing crimes on the premises of a housing complex for low-income residents. The evaluation team identified ten key elements of a crime prevention housing program that would be needed based on evidence of prior programs with a similar purpose that were effective.

Example of an Evaluation of the Essential Elements of a Housing Program

Foster and Hope (1993) wanted to identify the essential elements for preventing crime within a housing complex. Their evaluation focused on identifying a list of key elements found to be essential in the effectiveness of prior programs of a similar nature. They concluded that ten elements were essential:

1. A local housing office for the program
2. A local repair team
3. Locally controlled procedures for signing on and terminating tenants in housing units
4. Local control of rent collection and arrears
5. Tenants assume responsibility for caretaking and cleaning of the open space around units with the assistance of a locally supervised staff team
6. Existence of an active tenant advisory group with a liaison to the management of the program
7. Resources available for any possible small-scale capital improvements
8. Well-trained staff that delegate authority
9. The project manager is the key figure to be accountable for management of the program
10. A locally controlled budget for management and maintenance

In the housing example, the evaluators accumulated substantial evidence that the successful housing complexes in their city had ten essential elements. Housing complexes that were not totally effective were without all, some, or even one of the elements. As the elements suggest, some common themes included a housing management team with local control, realistic expectations of the tenants, availability of important resources, an active tenant advisory council, and a collaborative relationship between the council and the management team.

Is the Program Implemented as Intended?

Other types of questions address whether the program is actually implemented as proposed or intended. How a program is supposed to function may relate back to an initial grant proposal or other early planning documents. Implementation as intended could also be based on more current reports describing the policies and practices of programs that have been running for some time. Provision of a detailed description of a program as it is supposed to be implemented is a first step in this kind of evaluation.

A clear description of the program is needed prior to monitoring how a program is implemented. Therefore, it is often a good idea to begin with an accurate, written description of the program, whether articulated in an initial grant proposal or somewhere else. It is wise to describe a program in enough detail so that it can be replicated. An example of a program description is in an article about a visitation program for noncustodial parents (Fischer, 2002). The purposes of the program are to assist parents in establishing an access agreement with the custodial parent and in pursuing their legal rights and responsibilities as parents. The article documents the process of establishing and maintaining visitation agreements and identifies the principle barriers to establishing visitation. It includes a description of the policy and legal context for the program, a review of the pertinent literature, a description of a pilot program, a pilot process assessment, and a pilot outcome assessment. Data are also included on the factors associated with successful visitation. The program description came from several sources, such as case files, administrative records, and results of the pilot assessments.

Some further questions in attempting to find out whether a program is implemented as intended include the following:

- Are the clients being served the ones proposed or intended to be served?
- Are current staff members adequately qualified and trained to provide the proposed services at the required level of specialty and quality?
- Are the program's goals and objectives evident or identifiable in the way in which the program is implemented?
- What happens on a typical day in a program (e.g., a daily routine study)?
- How do staff from different disciplines collaborate or work together?
- How are the roles of BSW and MSW staff members differentiated and complementary?

Weinbach (2005) points out that new programs may need to ask different questions from those of older programs when it comes to how the program is being implemented. Newer programs may need to ask:

- Is the program at its anticipated stage of development?
- How many clients have been served to date?
- Is the program fully staffed with qualified people?
- How well known is the program in the community?
- How well have sources of client referrals been developed?
- In what ways is the program supported and in what ways is it being questioned within the agency and community?

According to Weinbach (2005), programs that have been implemented for a few years or more and are considered more mature may ask another set of questions:

- Do the services and programs appear to have the potential to achieve their objectives?
- Are the services and other activities of the program consistent with the program model?
- Is the program serving the clients for whom it was intended? If not, why?
- Is the program visible and respected in the professional and consumer community?
- How much attrition has there been among clients and staff?
- Do staff perceive that administrative support is adequate?
- How satisfied are clients with the program?

Often programs are not implemented as they were intended or proposed, or they may have gone adrift of their intended course. This can occur for several reasons. Perhaps the program approach or model was not adequately articulated and discussed. Perhaps the program goals and objectives were not fully developed, were crafted as unrealistic, or were displaced for some changing circumstances. Also, a program could decide to change course because of the changing needs and/or understanding about the client population. Finally, the people in charge of implementing a program could be different from those who proposed and planned it. In this case, if close collaboration did not occur between the two sets of people, a lack of continuity from the planning stage to the implementation stage is likely. Also, if all or most stakeholders are not involved at least in an advisory way in both stages, there may not be accountability to ensure that the planning decisions are implemented at a later time.

Example of an Overlooked Target Group

A Head Start program was established in a local community in which there was an important stakeholder group, a neighborhood civic organization. The organization was very concerned with needs of local children. This group wanted to make sure that families with the least available resources and the least ability to find an alternative program for their preschool children were given top priority. Once the Head Start program fully enrolled its cohort of children, the civic group decided to find out the social circumstances of the children and their families. To the surprise of some, they discovered that almost all the children were from very resourceful families with modest incomes that were likely to have access to comparable alternative programs. Therefore, the civic group raised its concern with the Head Start organization. When it received an unfavorable response, it pursued a lawsuit against the Head Start organization demanding that because the neediest families were the mandated target group they must be served. This lawsuit eventually ended up as a class action suit that resulted in a ruling that all Head Start programs in that city had to reserve a percentage of their openings for this neediest group of families.

Gardner (2000) offers an example of one way to create a description of a program involving a team of stakeholders. This program was developed using the logic model. One purpose of this exercise was to provide a clear program description; another was to more fully orient staff toward the program and its workings. At one point, some general questions were raised and discussed among all staff members, including "How would you describe how you go about working with clients?" and "What would be the important elements in the process of working with families?" Gradually, a diagram developed consisting of a series of boxes, each of which described a step in the process. Stage 1 described how families were encouraged to request services from this program. Stage 2 included helping families assess their strengths and the constraints they faced. Stage 3 involved goal setting. Stage 4 involved matching resources to family goals. How the family and staff worked to reach the goals was the focus of Stage 6, and Stage 7 involved completing the contract. The program description was then tested by asking some of the families, staff members, and other agencies how they perceived that the program actually worked using their experiences with it. Although the results of the interviews largely validated the proposed stages and principles that had been identified, the results also suggested the need to qualify and further refine some principles.

Monitoring a program's implementation can be done in several different ways. Sometimes agencies conduct staff activity studies using a list of prescribed activities, such as direct contact with clients, contact with other programs on behalf of clients, phone contact with clients, record keeping, staff meetings, and so on. In some instances, the studies may be interested in finding out whether too much time is spent on one type of activity, such as record keeping; in other instances, the interest may be in finding ways to increase time spent in direct contact with clients. These studies tend to be largely quantitative in nature (e.g., staff members tally the number of hours and minutes in each activity, each day, for a week or so).

Other evaluations attempt to find out more about the intricacies of the practice interventions provided to clients. The evaluations can be open-ended qualitative studies that identify what the social worker is actually doing on the basis of observations, videotapes, or analyzing journal entries recorded by the practitioners that describe what they are doing. Or the evaluations can be more deductive and quantitative by examining the extent to which prescribed activities reflecting a particular practice theory or practice model are implemented.

Exploration of the intricacies of a practitioner approach can be developed by prescribing an intervention protocol. For example, a protocol can be encouraged for medical social workers of a home-health program when clients manifest different types of problems. A frequently encountered problem in home-health settings are clients who are socially isolated, lack contact with friends and family, and are alone most of the time. In this case, a protocol could be to implement some or all of the following interventions:

- Provide a list of resources available to the clients that can reduce their social isolation.
- If clients are interested, assist with referral to a support group relevant to their interests/needs.
- Encourage activities appropriate to their medical condition.
- Explore and facilitate the clients' expression of interests in particular activities.
- Help clients express their feelings about themselves, their sense of satisfaction with their lifestyle, and any desire to change it.
- Help clients explore and resolve feelings related to social isolation, such as grief from loss, a recent loss of a previous health status, or an unresolved, conflicted relationship.

Once these and other activities are implemented, efforts can be made to document any evidence that the client has progressed toward specific outcomes, such as additional supports from other agencies, increased contact with others, and less time alone.

Program Quality

Although virtually all program implementation evaluations are interested in improving the quality of a program or practice intervention to some degree, some are especially known for their interest in program quality. When standards of quality are clearly defined and measurable, it is fairly easy to measure the performance of a program or practice intervention against these standards. In some cases, however, clearly defined, minimal performance standards are not defined or do not even exist. Also, quality evaluations primarily use qualitative methodologies, and measures tend to be subjective. Thus, quality evaluations are not as exact and predictable as one would hope.

Example of an Exercise on Evaluation of Practice Quality

Social work practice classes at the MSW level often can get into discussions about how to implement a particular practice theory or approach, such as the solution-focused or person-centered approach. An often fruitful way to explore such a question is to select a specific client case, real or made up, that one group could role-play (after preparation) using the solution-focused approach and another group using the person-centered approach. Other classmates could observe the role-plays and attempt to identify specific techniques and behaviors that reflected the respective approaches and those that did not. Afterward, the entire class could summarize the salient elements in each approach that manifested in the role-plays.

Some of the common models of quality evaluations described in chapter 4 included accreditation studies of programs and quality assurance evaluations. A fuller discussion of these types of evaluations will help illustrate the complexities of evaluating a program's quality.

Accrediting a Professional Program.   The process of accrediting a professional academic program, such as professional social work, is one form of quality control. The accrediting agencies propagate professional standards that academic programs are expected to adopt and implement. Member agencies typically are expected to prepare lengthy reports, referred to as "self-studies," to document how they meet these standards in their programs and in their administration. The self-study report is submitted to the accrediting agency, which assigns a team of accreditation officials to carefully review the self-study and conduct a site visit of the program. Site visits are used to find multiple sources of evidence that the member agencies are actually doing what they report in the self-study. Multiple sources of evidence include random samples of student records; informal observations; data on outcomes for graduates; and eliciting of the views of administrators, staff and faculty members, field instructors, and students. The standards of an accrediting agency tend to be broad and subjective.

Example of the Accreditation Process

The Council on Social Work Education expects all professional programs at both the BSW and the MSW level to prepare their students with content on social and economic justice. Programs are expected to show how they do this in the self-study and in each syllabus through lectures, outside speakers, assigned readings, assignments, and other methods. As long as the self-study and each individual syllabus shows how and where social justice content is covered and how students are expected to demonstrate that they understand and apply it in their practice, the standard is essentially met. However, this form of quality control is quite subjective and leaves open the possibility of a lot of unanswered questions. For example, what types of social justice are acceptable? How does the accreditation agency know that the content has actually been covered in every section of a particular course? How can faculty determine that students have embraced a belief system that supports this content? How can they know that graduates will actually use the content in their work once they have graduated?

Quality Assurance.   Quality assurance programs exemplify a focus on quality evaluations. Some agencies also sometimes refer to quality assurance as quality improvement or quality control. Quality assurance activities focus on a sampling of events and records that provide a snapshot of how the program and its staff members work. The key to quality assurance is determining whether an acceptable level of quality is reached. In a practical sense, the results of quality assurance data collection efforts can be immediately used to improve or fill omissions in a program. A case example was given in chapter 4 of a quality assurance evaluation of an agency providing residential programs for youths in foster homes. The example described the specific procedures that the agency used to conduct the evaluation.

Social agencies that have a quality assurance evaluation typically take a close look at several aspects of a program using multiple methods of data collection. These methods include staff peer reviews of a random sampling of client cases, a close-up review of some client records, inquiries into client perceptions and satisfaction, and observations of a few services. Quality assurance is usually conducted by a team of staff members, not agency administrators, who are employed either by the agency being evaluated or by another agency. Because the process involves staff members, there is likely a strong tendency that reviewers are supportive of staff members and possibly biased in favor of their viewpoints and practices.

Program Accessibility

How accessible is the program for clients and potential clients who are intended to be recipients? This is an important question to ask periodically. Access is a problem if the clients originally intended to be the recipients are underrepresented, tend to drop out, or are left out. Access is also an issue if a particular racial, ethnic, or cultural group that needs the program's services is underrepresented among the group of recipients.

If comprehensive client records are kept, it can be fairly easy to determine whether some groups are accessing the program and others are not, or if some use the program more than others. A first step in determining whether there are accessibility problems is to identify the types of people that the program has decided to serve. Next, determine the characteristics of the clients actually being served or those most likely to continue in the program beyond the initial session or stage. Finding the discrepancies between the characteristics of the two groups can reveal the characteristics of client groups that are underrepresented.

Exercise on Accessibility

Assume that you work for a family-counseling agency that has designed an outreach program to provide crisis-oriented family counseling to multiproblem families with young children. The program designers viewed the client target group as those without the financial resources or insurance coverage to contract services with private family therapists or fee-for-service agencies. When the staff members initially began accepting families, data were not systematically collected on the types of accepted families. What questions would you ask to find out whether the target group is being reached? Depending on what you find out, what steps would you take to monitor whether the target group will be assured of service in the future?

In the case of inaccessibility, the program sponsor may need to mount a more systematic effort to identify and recruit the originally intended target clients. Some specific questions on program accessibility that would be relevant to explore are the following:

- How are clients recruited? What is the marketing strategy, if any, in advertising the program? Do the strategies inadvertently favor or omit particular groups?
- How are clients selected at admissions? What specific criteria are used in selecting clients?
- How are clients assigned to specific program components (e.g., different staff teams)?
- How are clients assigned to different professional staff (e.g., what criteria are used)?
- Which groups of new clients are most likely to get beyond the first interview? Which do not?

Accessibility of programs is, in part, a diversity issue. Often, programs may be used primarily by people of one demographic characteristic, such as white and middle class, and used only minimally by other groups, such as Latinos or low-income earners. Over time, this demographic profile can become institutionalized and come to be viewed inadvertently by the wider community as the norm. In other words, people begin to assume falsely that the program must have been designed for this particular group. As a result, other groups may not even consider using this program because of the widely held view.

Example of Access Barriers to Prenatal Care for Low-Income Women

An important public health care priority is to improve prenatal care access for low-income women. A study (Cook, Selig, Wedge, & Gohn-Baube, 1999) interviewed low-income women in the postpartum unit of a large urban medical center about the barriers that they had experienced. Their perceived barriers included not wanting friends or family to know about their pregnancy, not having help getting to clinic appointments, a lack of trust in the health-care system, a long wait time at the clinic, no child care, feelings of depression or unhappiness about the pregnancy, fear that something could be wrong with the baby, feeling tired, and clinic overcrowding and inconvenient location.

Another example of a program sponsor that was sensitive to diversity issues but failed to follow through was a community group that wanted to serve adults with developmental disabilities who had little or no social contact beyond their immediate families. They were people who simply spent all of their free time in their family homes. The impetus for creating this program was that it would be uniquely available to isolated individuals in the city. The program would fit their special needs because there would be a cohort of professional staff members available trained to help them and an agency van to transport them to and from the program. However, the sponsor of this program, a group of parents with developmentally disabled members, made very little effort to channel their resources into special marketing, recruiting, and other forms of outreach. As a result, the new program was quickly inundated by other people with disabilities who were higher functioning and more independent. Once these people found out about the program, they adopted it as their own, and the staff members took the path of least resistance and went along with organizing their efforts around creating social opportunities for them. The original target group was forgotten largely because it did not have a vocal advocate; also group members turned out to be more difficult to recruit than had been originally thought.

Example of Observations of a Waiting Room: Some Simple Guidelines

Observations can often be helpful in determining how well an existing program is working. A waiting room of a large social service agency or a hospital is an interesting example. Longer waiting time for services has been correlated with them not returning to receive services. Waiting rooms can be an important part of a program, in that bad waiting experiences may discourage clients from returning. Some general guidelines for observing a waiting room are as follows:

- What do you see while you are sitting there?
- Are signs and brochures visible and helpful?

- How are the people greeted?
- Are different languages being used in the greetings when appropriate?
- How long do people seem to wait?
- How comfortable are the surroundings?
- Are specific toys and activities available for children?
- Is the noise level a possible problem for some who wait? How is this a problem?

It is important to keep in mind that the perceptions of those who have access problems or challenges are the most important source of information to investigate. Perceptions about access can vary considerably depending on who it is and what his or her relationship is to the program. As a program is being developed, stakeholders may feel that the program is truly designed to be available to all eligible clients, and that may be their intention. Yet the potential recipients of such a program may feel otherwise as a result of many factors. Access barriers to a program can result from many factors, including physical, geographic, psychological, cultural, and institutional barriers.

Physical Barriers.   Physical barriers can be evident in different physical structures within which a program is located. A non-disabled-accessible building is a good example. Barriers such as the absence of elevators, no information in Braille, high curbs surrounding a building, or no handicap parking spaces nearby can be especially problematic for many with physical disabilities including those in wheelchairs, the visually impaired, the hearing impaired, or the physically frail. Simply having a program located in a large building can pose barriers in itself, such as the need to take an elevator, to navigate confusing hallways, or to negotiate pedestrian traffic.

Geographic Barriers.   Geographic barriers can also pose serious access problems. A program that is not on a well-known, easily accessible, and safe street poses obvious barriers. Further, the absence of common public transportation routes that travel to and from the program site are barriers. Any program located outside a downtown area or outside the main section of a town can be fraught with barriers for many people. This can particularly be the case if certain clients do not have access to a car, cannot use public transportation on their own, or cannot walk a long distance. In many cases, well-known business and shopping centers may be the most accessible sites.

Psychological Barriers.   Psychological barriers are another challenge to program access. These barriers are often subjective and difficult to detect or even to get everyone to agree on. Psychological barriers can manifest in subjective things, such as whether a program is welcoming or sensitive to people's specific needs. Rudeness or aloofness may be factors. A center that does not return phone calls is enough of a reason to give up. Gay and lesbian people, for example, may be sensitive to subtle messages that appear judgmental or unwelcoming, such as an apparent lack of interest by a receptionist, an abrupt answer to a question, a stare or other uninviting look, or a long wait to receive services. The absence of employees of the same racial or ethnic group is another possible barrier for some. A program brochure might seem exclusive if it does not mention that a particular group is among those who are eligible for services. For example, would a family service agency provide counseling to a divorced couple involved in shared custody or to a gay couple? It is important for the agency to mention in brochures and other marketing materials that they would, to avoid the possibility that someone concludes they would not.

Psychological barriers are also evident, for example, in most programs that focus on mental health issues or are identified as mental health agencies. This is often the case because many people have misunderstandings about mental illness. Further, they are reluctant to admit that they or their family members have mental health problems or have a need for mental health services. Often a program sponsor that attempts to reach people with such sensitivities may consider locating the program in a school, community center, or house of worship to ward off this possibility.

A Study of Access Issues for African Americans' Use of Hospice

In chapter 2, a study was described that investigated why African Americans did not use hospice services proportionate to their numbers in a particular city (Reese, Ahern, Nair, O'Faire, & Warren, 1999). The researchers' activities began with a small qualitative study of African American pastors. This pilot study was followed by a larger quantitative study of African American hospice patients that documented their access barriers to hospice. Findings revealed that cultural barriers were evident in that African Americans described a preference for life-sustaining treatment (e.g., chemotherapy, resuscitation, life support) over palliative care. The respondents were also opposed to accepting terminality, planning for it, or discussing it with others. The findings also uncovered institutional barriers, such as a lack of knowledge of hospice services, a lack of trust in the health-care system, and a lack of a friendly face and diversity among health-care staff. The findings of the studies were used to facilitate a social action effort.

Cultural Barriers.   Cultural barriers are in some ways like psychological barriers. They can be subjective, subtle, and difficult to detect and agree on. Similarly, they are extremely important to overcome. As our society becomes more diverse, program sponsors are increasingly challenged to make special efforts to be sensitive to the cultural aspects of clients and potential clients. If a program wants to be inclusive in this regard, special considerations must be given to preparation for work with African Americans, Latinos, low-income clients of all ethnicities, and recent immigrants from around the world. Each of these groups and subgroups has cultural beliefs, practices, rituals, and sensitivities that are important to consider in planning and carrying out a program.

Barriers to Using a School Program

Child Trends (Kennedy, Wilson, Valladares, & Bronte-Tinkew, 2007) conducted a study of barriers to low-income children and adolescents using after-school programs. They identified five types of barriers:

1. *Safety, Transportation, and Cost*: Unsafe neighborhoods, the cost of after-school programs, and problems getting to and from a program are persistent barriers that limit participation for many children.
2. *Family responsibilities*: Many adolescents have other responsibilities, such as babysitting younger siblings, preparing meals, or taking care of household chores that prevent them from participating.
3. *Desire or need to work*: Many older youths take on part-time or even full-time after-school jobs.
4. *Lack of identification with staff members*: Trusting relationships between youth participants and staff members are a central feature of these programs. Children and youths often prefer staff members who are similar to themselves in race, gender, and experience, but the most important consideration is that staff care about children and youths and can connect with participants.
5. *Lack of interest in organized activities*: Adolescents, more so than children, often have little or no interest in activities offered through after-school programs. Adolescents frequently cite boredom, a desire to relax and hang out with friends, and dissatisfaction with program activities as reasons that they would rather not participate.

Child Trends also listed numerous ways to overcome each barrier. A few examples include partnering with the schools and community-based organizations, helping parents form partnerships to support the program, incorporating vocational and apprenticeship activities into programs, hiring teenage participants to take on paid roles, recruiting program alumni to serve as volunteers and staff members, and varying activities on a daily and monthly basis to maintain interest.

A group service, for example, that emphasizes open sharing, self-disclosure, equality, and participation by all will likely find resistance from some cultural groups because of their emphasis on patriarchal families, hesitations to self-disclosure, varying beliefs about how anger should be expressed, how animated they can be in a lively discussion, how much they can confront others, how they perceive authority figures, and what they choose to talk about (Reid, 1997).

Institutional Barriers. Finally, institutional barriers are important to consider in almost every program. Such barriers can overlap considerably with cultural barriers. They could be such things as a lack of knowledge about the services provided by a program. In this regard, how well does an agency brochure or flyer explain the purpose of a program in a language that can be understood by client groups? Also, is the program material provided in languages other than English in communities in which there are groups of people who speak English as a second language? A lack of diversity among the staff members and volunteers could be another factor that discourages some people from seeking out a program's services. As the earlier cited study of access to hospice indicates, a face that is similar to your own may be synonymous with being a friendly face. Any of these factors could be barriers; one way to determine how problematic they are is to openly discuss them with people of these cultures.

We should keep in mind that accessibility barriers can go beyond the factors described here. They could be any of several things that we might suspect but cannot identify from those who hesitate to use services. In many instances, we do not know what the barriers are that keep some people from using a program or service. Yet we know that some people who need a program do not use that program. Further, we always need to be sensitive to and vigilant in seeking to learn what might get in the way of people engaging with and fully using a program.

Client Satisfaction Studies

Client satisfaction studies investigate how satisfied clients are with the services they receive. Such studies are extremely important to conduct. They reveal clients' perceptions of the services they are receiving, what they feel works, and what may be problematic. These studies can help pinpoint what was helpful to clients, where there might be a breakdown in services, and where improvements may need to be considered. Client satisfaction questions also offer a fuller picture of the interface between the clients and their service provider. They help agencies determine how each party (client and social worker) perceives what is happening and any discrepancies between the two. In this case, a concurrent study of the social worker's perceptions would also need to be conducted using the same or similar questions.

There is often a close correlation between whether clients are satisfied with a program and whether the program is effective in helping them. This is likely to be the case because if clients are not satisfied with the services they receive, one of several possibilities is likely. Dissatisfied clients may not trust their providers or the services they are offering, and therefore they may not fully engage in using them. Dissatisfied clients may throw out various obstacles to receiving services, such as withholding information, minimizing participation, avoiding in-depth interventions, sporadic attendance, or even discontinuing use of the program.

In addition, client satisfaction studies can reveal, in part, how effective programs are, if client satisfaction is viewed as a necessary though not sufficient condition for claiming program effectiveness. It is the author's view that if there is an absence or low level of client satisfaction generally, it is difficult to conclude that a program has been effective in helping them. Involuntary clients may be an exception, in that their lack of satisfaction is likely to be related to their involuntary status. In this case, a report of program dissatisfaction presumably relates more to their status than to any of their accomplishments or progress. In some studies, client satisfaction scores are even viewed as an outcome measure of success. In summary, the client's perceptions are always important to consider, even though they are a subjective viewpoint that is influenced by their perspectives and biases.

Satisfaction of Clients in an Inpatient Psychiatric Facility

Baker, Zucker, and Gross (1998) report that client satisfaction studies are rare among inpatient mental health patients. Their 770 clients had serious and persistent mental illness, and in most cases had schizophrenia and were involuntarily hospitalized. The authors explore, among other things, clients' perceptions about the different treatment modalities used, treatment goals, and the philosophy of treatment. The authors discuss several specific issues revolving around conducting client satisfaction surveys with this type of population, including considerations of what aspects of satisfaction should and can be measured, whether such surveys can reflect client stability in satisfaction, and whether the results can be used for program improvement.

Although client satisfaction studies are important to have as a component of virtually every program, they do have their weaknesses. As already indicated, clients' perceptions are bound to be subjective and perhaps biased. They can also be difficult to interpret. If you were to ask ten clients, "How satisfied are you with social work services?" what would it mean to each client? One person may associate "satisfaction" with one image, while another associates it with something altogether different. For example, satisfaction or lack of satisfaction in a social worker's help could mean any number of things:

- Liking or disliking some characteristic of the social worker
- Being unhappy with the initial waiting period
- Feeling angry or disappointed about what the social worker said during a recent session
- Being disrupted by a change to a new social worker
- Being grateful that the social worker helped them find a resource
- Being pleased that the current social worker is not judgmental like the previous one
- Being comforted that the social worker listens intently

The list of possible interpretations can be almost limitless, which suggests that we may never know what clients mean when they check a particular response category of a satisfaction survey.

A related example of a weakness in client satisfaction studies revolves around interpreting what the word *satisfaction* means to the clients who fill out a survey. Because the term is ambiguous, it will likely need to be defined. It could be interpreted in various ways, for example, as "no major complaints," "being acceptable," or "being preferred over similar services of competing agencies." *Satisfaction* to some may mean a program or service that meets a very high standard overall, such as being exceptionally well delivered, having almost every aspect done well, being reasonable in cost, and being offered at the best time and at a convenient location for the client. In contrast, to others the standard of satisfaction may be very low, such as simply being pleased to receive an opening in the program and being treated in a friendly way. Again, a client satisfaction study may never uncover what standard of satisfaction the respondents use.

Of course, one could respond to the point about the ambiguity of satisfaction by saying that it does not matter what the standard is. It is all about perception and the perceiver. If the client perceives the program or service as satisfying, then that is all that counts, particularly if satisfaction means they will continue to use the program and continue to engage the provider in the helping process.

Options for Determining What Satisfaction Means.   Keep in mind that there are options for exploring a client's satisfaction in more detail or depth. One option is to use a questionnaire format that asks forced-response satisfaction questions for each of several aspects or dimensions of the program and its services. It is up to the evaluator to decide which program dimensions are most important to include in the study. Examples of program dimensions include asking whether clients are satisfied with the agency's fee schedule, the extent of the waiting period, the psychological accessibility of the agency, whether services are available at convenient times, the friendliness of the receptionist, the social worker's ability to listen, and the social worker's ability to help them find solutions to their problems. When analyzing the responses to these questions, the evaluator can zero in on the dimensions of the program that are more and less satisfying by comparing them. Further, if one or two dimensions are particularly troubling for clients, they can be singled out and addressed in this type of instrument, which may lessen the impact that the troubling feelings have on their responses to questions about the other program dimensions.

The Dimensions of Satisfaction Use by a Nursing Home Admissions Department

Family members were asked five questions about their satisfaction with admissions when admitting their loved one to a nursing home (Huntersville Oaks Nursing Home, 2005). These five questions addressed the following five dimensions of admissions:

1. Support provided
2. Information regarding financial issues
3. The orientation to the nursing home
4. The amount of information provided
5. Overall assistance given

A five-point Likert scale (excellent, very good, good, fair, poor) was used to frame the questions.

Typically, a client satisfaction questionnaire with forced-response questions has one or two open-ended questions at the end of the instrument. The questions provide an opportunity for the respondent to comment on something that other questions did not address. The open-ended questions could be simply stated as, "Please share any additional comments," or "What are you satisfied with the most?" and "What are you least satisfied with?"

Example of Another Way to Explore Client Satisfaction

In the case of one client satisfaction study (Dansky, Colbert, & Irwin, 1996), two additional questions were asked: "Would you recommend this program to a friend" (yes, not sure, no), and "Would you return to this agency in the future if the need arose" (yes, not sure, no)." Both questions get at client satisfaction with respect to telling others and returning in the future.

Another option is to use an unstructured interview format with open-ended questions about satisfaction. In this case, clients would be encouraged to respond to the questions in their own words as naturally as possible. Probing would be added as needed when clients' responses were not fully clear or needed elaboration. A qualitative interview may take a fair amount of time, perhaps an uninterrupted period of an hour, in a place that feels hospitable to clients. An interviewer could be someone known by the clients or a stranger. Both choices have advantages and disadvantages. A person who is known to clients and identified with the agency sponsor would be able to establish rapport more quickly and possibly ask questions within the context of the specific helping process. A disadvantage of using a familiar interviewer is that clients may be hesitant to share negative responses for fear of jeopardizing their standing as clients. A stranger may have more challenges establishing rapport because he or she would be unfamiliar to the clients; a stranger, though, may also have advantages eliciting an honest set of responses if clients are assured that their responses will be kept confidential.

Occasionally, a qualitative questionnaire has been used to determine satisfaction. In one study, forty children of divorced parents were asked to share their perceptions of a family-in-transition program in which they participated (Oliphant, Brown, Cambron, & Yankeelov, 2002). They were asked to respond to open-ended questions about the usefulness of the program in helping them cope; their feelings, experiences, and ideas about the program; and additional topics that they would have liked to have covered. They were also asked to list specific things that helped them. A qualitative questionnaire, while relevant with many types of clients and in a variety of circumstances, may also be too open ended, time consuming, and challenging to complete. A lower response rate may also result. Another option, of course, is to combine two or more methods. Possibly the structured questionnaire could be administered first, followed by an unstructured interview.

The decision about which type of instrument to use needs to consider the people being studied, the costs, and time available. For example, the best fit for a satisfaction study of people who are unable to read would be an interview rather than a questionnaire, whereas a phone interview or a mailed questionnaire may be the best fit for a regional study of clients who live some distance from the evaluator.

Example of a Client Satisfaction Interview for Children

Prior, Lynch, and Glaser (1999) reported on a client satisfaction interview with children who were in a child sexual abuse program. The interview schedule used included both quantitative and qualitative questions. The children were asked to rate the social work services on six dimensions (listening and talking, providing information and explanation, social worker's attitude and demeanor, continuity and accessibility, for whom the services were for, and special occasions) using a three-point scale of positive, neutral, and negative. In each of these cases, the children were asked to elaborate on their answers. For example, one thirteen-year-old girl elaborated on her positive response about the social worker listening by saying, "If I didn't want to answer, which I sort of had to, she wouldn't force me to, she'd just go on to the next question, she wouldn't ask me to think."

Administering and Collecting a Client Satisfaction Instrument. It is often wise to alert clients that a client satisfaction survey is coming before it is actually handed out. Some agencies send a note or a postcard out to a client informing them of the study, explaining the purpose of the survey, stating how important clients' feedback is in evaluating the program's effectiveness, emphasizing confidentiality, and thanking them ahead of time. One agency even offered to give clients a small gift the next time that they came to the agency as an incentive for filling out the survey. Such gestures often may be important in maximizing clients' interest in participating. Further, such preparatory steps are often viewed as signs of courtesy and recognition of the value of clients' time.

Example of Multiple Use of Satisfaction Surveys

An agency providing group homes to people with developmental disabilities regularly uses several satisfaction surveys to obtain feedback on how the agency is doing and how it can improve its programs (Lori Gougeon, executive director of Residential Support Services, Charlotte, NC, personal communication, Jan. 21, 2005). This agency has a client satisfaction interview that is conducted with every client annually, using students and volunteers as interviewers. They also have a satisfaction questionnaire administered voluntarily to staff members and another questionnaire administered to all family members of clients. Finally, the agency conducts an annual satisfaction interview with several key community representatives who are familiar with the agency. The community representatives vary each year and have included representatives of other agencies, landlords and employers of clients, regular volunteers, leaders of civic associations, church members, and store clerks.

How the client satisfaction study is administered is also important to consider in order for the evaluator to have valid and reliable data. The person administering the questionnaire or interview needs to be well prepared and trained. In this regard, the person assigned to hand out a questionnaire to the clients is often not directly involved in the evaluation process for practical reasons. Usually it is not realistic for the evaluators or their assistants to be available to give it out to every client. Those assigned to hand it out could simply be asked to hand out the survey and remind the client to fill it out and return it. They could be a receptionist, secretary, a volunteer, another staff member, or even a manager who is uninformed about it.

In one example the author encountered, a receptionist at a medical clinic handed him a patient satisfaction questionnaire and asked him to fill it out before he even saw his physician. The receptionist apparently did not know what the questionnaire was all about. So the author filled it out imagining what the visit with the physician would be like. He did not contest this inappropriate request so as not to avoid any delay in seeing the physician.

Other examples of mistakes and overt biases that have been evident in administering client satisfaction surveys include identifying clients to fill out a survey only after they have communicated a favorable verbal impression of the program provider, failing to adequately explain the purpose of the satisfaction survey, placing completed surveys in an open pile that violates privacy rights, requiring clients to fill out the survey rather than giving them the choice to participate, and looking over the results of clients' surveys in their presence.

What Students Learned from Conducting a Satisfaction Interview

Four graduate students conducted client satisfaction interviews with several people with mental retardation who lived in group homes. Afterward, they shared their experiences and what they learned with their class. Among the things that they learned were the following:

- Open- and closed-ended questions elicited very different, sometimes contradictory responses.
- Their probe questions following interview questions can easily influence the nature of their responses, suggesting that probes should be standardized.
- The importance of meeting in private because some of the questions were about their daily lives on a very personal level.
- The location of the interview in group homes made a big difference in responses (choices were the living room, the person's bedroom, and the office where the staff member usually works).
- Sometimes it was difficult understanding the respondent's speech, so a staff person assisted. In these instances, it became quite evident how much the staff member became an "interpreter" by speaking for the respondent, interfering with what he or she said, and having an influence merely by being present.
- Some questions such as "What makes you happy?" brought more meaningful responses than most other questions.

Maximizing the chances of a high response rate by clients is another factor to consider. Because interviews are conducted with an interviewer present, their response rates are usually much higher than when using a questionnaire. How a questionnaire is introduced is critical. In terms of informed consent, all the necessary aspects of informed consent (e.g., purpose of the survey, confidentiality or anonymity, option to not participate, explanation of how results will be used, any potential harm or benefits from participation) should be shared, as both an introduction stated on the questionnaire and verbally by the person who administers it. Having a relatively quiet and private location for filling out the questionnaire is also important.

Another issue is how the survey is to be returned. Is it to be returned by mail? If so, it is necessary to include a self-addressed, stamped return envelop, with a reminder in large print to return it within a specific time, not to exceed seven to ten days from receipt. Furthermore, a follow-up reminder card or call helps increase response rate in many cases. If the questionnaires are to be completed at the agency site, allowing time to fill them out and having someone designated to collect them are necessities.

Studies of Staff Members and Volunteers

Because staff members are central to most program activities, it is not surprising that there are numerous purposes of evaluations to document their views, attitudes, and actions. The specific evaluations introduced in this section focus on the program as the unit of analysis and are not intended as evaluations of the performance of individual staff members. Some of the program-related evaluations overlap with quality assurance activities, particularly those that obtain snapshots of program activities involving staff such as specific client cases and reviews of client files that reflect staff members' activities.

The list of purposes for evaluating staff members, presented subsequently, is not exhaustive but is intended to introduce several purposes that are often of interest to social agencies. Many of these types of evaluations can focus on volunteers and on staff members. Therefore, keep in mind that each described type could just as easily focus on both staff and volunteers or just volunteers.

Some Purposes of Staff and Volunteer Evaluation Studies

- Overall, do staff members have the recommended credentials to meet expectations of the services that they provide?
- Do the services they provide meet the requirements of the respective programs?
- Is there evidence that these services approximate best practices?

- Do staff members meet equal employment opportunity and other diversity standards?
- How do staff members use their time on the job?
- How satisfied are staff members with their working conditions?

Meeting Recommended Credentials.   Some important evaluations attempt to document the extent to which staff members implement the actual services defined in programs. Such evaluations involve at least two domains: determining whether staff members have the qualifications to provide a program's services and determining whether they actually implement these services. Having qualified staff is obviously the easier of the two to evaluate. In this case, the staff qualifications identified during the planning stage as necessary to implement the services of the program can be compared to the qualifications actually held by the current staff members delivering services. The qualifications could include several different characteristics, such as the disciplines of staff members, level of education and professional degrees, professional licenses, previous work experiences and positions held, any specialized skills, and experiences with specific populations (e.g., children). A further question about qualifications could be asked as well. What evidence is available to indicate that the staff qualifications identified in the planning stage are both necessary and sufficient to provide the needed services?

Meeting Requirements of the Program.   Determining whether staff actually implement services is a more challenging evaluation question. Several specific questions can arise when considering this question:

- How is the overall program approach described and defined? How can it be identified and measured when observing staff members' actual practice?
- Is the expertise of the staff members evident in some way in the actual implementation of the program's services?
- What roles do staff members play? What roles are clients expected to play?
- What specific practice theories, if any, are emphasized in this program approach?
- How can the application of these theories be identified and measured when observing the staff members' actual practice?

Best Practices.   Once a theoretical approach and all its dimensions or components are defined, along with procedures for implementing them, standards can be set to ensure that the approach is implemented in a professionally acceptable way. Best practices are pertinent here. Best practices is a concept that represents the highest standards possible for a specific area of professional practice. Best practices are partially established by evidence-based research demonstrating that a practice approach is effective in helping specific client populations. An important way to establish best practices is through peer-reviewed professional journals articles published and disseminated by researchers and practitioners.

Diversity Standards. Diversity evaluations can be relevant as well. Every so often, it is a good idea for agencies to take a closer look at the demographic characteristics of their staff members and volunteers to determine whether they are similar to the demographic characteristics of the client population. In addition, it is a good idea to determine whether these characteristics take into account projected changes in the client population over the next five to ten years. Having a diverse staff cohort, one that roughly approximates the demographic characteristics of the client population, is a meaningful ideal to pursue. Equal employment strategies can be helpful in reaching this ideal. The more genuine and rigorous the effort that goes into implementing equal opportunity standards in recruitment, hiring, and retention, the more likely it is that the agency will recruit diverse staff members and volunteers. Demographic characteristics of importance should include race, gender, ethnicity, social class, religious affiliation, age, regional background, marital status, having children or not, sexual orientation, and other characteristics related to the needs of specific populations. Although this type of evaluation is not intended to support the notion of pairing clients and social workers on the basis of similar background characteristics, the collective diversity of a cohort of staff members can provide a visible signal to many with a minority status that they belong there or are welcomed as recipients. In addition, the more varied the backgrounds of staff members and volunteers overall, the greater their capacity will be to plan and implement a culturally sensitive and effective program.

Use of Staff Members' Time. Staff members' use of their time can be another focus of an evaluation. Administrators sometimes wonder how their employees spend their time. For example, how much time in a week, on average, do staff spend in direct contact with clients, in meetings, in collaborating both with other in-house staff and staff of other agencies, in record keeping, and so on. Often staff members are thought to see too few clients, and there may be a question about how they could use their time differently. Generally, it is wise to use the time of staff members and volunteers, particularly in a human services environment with limited resources, in the most efficient way. Efficiency in itself tends to increase the outputs and outcomes for programs.

Working Conditions of Staff. How satisfied are staff members with their working conditions? This is an important question that many agencies often downplay. The rationale for minimizing its importance can vary. Some administrators may say that staff are paid to provide their services, so why emphasize their satisfaction? Other administrators may feel that seeking to satisfy staff members could weaken their own authority. This rationale may be especially important to a top-down administrator who does not encourage staff participation in major decisions of the agency.

Nevertheless, studies have found a strong correlation between staff contentment with their working conditions and their productivity and retention. Agencies with low staff morale are usually among those with high staff turnovers. Mor Barak, Nissly, and Levin (2001) conducted a meta-analysis of twenty-five studies on retention and turnover of staff and their antecedents. The studies reported a range of staff turnover in the agencies studied of 30 percent to 60 percent in a typical year. Among the contributors to staff turnover were burnout, job stress, a lack of support from coworkers and supervisors, and other organizational conditions. Therefore, paying close attention to staff satisfaction with work conditions can be important, and staff satisfaction evaluations are among the ways to investigate such issues.

Some of the issues revolving around working conditions and morale that make sense to periodically investigate include salaries and annual salary raises, availability of medical coverage for employees and family members, retirement benefits, workload issues (e.g., size of caseload), availability and quality of their supervision, opportunities for advancement, support for professional licensing, openness of administrators to staff members' views on programs and personnel matters, availability of useful in-service and out-sourced training opportunities, reasonable vacation and sick-leave policies, other family-friendly policies, and incentives and rewards for doing exemplary work. At least one study also found that the challenges imposed by some client groups, such as clients with mental illness, also affect job satisfaction (Acker, 1999).

Evaluations of Practice Processes

Many of the preceding types of evaluations could naturally focus on either programs or practice, even though the discussion so far has been mostly on programs. For example, linking client problems with the practice approach is relevant, as some practitioners may apply a rigid approach with every client rather than vary their practice to clients' individualized needs. In this regard, one purpose of a practice evaluation might be to explore variations in the implementation of a practice approach and how variations may be linked to different client needs. It may well be that many staff members decide to use a specific practice theory without varying it to what clients need. For example, one client may benefit from an approach that helps them gain insight into their problems using a cognitive behavioral approach, while another may need more emphasis on support and not benefit from insight.

Monitoring Practice

Practice quality is closely related to program quality, as the quality of an overall program depends on the quality of each service component, which often comprise the services of individual staff members. Monitoring practice is a discipline that can help practitioners improve what they do. Social work practitioners often monitor the quality of their practice; some of their efforts may not even be considered evaluations.

Process recordings are an example. Supervisors and practice teachers often request process recordings of new staff members and field students to find out what happens in their interviews. The recordings are then carefully reviewed in a supervisory session to explore the appropriateness of the social worker's responses to the client's comments. Often the recordings are helpful for revealing missed opportunities for the worker to respond to the subtle messages and emotional reactions of clients. The supervisory discussions can be very useful in helping new workers and students become more disciplined in how they use themselves in practice situations and in providing supervisors with enough information to be satisfied that clients receive satisfactory help.

Direct observations of practice through a two-way mirror or by videotaping and audio taping interviews are other ways to evaluate practice interventions through the supervisor-worker relationship. Other devices such as case summaries and personal logs of staff members can also be used to help practitioners monitor their own practice and receive helpful feedback from a supervisor. Discussion of case summaries of sessions can lead to planning future interviews and to modifications in a worker's approach.

Case managers carry a specific role that emphasizes monitoring the practice of other providers of service to a client (Frankel & Gelman, 1998). Social workers at the BSW level are especially equipped in their education to fill these positions. Case managers typically locate services for their clients, negotiate and facilitate contracts with agencies offering services, and monitor the range of services provided to the clients to ensure that they are appropriate to their needs and provided in a high-quality way.

Practice Accessibility

Problems of practice accessibility are inherent in an individual's practice, as they are in programs. Practitioners frequently face no-shows and early dropouts among their clients, which often points to accessibility barriers that need addressing. For example, prospective clients may explore the services of a practitioner by phone and agree to come to an initial interview. Yet they may neither show up nor call in to explain. Often clients come to an initial interview or the first session of a group but do not return again. Unless these no-shows and early dropouts are followed up in an attempt to find out what happened to them, practitioners cannot know whether accessibility barriers existed that could be overcome.

The Wrong Motives for Dealing with "No-Shows"

One mental health agency decided to address its high number of no-shows with two strategies. First, clinicians were encouraged to double schedule appointments in hope that at least one of the two clients scheduled for each time slot would show up. If both clients showed up, the program director promised to find someone to meet with the second client. The other strategy was to employ a decision committee, which a client who had missed three or more appointments had to talk to before being scheduled for another session. The decision committee was used to stress clients' responsibility to attend all appointments and to inform clients that additional sessions would not be offered if they missed another session. The decision committee was not used to seriously explore the clients' reasons for no-shows. Both strategies were motivated by an administrative need to generate a maximum number of client reimbursements for the private-for-profit agency.

No-shows and dropouts can result from accessibility barriers, which should be carefully considered and addressed. Otherwise, the circumstances that cause or exacerbate the barriers could easily continue for prospective clients in the future. Some types of clients may easily use the services of a practitioner or program (e.g., a middle class, married client, experienced in using a multitude of services, and/or who generally copes well with and manages personal issues). Others, possibly racial or ethnic minorities, low-income families, recent immigrants, single mothers, unmarried and inactive fathers, older lesbians, people with AIDS, people with chronic mental illness, and people with numerous other challenging characteristics are known to have been excluded or discouraged from using services. Studies have shown, for example, that no-show behavior can be correlated with low income (e.g., Allan, 1988), lower socioeconomic status (e.g., Lefebrve, Sommerauer, Cohen, Waldron, & Perry, 1983), age (e.g., Carpenter, Morrow, Del Guadio, & Ritzler, 1981), and substance abuse (e.g., Paolillo & Moore, 1984), among other factors.

Concluding that clients and prospective clients are simply resistant or unmotivated to use services is a frequently given excuse and a superficial way to ignore some of the more complicated and valid explanations. Some more valid explanations can be explored by considering the types of barriers described previously (e.g., physical, psychological, cultural, geographic, institutional).

Practitioners are encouraged to devise a plan to address accessibility barriers when they face a considerable number of no-shows or dropouts. Meyer (2001) offers some suggestions. One barrier may be the wait time before a first visit, as the longer the wait time to obtain a first appointment, the less likely a client is to keep the next appointment. Thus, workers should minimize any wait time initially or before any session. Another barrier could be the expectation of employers that clients accomplish speedy outcomes as a result of the growing pressures that assistance be short term and address only immediate problems.

Another concern, according to Meyer (2001), may be that the client's problems with service providers in the past were barriers because former providers may have been unresponsive or unhelpful. In this case, special efforts may be in order to help clients openly talk about their negative past experiences, and they may need to be reassured that such experiences will not be repeated. Another suggestion is that the practitioner demonstrate the qualities of the therapeutic relationship from the very first contact, whether by phone or in person; these qualities include reliability, trustworthiness, calmness, respect, good listening, warmth, empathic responses, and not rushing. Well-thought-out and sensitive follow-up efforts are also encouraged when a client does not show up for an appointment. Such inquiries could include asking a client in a direct but nonjudgmental and caring way why he or she missed the appointment and exploring how the client wants to proceed.

Staudt, Bates, Blake, and Shoffner (2004) offer further suggestions for preventing no-shows. Besides emphasizing with clients such central practice qualities as conveying a nonjudgmental attitude and clearly explaining the confidentiality policy, they suggest some helpful practice notions that could enhance the possibility that clients will return for their second and later interviews. These practice techniques include contracting for a set number of sessions, eliciting what the client wants to get out of treatment, asking clients what might prevent them from returning, and educating clients about their role and the role of the social worker.

Are the Clients Satisfied?

Obtaining feedback from clients on their satisfaction is important to consider not only in monitoring programs but also in practice. Social workers can be encouraged to periodically have informal discussions with clients and/or ask them to fill out questionnaires to elicit their feedback on how helpful the services have been and what can be done to improve them. A social worker can ask clients several basic questions, such as the following:

- How satisfied are you with the services that you have been receiving?
- Are you feeling satisfied generally? In what ways?

- How might you be feeling dissatisfied or disappointed? In what specific possible areas?
- What am I doing that is helpful to you? How is it helpful?
- What additionally would you like me to do?
- What am I doing that is not helpful to you?
- How am I helping you reach your goals?
- How do you feel about the session today (a good overall question at the end of each session)?

Client Satisfaction Using a Focus Group

A graduate student (Borys, 2006) decided to conduct a client satisfaction study to find out what aftercare residents of a substance abuse agency for women thought were the strengths and weaknesses of their program. She used a focus group format and asked the following questions:

1. What do you feel are the strengths of the program?
2. What do you see as some areas that need to be improved?
3. What part of the program have you struggled with the most?
4. If you could change anything about the program, what would it be?

In brief, a general consensus was reached about bringing back a residential program that had been discontinued; providing more advocacy for housing, jobs, and day care; having a supportive staff; and involving board members more with the residents, including being more of an advocate for them.

Client satisfaction is especially important to explore at the time that a client is terminating services. Yet it is strongly advised that client satisfaction explorations also occur periodically while services are still being offered. In this way, changes can be incorporated into a worker's practice during future sessions. In addition, periodic client satisfaction conversations can create greater bonding with clients because clients feel they are being heard and that their voice is important.

Key Terms
Best Practices
Client satisfaction
Cultural barriers
Geographic barriers
Institutional barriers
Link between client problems and program

Monitoring practice
Physical barriers
Practice accessibility
Program accessibility
Program implementation
Program quality
Psychological barriers
Quality assurance
Quality control
Quality improvement
Staff morale and satisfaction

Discussion Questions and Assignments

1. Identify what you think are the key elements of a program at your field agency that are necessary for it to be effective in addressing the causes of clients' problems. Then ask three different staff members to identify how these elements are present and operable in the program.
2. Review the factors of the larger context of a program in chapter 1. In your opinion, which factors are essential for the effective functioning of a program? Which are optional? Give reasons for your answers. Which factors are essential for accountability? Which are important in responding to the sociocultural characteristics of a program? Give examples.
3. Assume that you work for a child welfare agency that had previously provided protective services in instances of child neglect. Now the agency is preparing to provide secondary prevention services to families who may be most prone to neglecting their children as a result of a range of problems. Identify a list of questions that can be asked to determine which families would be most qualified to be clients of this secondary prevention program.
4. You plan an education symposium on preventing strokes for the older adults in your community and hold the symposium at the local hospital. You are pleased that the symposium has a good turnout of older and middle-aged adults but as you look around the room you see almost no African American adults present. You know that African Americans have a higher incidence of stroke than other ethnic groups. Design a plan for another community education program that will reach this underrepresented group of older adults.
5. Review the two strategies to address no-shows in "The Wrong Motives for Dealing with No-Shows." What is ethically wrong with these strategies? How, if at all, could either strategy be modified in some way to make it ethical and possibly effective?

6. A. Conduct a role-play of a conversation between a social worker and a client after meeting for five sessions. Conduct an informal client satisfaction exploration. You can use some of the questions found in the chapter or the following questions in the interview.

   - Generally, how are we doing?
   - How am I doing?
   - What's helpful?
   - What's not so helpful?
   - What would you like to have that you are not getting?

   B. Now add the following variations in separate interviews:

   - A client is Asian American and tends to defer to the person in authority.
   - A client is Southern and tends not to want to directly question the person in authority; the client tends to be less direct and less open but has some complaints to share.
   - Vary the client's age (e.g., young adult, older adult).
   - A client is the victim of domestic violence.
   - A client is a perpetrator of domestic violence in an involuntary setting.

7. This *major class assignment* is to be completed by choosing *one* of the two types of practice evaluations described:

   1. *Monitor your interventions*: Work on monitoring and improving your interventions through self-reflection (e.g., What theoretical approach are you aware that you use? How well are your interventions implemented? What have you done that worked well? What needs improvement?).

      Tools to consider: (a) process recordings of a few interviews, (b) summaries and personal impressions of a few interviews, (c) video or audio recordings of interviews.

   2. *Determine client satisfaction*: Determine whether your client is satisfied with your interventions (e.g., Is your client satisfied with the services that you have provided? In what ways? To what extent? In what ways is the client dissatisfied?).

      Tools to consider using: (a) client satisfaction forced-response interview schedule, (b) client satisfaction qualitative interview, (c) client satisfaction questionnaire?.

Steps to Complete the Assignment

1. Identify *a need for a practice evaluation* in your field agency and a client system that can benefit from an evaluation. Inform the client about the evaluation and encourage her or him to participate.

2. Select the *type of evaluation and specific tool* that most readily fits your client situation from the preceding list. Feasibility is an important consideration in your selection if you have limited time. For example, consider the number of likely sessions in which you will see your client, the overall amount of time that your agency will serve the client, and any difficulty you may have in identifying a measurable goal(s) for the client.

3. Use your *field instructor as a consultant*. Discuss the assignment thoroughly with your field instructor to make sure that she or he understands the assignment and the evaluation tool that you will use. Give the field instructor a copy of the assignment.

4. *Obtain informed consent* either in written or oral form. Make sure that the client understands all pertinent issues of informed consent (e.g., purpose of the selected tool; how it works; how the client, worker, and agency can benefit; expectations you have for the client in participating in the evaluation; informing the client if this is a course assignment to be turned in; ensuring confidentiality; reminding the client of the option to say no or withdraw after the evaluation begins). Whenever your field agency has a protocol for obtaining informed consent, use it to complete this assignment.

5. *Formulate and implement your practice evaluation*. Follow the specific steps below that fit the type of evaluation you decide to focus on.

A. *For monitoring your interventions*:

1. Identify your purpose as specifically as you can (e.g., What specific things do you want to consider in more depth about your interventions or What questions do you want to answer about your interventions?).

2. How will you go about monitoring your interventions (e.g., Will you use process recordings or case summaries of a few interviews with a client? Will you tape-record interviews?).

3. Select a way to analyze your qualitative records, such as a simplified version of a theme analysis.

B. *For client satisfaction evaluations*:

1. Construct an interview schedule or a questionnaire. It can be structured, semistructured, or unstructured.

2. Include questions in your instrument that explore how to address any perceived dissatisfactions raised by the client.

3. Pretest your instrument with a client or someone similar to a client.

4. Conduct the interview or administer the questionnaire to the client.

5. Discuss the client's views about how helpful the instrument is.

6. Describe what you have learned about evaluating your practice from this assignment and what advantages and limitations you see in using this tool. Complete step 6 for both monitoring and client satisfaction evaluations.

References

Acker, G. M. (1999). The impact of clients' mental illness on social workers' job satisfaction and burnout. *Health and Social Work*, *24*(2), 112–119.

Allan, A. T. (1988). No-shows at a community mental health center: A pilot study. *The International Journal of Social Psychiatry*, *34*(1), 40–46.

Baker, L., Zucker, P., & Gross, M. (1998). Using client satisfaction surveys to evaluate and improve services in locked and unlocked adult inpatient facilities. *Journal of Behavioral Health Services Research*, *25*(1), 51–68.

Borys, L. (2006). *Focus group assignment for a program evaluation course*. Unpublished manuscript, University of North Carolina at Charlotte.

Carpenter, P., Morrow, G., Del Guadio, A., & Ritzler, B. A. (1981). Who keeps the first outpatient appointment? *American Journal of Psychiatry*, *138*, 102–105.

Cook, C. A., Selig, K. L., Wedge, B. J., & Gohn-Baube, E. A. (1999). Access barriers and the use of prenatal care by low income, inner-city women. *Social Work*, *44*(2), 129–139.

Dansky, K. H., Colbert, C. J., & Irwin, P. (1996). Developing and using a patient satisfaction survey: A case study. *Clinical and Program Notes*, *45*, 83–88.

Dudley, J. R. (2005). *Research methods for social work: Becoming consumers and producers of research*. Boston: Allyn & Bacon.

Fischer, R. L. (2002). Gaining access to one's children: An evaluation of a visitation program for noncustodial parents. *Families in Society: The Journal of Contemporary Human Services*, *83*(2), 163–174.

Foster, J., & Hope, T. (1993). *Housing, community and crime: The impact of the Priority Estates Project*. London: HMSO.

Frankel, A. J., & Gelman, S. R. (1998). *Case management: An introduction to concepts and skills*. Chicago: Lyceum Books.

Gardner, F. (2000). Design evaluation: Illuminating social work practice for better outcomes. *Social Work*, *45*(2), 176–182.

Huntersville Oaks Nursing Home. (2005). Nursing home admissions satisfaction survey. Huntersville, NC: Author.

Kennedy, E., Wilson, B., Valladares, S., & Bronte-Tinkew, J. (2007). Improving attendance and retention in out-of-school time programs. *Child Trends*, Publication 2007-17.

Lefebrve, A., Sommerauer, J., Cohen, N., Waldron, S., & Perry, I. (1983). Where did all the "no-shows" go? *Canadian Journal of Psychiatry*, *28*, 387–390.

Martin, L. L., & Kettner, P. M. (1996). *Measuring the performance of human service programs*. Thousand Oaks, CA: Sage Publications.

Meyer, W. S. (2001). Why they don't come back: A clinical perspective on the no-show client. *Clinical Social Work Journal*, *29*(4), 325–339.

Mor Barak, M. E., Nissly, J. A., & Levin, A. (2001). Antecedents to retention and turnover among child welfare, social work, and other human service employees: What can we learn from past research? A review and metanalysis. *Social Service Review*, (December), 625–661.

Oliphant, E., Brown, J. H., Cambron, M. L., & Yankeelov, P. (2002). Measuring children's perceptions of the 'Families in Transition' Program (FIT): A qualitative evaluation. *Journal of Divorce and Remarriage, 37*(3/4), 157–164.

Paolillo, J. G., & Moore, T. W. (1984). Appointment compliance behavior of community mental health patients: A discriminant analysis. *Community Mental Health Journal, 20*(2), 103–108.

Pawson, R., & Tilley, N. (1997). *Realistic evaluation.* Thousand Oaks, CA: Sage Publications.

Prior, V., Lynch, M. A., & Glaser, D. (1999). Responding to child sexual abuse: An evaluation of social work by children and carers. *Child and Family Social Work, 4,* 131–143.

Reese, D., Ahern, R., Nair, S., O'Faire, J., & Warren, C. (1999). Hospice access and use by African Americans: Addressing cultural and institutional barriers through participatory action research. *Social Work, 44*(6), 549–559.

Reid, K. E. (1997). *Social work practice with groups: A clinical perspective* (2nd ed.). Belmont, CA: Thomson Learning–Brooks/Cole.

Staudt, M. M., Bates, D., Blake, G. H., & Shoffner, J. S. (2004). Practice evaluation: Moving beyond single system designs. *Arete*, (September), 71–78.

Weinbach, R. W. (2005). *Evaluating social work services and programs.* Boston: Allyn & Bacon.

Part V

The Outcome Stage

Chapter 9

Outcome Studies: Is the Intervention Effective?

How do we know that our program really helps clients?

To many people, the evaluation of programs and practice essentially means evaluating whether the intervention resulted in positive outcomes for clients. Outcome questions have a familiar ring to them: Did the clients reach their goals? Did they make significant progress? Is there evidence that the program made a difference in their functioning?

Although outcome studies are presented as one of three general types of evaluations in this text (i.e., planning, implementation, and outcome), it must be said that they are ultimately the most important type. If progress on clients' goals is not evident at the completion of a program, a provider will have difficulty justifying the program's continuation. This is the case no matter how well the program was planned, how qualified the staff members who provide services are, and even whether the program's quality is superior. This is also true for practice interventions. If practice interventions do not lead to substantial gains for clients in the intended areas, then the intervention needs major modifications or should be discontinued and replaced with another approach.

This chapter describes the critical ingredients in outcome evaluations, including two basic elements: a clearly defined intervention and measurable client outcomes. Several types of evaluation designs used in outcome evaluations are presented. The advantages and limitations of each design and what each can claim are described, with examples of outcome evaluations to help explain the relevant concepts.

Figure 9.1 provides an overview of many of the types of evaluations and related activities that are important during the outcome stage. As figure 9.1 indicates, many of the activities are not evaluations but have an obvious impact on the conduct of outcome evaluations because they are instrumental in analyzing, interpreting, communicating, and disseminating results. All the types of evaluations listed in figure 9.1 are described in some detail in this chapter, and later chapters address many of the related activities.

The Nature of Outcomes

Program and practice outcomes can focus on many things. Outcome measures may be identified for staff members' performance, material resources,

FIGURE 9.1   Spectrum of Activities Involved in Outcome Stage

---

Outcome Stage
(Determining Effectiveness)

Types of evaluations

1. Pre-experimental designs
2. Experimental and quasi-experimental research designs
3. Cost-benefit analysis
4. Single-system designs
5. Goal Attainment Scale
6. Target Problem Scale
7. Sequencing Blocks

Related activities

8. Analyzing the data
9. Interpreting the results
10. Communicating with the stakeholders about the results and what they mean
11. Communicating with client groups, the community, and relevant agencies about the program
12. Other forms of agency public relations
13. Preparing new grant proposals in response to the results

---

recruiting of more clients, or other concerns. Ultimately, however, the outcomes for clients are the focus of human service outcome evaluations. Outcomes typically are the goals of clients and measure whether the goals have been reached. Chapter 7 described how to identify, describe, and measure goals.

Outcomes Are Not Outputs

The outcomes of clients, which are the ultimate interest of a program or practice evaluation, have several distinct characteristics. Unfortunately, most agencies focus almost exclusively on outputs rather than outcomes in their performance reports that are available to the public. For example, an agency report may focus on the number of staff hours of counseling provided, the number of clients who use services, or the costs of a particular program.

Excerpts from an Annual Report of a County Government

The following statistics are from the annual report of the Cabarrus County (2007) government:

- 322,000 people visited county-operated parks.
- 14,706 people participated in athletics, competitions, and other recreational events held in county parks.

- 7,801 calls and personal contacts came into the Veterans' Services office.
- 976,939 miles were driven by county vans.
- 81,847 rides were provided to disabled and or elderly residents by the county transportation service.
- 35,335 individuals visited the Department of Social Services for services or assistance.
- 5,085 families in a crisis situation received assistance through the Department of Social Services.
- 3,885 children were protected from abuse, neglect, or dependency through provision of child protective services.

Note that all of these indicators are outputs, even though some may be misrepresented as outcomes. The last output in the preceding example, "children were *protected* from abuse, neglect, or dependency" is incorrectly stated and should be phrased as "children were provided with child protective services." The agency did not have any evidence from a follow-up inquiry to conclude that the children were protected.

Outcomes Ultimately Focus on the Clients, Not Staff Interventions

A frequent problem for many who are new at crafting outcomes for clients is the confusion of client outcomes with outcomes for the staff who are helping them. For example, "The client will be referred to X agency for assistance whenever the program cannot help her." Note that this statement refers more to what a staff member will do than to what the client does. Many stakeholders may think that the goals of the staff members are outcomes. In a sense they are, but outcomes for staff activities are more appropriately referred to as the means of achieving goals.

Articulating and documenting outcomes for staff activities can be helpful, especially because client outcomes usually depend on the success of staff in reaching their goals. Outcomes for staff members can be viewed as an appropriate evaluation focus at the process stage, such as when we ask whether staff members use evidenced-based practice theories or provide quality services. Nevertheless, these outcomes are not the end results sought for clients.

Quiz: Are These Outcomes for Clients or Staff Members?

Try to pick out which of the following outcomes or goals are the clients' and which are the staff members'.

1. The clients will be transported to the grocery store in the agency van every Monday.
2. The clients will purchase groceries for the evening meal.

3. The client will have access to a planned meal written out on a piece of paper.
4. The client will pay for the groceries using the money available for shopping.
5. The clients will have enough money to buy the groceries.

The correct answers to the outcomes in the preceding quiz are that nos. 2 and 4 focus on clients and the others focus on staff members. The fifth outcome could be intended either for the clients or for staff, depending on who has control over the funds for shopping; unfortunately, it is presented in an ambiguous way. Overall, the five examples show how dependent client outcomes are on staff outcomes.

Outcomes Are Directly Linked to the Interventions

It is important that the link between outcome measures and the intervention used to affect them be readily evident according to the logic model. This should be the case both conceptually and practically. Often, having a commonsense approach to understand the intervention helps in the crafting of realistic outcome measures. For example, the community organization mentioned in chapter 7 that wanted to reduce the number of divorces in the community within the first few years of marriage decided to offer a premarital weekend retreat format at several different houses of worship to help couples become better prepared for their marriages. The retreat curriculum included five major components: communication between the couple, having realistic expectations of a partner, finances, health issues, and sexuality and intimacy. The sponsoring organization recruited speakers who had expertise in each topical area to lead the components. On the basis of this information, the evaluator devised a pretest-posttest measure of outcomes for the retreat based on what could be realistically expected from participation in each retreat component. Specific questions were devised on the basis of the specific objectives of each speaker. For example, the topic of having realistic expectations of your partner included questions such as, "Do you know what your spouse expects of you?" "Do you and your partner know how to resolve conflicts when they arise?" and "Do you know how to meet your partner's needs?" The response categories were "yes," "sometimes," and "no."

Outcomes Are Determined at Different Points in Time

The point in time to measure a client outcome is an important factor to consider. For example, outcomes can be measured when a client completes a program or at some future time. Outcomes can be short-term (e.g., when a client completes the program), intermediate (e.g., three months later), or long-term (e.g., twelve months later). The time selected and the specific outcome expected depend on the amount of time realistically needed for the program to have such an impact.

Example of Outcomes at Different Points in Time

A crisis center for transient youths decided to use short-, intermediate-, and long-term outcomes for the youths they sheltered. Their outcome measures were as follows:

Short term: reduction in runaway behavior, physically aggressive behavior, and serious physically aggressive threats while residing at the crisis center.

Intermediate term: residence in a safe, least restrictive environment for two months after discharge and increase family access to community services.

Long term: residence in a safe, least restrictive environment for six months after discharge, increased school attendance, and reduction in involvement with the juvenile justice system.

Unfortunately, most evaluations are set up to measure client outcomes only when clients complete the program or otherwise terminate from the agency. This is an important time to measure outcomes, as it provides a measure of how much change occurred while the client was in the program. Yet this single short-term measure usually reveals little, if anything, about the long-term effects of a program. Inpatient programs for drug-addicted clients, for example, are often criticized for not providing a long-lasting impact on recovery. Clients who leave a program may be drug free, but the true test of their success is likely determined over time, once they return to their community and reconnect with their social supports, both previous and new. Unfortunately, many substance abuse programs do not conduct a follow-up evaluation to determine whether their services led to long-term recovery or a return to addiction and a lifestyle that supports addiction.

Varied Ways to Measure Outcomes

Martin and Kettner (1996) identify what they perceive as the four kinds of outcome or performance measures: numeric counts, standardized measures, scales of level of client functioning, and client satisfaction indicators. Numeric counts are generally used to measure client conditions, status, and behaviors. Examples include attendance at school, frequency of drinking alcohol, and numbers of violent and other antisocial behaviors. Standardized measures usually measure such things as client feelings, attitudes, and perceptions. Examples of such scales include self-esteem, clinical anxiety, hope, and happiness. Level-of-functioning scales measure client and family functioning. Examples include scales of adaptive behavior, employment behavior, wellness, and social integration. Martin and Kettner (1996) also refer to client satisfaction as an outcome; however, they view client perceptions of the services received as only an intermediate outcome, not a final one.

Child Welfare Outcomes Document on the Internet

The U.S. Department of Health and Human Services' Children's Bureau includes child welfare outcomes as part of its annual report to Congress. Now in its fifth year, the report provides data on states' performance in meeting the needs of children and families who come into contact with the child-welfare system. Two federal data-reporting systems are used to gather data on seven outcomes: reduced recurrence of child maltreatment, reduced maltreatment in foster care, increased permanency for children in foster care, reduced time in foster care to reunification, reduced time in foster care to adoption, increased placement stability, and reduced placement of young children in group homes and institutions. Additional information from the Child and Family Service Reviews provides context for the results observed in each state. The full report can be downloaded from the Web site www.acf.hhs.gov/programs/cb/publications/cwo. htm. A booklet containing the executive summary and a CD of the full report is also available. All can be obtained from the National Clearinghouse on Child Abuse and Neglect Information, at 800-394-3366 or by e-mailing nccanch@caliber.com.

Practical Measures of Outcomes

Ideally, virtually all agencies have client outcomes that they are helping clients accomplish. Because the outcomes are the ultimate reason for the agency's existence, it makes sense to keep them at the forefront of their work, their conversations with clients, their sources of referrals, and their education of the general public. One agency, for example, does just that. Community Choices Inc. (2006) helps pregnant women addicted to alcohol and/or drugs by offering group treatment. The outcomes of the agency are evident in much of its material, including the brochure handed out to prospective clients and referral agencies. Outcomes that they highlight for clients are becoming drug free; maintaining or regaining custody of children; having a healthy, drug-free baby; becoming self-sufficient; finding a job; finding permanent housing; improving parenting skills; and feeling better about themselves. The open and direct communication about the outcomes has many benefits, including helping the women identify what they want or need, self-selecting the agency as a result of desired outcomes, and communicating the agency's purpose and intentions to the general public.

Outcome Indicators Used for Clients in a Domestic Violence Agency

The following indicators are from White (2005):

- Homicide rate (chosen by the county government)
- Perceived degree of safety
- Knowledge of a safety plan that could be used in an emergency
- Acknowledgment of a broad definition of domestic violence
- Favorable responses to client satisfaction questions
- Referral contact rate (when client follows through and contacts another agency he or she is referred to)
- Recidivism rate (returning to agency a second time or more)

Litzelfelner (2001) gives another example of a need for practical outcomes when the overall goal of a program is not measurable. She points out that the goal of child protective services to protect children from abuse is not usually measurable. Abuse and reabuse of children is often undiscovered or unreported. She offers what she views as practical alternative measures in a set of four general areas related to child abuse: child safety, child permanency, preserving families, and child health and development. For each area, she identifies several measurable objectives and activities to reach the objectives. For example, for child safety, she suggests two objectives as examples: (1) 90 percent of children served will not reenter the system within two years following their initial discharge (based on reports of the agency's home visit and case management services), and (2) each quarter, 85 percent of caregivers participating in the parent education program will demonstrate three nonphysical behavior management techniques during the agency's home visits.

As an exercise, identify the weaknesses in this approach to measuring child abuse. Then develop an alternative approach that could be another way to measure child abuse.

Outcomes can also be measured by qualitative methods. One student who was working with a group of emotionally disturbed children in a public school decided to use journaling to measure progress on their personal goals related to self-esteem (McLean, 2007). She encouraged her group members to keep an ongoing journal of their impressions discussed in the group. They were given ten minutes at the end of each session to write about their impressions. During most sessions, members were asked to journal on the topics that had been discussed, such as, What are the benefits of self-esteem? or How can mistakes be opportunities for growth? Journaling during the first and last sessions was used to evaluate their progress in working on their personal goals. During the first session, members were asked to journal on their goals and expectations for the group. The topic for them to focus on was, What do I want to get out of this group? The final session was used to journal on the topic, How has the group changed my self-esteem? Quantitative ratings were also used to evaluate their progress on goals during the last session.

Criteria for Choosing Outcome Measures

What determines whether an outcome measure is adequate or acceptable? Martin and Kettner (1996) offer seven criteria: the outcome measure's usefulness, validity, reliability, precision, feasibility, cost, and unit costs.

Usefulness

First, the measure needs to be useful and relevant to stakeholders. This is a commonsense criterion that raises an important question: How will the outcome measure be useful? Will it offer helpful information to stakeholders to support the program or assist them in improving, expanding, or even reducing it?

Validity

Is the outcome measure valid? Validity is one of the two psychometric standards for determining whether a measure is satisfactory. Validity refers to whether the outcome measure reflects what it is supposed to measure and whether it does so accurately. Accuracy is the key issue. The more valid that a measure is, the better it is. For example, an outcome measure for father involvement should include several different functions or activities, not just one. Some will involve direct contact with their child (e.g., how many direct contact hours in an average week, quality of the specific activities), and other functions may involve no contact but direct responsibilities (e.g., attending a parent-teacher conference, arranging a dental appointment for the child). From this example, it is clear how complex outcomes like father involvement are and the enormous challenges they pose for creating accurate measures. Father involvement requires at the very least a certain amount of contact; and the quality of that contact, whether direct contact or indirect responsibilities, is also important to consider.

Reliability

The third criterion for choosing an outcome measure is reliability. Reliability is a second key psychometric standard in determining whether a measure is satisfactory. Reliability refers to the internal consistency of the measure. It asks two questions: whether the measure of the outcome consistently measures it from one time to another and whether the measure is consistently applied among different people (e.g., do different clients consistently understand the measure in the same way?). Reliability is weak if the questions asked in a measurement instrument are ambiguous, with words likely to be understood and interpreted differently at different times or by different respondents. For example, satisfaction with a program can be interpreted in many ways.

Precision

Precision is the fourth criterion. Precision refers to how well the outcome measure captures the incremental changes in clients' condition, either quantitatively or qualitatively. Quantitative measures are at the interval, ordinal, or nominal levels. Qualitative measures are at the prenominal level. For example, incremental quantitative measures are the number of times truant children attend school (interval level) and their average letter grade (ordinal). An example of an incremental qualitative measure is the subtle variations in how a parent uses nonviolent strategies in disciplining their children.

Feasibility

A fifth criterion in deciding on outcome measures is their feasibility. Is the measure viewed as practical and acceptable to all stakeholders? Some may be opposed to a measure because it is at odds with their cultural values or ethics. For example, a measure of assertiveness needs to take into account the ways that various cultural groups view confrontation with authority. Feasibility may also be a problem if it is likely to demand a lot of the attention and time of staff members in explaining or administering it.

Cost

The cost of an outcome measure is another criterion. Does the measure require some major start-up or maintenance costs? Another possible cost factor is the purchase of any standardized scales owned by other people or organizations.

Unit Cost Reporting

Unit cost reporting is the final criterion. Can the measure be described as a cost per unit of outcome? For example, the cost of a client graduating from a program could be used as a cost per unit of outcome. Numeric counts lend themselves to this type of cost more than other measures, such as standardized scales, do.

Outcomes and Program Costs

Sometimes outcome studies are conducted that focus directly on costs. Some refer to these evaluations as cost-benefit or cost-effectiveness evaluations. Cost-related evaluations are increasingly important to consider, given the diminishing funds for human service programs and the increasing call for financial accountability. One ethical dilemma with cost-benefit studies is that it is too difficult to directly translate the benefits of a program, such as reduced child abuse or treating and managing severe mental illness, into financial savings. Although immediate financial savings are evident in such things as fewer health-care visits and avoiding legal costs in a court case, the benefits of protecting a child from harm go well beyond material factors and may have implications for the life of the child and for the child's offspring. In brief, although fiscal matters have obvious value, their value is limited and should be subordinate to the value of basic human needs.

Cost-effectiveness evaluations, similar to cost-benefit studies, may have more utility in human service programs than cost-benefit studies. In this case, the client outcomes resulting from a program can be analyzed according to cost. The cost, for example, of obtaining adoptions, on average, for special needs children could be considered in terms of costs. The costs could then be compared to the costs of such an outcome in the previous year, or two different programs could be compared on the basis of the costs incurred in completing a successful adoption.

It is complicated but possible to calculate costs in a human services program. For example, one could categorize costs into direct (e.g., staff salary) and indirect (e.g., secretarial salary, telephone bills). Costs could also be divided into fixed (e.g., building maintenance) and variable (e.g., salaries), and recurring (e.g., rent) and nonrecurring (e.g., equipment). Determining the costs of providing services to an average client must take all of these costs into account, which sometimes becomes a real challenge to figure out. For example, in the 1970s, with deinstitutionalization of people with mental retardation, some legislators wanted to argue in favor of either community-based services or institutional services according to which had lower per capita costs. This exercise led to the discovery that it was easier to calculate the per capita costs of community-based services because they were discrete (e.g., residential, vocational, recreational). In contrast, the cost of institutional services, encumbered by extensive capital costs such as maintenance of buildings and grounds, were more difficult to calculate accurately.

Evidence-Based Interventions

Once the outcome measures have been carefully selected for an evaluation, another challenging task is to demonstrate that the measures are logically and empirically linked to the intervention that will be used. Interventions that are empirically linked to important outcome measures are evidence-based interventions. This raises a critical point about evidence-based interventions—they are interventions that have, to some degree, a demonstrated causal relationship to particular client outcomes.

Evidence-based interventions were defined in chapter 2 as integrating individual practice expertise, the best-available external evidence from practice research, and the values and expectations of clients (Gambrill, 1999, p. 346). This definition suggests that *evidence-based* should not be either defined simply by one criterion or based on solely one source. Instead, the interventions should have multiple factors in common. One such factor, a necessary one, is that evidence-based interventions have the best evidence available that they are effective in helping clients, and strong evidence is available to support the claim in the measures of client outcomes. Thus, we can say that evidence-based interventions should be grounded one way or another in outcome evaluations of some form.

O'Hare (2005) describes four important characteristics of evidence-based practices: they use critical-thinking skills, obtain scientifically credible evidence, seek multiple sources of evidence whenever possible, and seek diversity-sensitive evidence.

1. Critical-Thinking Skills

Critical-thinking skills are used to determine whether an intervention is evidence based. Critical thinkers are natural skeptics about how well an evaluation is conducted, whether someone else's evaluation or one's own. Critical thinkers are also skeptical about whether their interventions actually work. As mentioned in chapter 1, Gibbs and Gambrill (1996) identify several types of problems that evaluators experience when they fail to be critical thinkers, including the selection of weak or inappropriate interventions.

2. Scientifically Credible Evidence

Evidence-based interventions must have documentation that is scientifically credible. This means, in part, that there is scientific evidence of a causal relationship between the intervention and clients' outcomes. Such evidence for programs is most likely to come from group designs, especially experimental and quasi-experimental designs, which are known to be superior to other evaluation strategies (Cook & Campbell, 1979). Evidence for practice interventions is most likely to come from a version of a single-system design, especially a design that controls for as many extraneous influences as possible.

Scientifically credible evidence and critical thinking share many common values. Both approaches involve skepticism. Both carefully distinguish between questions of fact and questions of value. Both use caution when inferring what may have caused improvement in the client outcomes and when making generalizations to other client groups, and both emphasize the need for measurement in the identification of clients' needs, interventions, and outcomes. Finally, both perspectives are likely to continually ask, Does this intervention work?

3. Seeking Multiple Sources of Evidence

Triangulation, a process of using multiple methods to measure something, is also important to evidence-based interventions. Evaluators who obtain two or more measures of an outcome for comparison triangulate the findings. The process also adds confidence that the two measures are valid because of their similarity. The more sources available that document that the intervention has a causal relationship to client outcomes, the better. An example is to find out the frequency of a nonresidential father's contact with his children in an average week by seeking a report from two or more sources (e.g., the father, the children's mother, the father's current partner).

Criterion-related validity is another way to triangulate the findings of an evaluation. Criterion-related validity is a means of determining whether the scores of an outcome measure are valid by correlating the scores with those of another measure of the same construct (Babbie, 2001). The other measures of the same construct are external criteria. For example, an external criterion could be a behavioral indicator that correlates with a verbal response of a client to an interview question. If a short-term outcome measure of an evaluation is regular attendance at a drug treatment program, the evaluator could compare the client's report of his or her attendance with a report of attendance obtained from the drug treatment agency. In another example, the outcome measure could be a depression scale developed by an agency, and the scores could be correlated with the scores of the same clients using a well-established measure like the Beck Depression Scale (Beck, Steer, & Brown, 1996).

4. Evidence Is Diversity Sensitive

If there is evidence that a program or practice intervention is effective with one group of people, it is extremely important not to automatically conclude that it will be effective with other groups. This is a fallacy that has resulted from the misuse of previous findings, especially evidence that a particular approach helps white, middle-class men and generalization of its effectiveness to people of other races and social classes, as well as white women. Evidence must be obtained skeptically for each group before arrival at such a conclusion. The issue of generalizing the results of a group design to other people is the external validity of the group design.

Thyer and Meyers (2003) recommend that the most realistic way to generalize the results of a group design to other client groups is to use the process of replication. Replication involves repeating a group design with different client groups and at various times. If the results of a group design reveal that an intervention works for one client group, the intervention could be tried with a different client group that has similar characteristics. If the same result occurs, a claim that the intervention is effective would be somewhat strengthened. This could be followed by further replication, such as with similar clients in another agency or by other evaluators with similar clients in other geographic areas. Also, if the results of the group design indicate that an intervention is effective with a group of men, the intervention could be tried with a group of women. Or if an intervention works for young-adult clients, it could be tested with middle-aged adults. Repeated replication of a group design can be extremely valuable in exploring the extent to which an intervention can be generalized to others. Such replication can also be used to determine the limitations of an intervention and the characteristics of clients with whom it may not work and with client circumstances that are contraindicated.

Example of Setting Standards for Evidence-Based Practice

Harding and Higginson (2003), in a systematic review of articles from relevant professional journals, found twenty-two interventions for helping cancer and palliative care patients and their caregivers. They analyzed the twenty-two interventions on the basis of the type of patient and caregiver populations, the evaluation design used, and findings. They graded the evaluations as follows:

Grade I   (strong evidence): randomized control trials

Grade II   (fairly strong evidence): group designs with a comparison group

Grade III   (weaker evidence): retrospective or observational studies

Grade IV   (weak evidence): cross-sectional studies, Delphi exercises, consensus of experts

They concluded that there were a lack of outcome evaluation designs used to evaluate the effectiveness of the interventions. Instead, most articles contributed more to understanding feasibility and acceptability issues than to effectiveness. The authors encouraged programs to conduct more experimental and quasi-experimental designs to determine whether interventions effectively helped cancer patients and their caregivers.

Decisions on the sources of evidence for social work evaluations are important. Evidence can come from the reports and experiences of administrators, staff members, and faculty; clients' records; observations that document evidence; interviews and questionnaires that document perceptions of evidence; case examples of clients; other types of recordings; and scientific studies. Sources will vary in relevance and importance depending on their purposes. Evaluation has been conceptualized in this book as occurring at the input, implementation, and outcome stages of program and practice development. Using this framework, the types of sources of evidence used in the various stages will differ. Evidence-based interventions that follow are concerned with interventions in which there is scientifically credible evidence of a causal relationship between the intervention and clients' outcomes.

Determining a Causal Relationship

How do we know whether the program or practice intervention was the cause of the progress in client outcomes? The answer to this question is complicated. Three conditions must be met before a causal relationship can be claimed. The first condition is that the program (or practice) intervention must precede clients' improved outcomes. This condition makes sense: a provider could not ethically claim responsibility for clients' progress if the progress occurred prior to the introduction of the program.

The second condition needed to claim a causal relationship is that an association is found between the introduction of the intervention and the client's improvement in his or her outcome measures. An association means that the client's improvement becomes evident after the intervention is implemented. To be able to determine whether improvement occurs in the outcome measure during the period of implementation, we need to obtain a measure of the outcome both before (i.e., pretest measure, or baseline measure) and after (i.e., posttest measure) the intervention is introduced.

An association between the intervention and clients' outcomes can be determined through one of two methods: a test of statistical significance or an established standard of clinical significance. Statistical significance can be calculated by applying a statistical test, which determines whether the probability of an association is high enough to claim significance. Usually, a probability of 95 percent is expected, with the likelihood of error at 5 percent.

Clinical significance is defined by clinical criteria established by a professional group or agency. In this case, the amount of improvement in client outcomes is satisfactory when it meets the established clinical criteria. Clinical significance may be preferred over statistical significance in many circumstances, as it is based on clinical judgment, not mathematical probability. However, statistical significance is usually expected in summative evaluations when evidence of a program's impact is expected to be based on scientific principles.

To illustrate these points, consider the example of a recovery group of clients with substance abuse problems. The group has as its desired outcome reduced alcohol consumption. Assume that the recovery group is a weekly treatment group that emphasizes cognitive behavioral therapy and a modified version of the twelve-step program of Alcoholics Anonymous. The blood-alcohol level of group members is the measure used to determine whether there is improvement. If statistical significance is the standard to be used, then there is a statistically significant difference between pretest and posttest scores of the average blood-alcohol level of group members. A statistical test, such as a t-test, can tell us whether the two measures were significantly different according to probability theory. The various types of t-tests and other statistical tests that can be used to determine statistical significance are discussed in the next chapter.

Let's determine whether group members improved significantly according to clinical criteria. The agency sponsoring the group intervention has a clinical standard based on the definition of satisfactory improvement reported in the professional literature. The agency has found studies that have reported that an intervention is not fully successful until a person totally withdraws from the substance. Therefore, the agency decided that clinical significance would not be fully achieved until the group members totally withdrew from drinking; in other words, the members would not show enough improvement if they fell short of this high standard.

The third condition for claiming the intervention is the cause of the client's improvements is the most difficult to achieve. This condition is the claim that the improvement occurring in the clients' outcome measure is due, at least in part, to the program intervention. We need to consider that many other factors, such as a change in family circumstances or joining an Alcoholics Anonymous support group, have an influence on the outcome as well. Usually, an intervention is not expected to be totally responsible for clients' improvement. If we are interested in determining how much of the improvement is due to the intervention, we would have to use an experimental design. A less dependable method is a multiple regression test, which is discussed in the next chapter.

Using the example of the recovery group mentioned previously, an experimental design could be used that includes an experimental group (i.e., clients in the recovery group) and a control group (i.e., another group randomly selected and assigned to receive traditional individual services). If the outcome scores of the experimental group members (their average blood-alcohol level) changed significantly from pretest to posttest and the outcome measure of the control group members changed less or not at all, then it can be claimed that the intervention provided to clients had a causal influence. The amount of influence that it had on the recovery group members is determined in two steps. First, the change in the members' outcome score from the pretest to posttest is calculated as the amount of change that occurred in the group. This change would then need to be reduced by the amount of change, if any, that occurred in the outcome measures for the control group.

Quasi-experimental and pre-experimental designs can also be used to explore whether a social work intervention has a causal influence on changes in client outcomes. In such cases, only tentative conclusions can be made about the intervention's influence or impact. However, in most cases, an experimental design cannot be realistically used for ethical reasons, as field-based evaluations are not amenable to the controls that an experimental study requires. Quasi-experimental, pre-experimental, and experimental designs are reviewed next for program interventions.

Group Designs for Programs

Several group research designs are available for conducting outcome evaluations of programs. These designs are known as group designs because they measure the impact of an intervention on a group of clients, not on one client. Two overall categories of designs are possible in an evaluation study: cross-sectional and longitudinal. A cross-sectional design collects data from participants at one time only, and a longitudinal design collects data from research participants at two or more times. Longitudinal designs provide the most powerful evidence of a causal relationship between a program intervention and client outcomes.

Internal and external validity are important standards to use when evaluating the strength of a group design. Internal validity addresses whether the intervention and not other factors is responsible for improvement in the client outcome variable. Several extraneous variables could be responsible for improved outcome in addition to or instead of the intervention. For internal validity to be strong, for example, factors independent of the intervention present in clients' lives (e.g., receiving services from another professional agency, joining a self-help group) could be responsible for improvement in the outcome measure in addition to or instead of the intervention.

External validity addresses the issue of generalizing the results of a group design to other people. In this case, if the participants in the group design were randomly selected from a large population (e.g., a client group of one hundred or more), generalizations to the larger group are possible. However, if participants selected for the group design were drawn from a smaller population or were selected using nonprobability sampling, generalizations are not advisable.

Experimental designs, quasi-experimental designs, and some pre-experimental designs are longitudinal designs that can be used to explore a causal relationship between a program and its impact on client outcomes. Several group designs are described in Campbell and Stanley (1963). Six designs are highlighted here because they are among the most practical ones for outcome evaluations of programs in human service agencies:

Pre-experimental Designs

1. One-group posttest-only design
2. One-group pretest/posttest design

Quasi-experimental Designs

3. One-group pretest/posttest design with a comparison group
4. Time-series design

Experimental Designs

5. One-group pretest/posttest design with a control group
6. Posttest-only control group design

All of these group designs can be used to explore the impact of a program on a group of clients, whether the intervention focuses on individual, family, small group, or community services. All of these designs require that there be a clearly defined program intervention that can be replicated and at least one client outcome measure. These are the central elements of any group design. Other elements are included in some of these designs and not others.

Concepts Relevant to Group Designs

Clients' outcomes: outcome measures of what clients are to achieve

Program intervention: an intervention defined clearly enough to be replicated

Pretest or baseline measure: a measure of an outcome for clients prior to the intervention

Posttest measure: a measure of an outcome for clients after implementation of the intervention

Comparison group: a group of clients in a group design similar but not identical to the group receiving the program intervention; the group does not receive the program intervention

Control group: a group of clients in a group design considered identical to the group receiving the program intervention, based on either random selection and assignment or matching; the group does not receive the program intervention

Let's look at each of the six group designs and the concepts incorporated into each one. Diagrams of each design are also included in table 9.1 (where *X* symbolizes the program intervention, *O* represents a measure of the client outcome, and *R* indicates that the two groups were randomly selected and randomly assigned).

TABLE 9.1   Pre-experimental, Quasi-experimental, and Experimental Designs

Diagram	Description
X O_1	1. *One-group posttest-only design*: intervention followed by a posttest measure of client outcome
O_1 X O_2	2. *One-group pretest/posttest design*: intervention preceded by a pretest measure and followed by a posttest measure of client outcome
O_1 X O_2 O_3 X O_4	3. *Pretest/posttest design with a comparison group*: pretest/posttest design with a comparison group that does not receive intervention
O_1 O_2 O_3 X O_4 O_5 O_6	4. *Time-series design*: multiple measures of client outcome before and after the intervention
R- O_1 X O_2 R- O_3 X O_4	5. *Pretest/posttest design with a control group*: pretest/posttest design with a control group that does not receive intervention
R- X O_1 R- O_2	6. *Posttest-only control group design*: a posttest-only design with a control group that does not receive the intervention

One-Group Posttest-Only Design

Pre-experimental designs are often important to consider initially because they are easy to implement and take less time than stronger designs. This design involves collecting data at only one point in time after implementation of the intervention. Thus, this is a cross-sectional rather than a longitudinal design. During time 1 the intervention is introduced, and during time 2 the posttest measure of client outcome occurs.

This design is a good one for a beginning exploration of program impact, and it can simply answer the question of whether it is *possible* that the program had an impact. A one-group posttest-only design has several weaknesses. Most important, there is no pretest measure to determine whether any improvement occurred during the time of the intervention. Furthermore, none of the extraneous influences (e.g., environmental changes) are controlled for. An important conclusion derived from this design if the client outcome measure is not positive or favorable is that the intervention does not work.

One-Group Pretest-Posttest Design

The pretest-posttest design builds on the previous design by adding a pretest measure before the initiation of the intervention. This design, like the first one, is pre-experimental. However, it is longitudinal because data is collected from the clients at two different times—before and after the introduction of an intervention. The design is helpful in revealing how much improvement occurred between the pretest and the posttest. During time 1, the pretest score of the outcome variable is measured, during time 2 the intervention is introduced, and during time 3 the posttest score of the outcome variable is measured.

An example of a pretest-posttest design was described earlier in this chapter. The community organization that sponsored the premarital weekend retreat to reduce the number of divorces in the community was essentially interested in determining whether participants made progress between the time that the retreat began and ended. The pretest-posttest design served that purpose and helped them further refine the curriculum offered.

With this design, we can only determine whether improvement occurred during the time that the program was introduced, not whether the program was necessarily responsible for any change in the client outcome measure. The most important weakness of this design is that it does not have a comparison or control group to control for extraneous influences.

Example of an Evaluation with a One-Group Pretest-Posttest Design and a Qualitative Component

The purpose of an evaluation conducted by Courtney Lynch (2007) was to explore the impact of an independent-living skills-training program on the resilience, social support, and life skills of sixteen ethnically diverse foster-care teenagers. The teenagers' scores on standardized measures of resilience, social support, and life skills were compared before and after they participated in the training program. The improvements in scores from pretest to posttest were found to be statistically significant for social support but not for resilience and life skills. In a qualitative component of the mixed-methods study, the youths' descriptions of the same constructs of social support, resilience, and life skills were, in most cases, consistent with scores on standardized measures. Most of the youths had difficulty describing and recollecting life skills information, such as managing money and locating appropriate housing, which was consistent with scores suggesting that they "mastered" only about half of the life skills items.

Pretest-Posttest Design with a Comparison Group

The pretest-posttest design with a comparison group builds on the two previous designs. It is longitudinal in nature, as data are collected of the client outcome measure both as a pretest and as a posttest. However, another group *similar* to the first group is organized as a comparison group that does not receive the intervention. This design compares the progress of both groups during the intervention period. As table 9.1 indicates, the design is diagrammed with two different groups: one that receives the program intervention and the other that does not. At time 1 a pretest score of the outcome variable is measured for both groups, and during time 2 the intervention is introduced for the group assigned to receive it and nothing happens for the comparison group. The comparison group could receive services that are usually available as an alternative to nothing. At time 3 a posttest score of the outcome variable is measured for both groups.

Example of Pretest-Posttest Comparison Group Design

Engagement services during the intake period were introduced to female clients in a substance abuse treatment program as a motivational strategy to draw them into treatment (Comfort, Loverro, & Kaltenbach, 2000). An evaluation was conducted to determine whether the engagement services resulted in an increased use of treatment services. The evaluation used a pretest-posttest design with a comparison group. The engagement services involved an engagement specialist offering van transportation to the agency and child care during intake interviews, and making telephone calls to remind clients of intake appointments. Although transportation and child care were always offered to the group, members infrequently used child care in particular. Nevertheless, the results revealed that clients receiving engagement services were more likely than those in the comparison group to use treatment services.

A comparison group can be drawn from a larger pool of clients, such as those on a waiting list or clients who are receiving traditional services during the time of the study. This type of design can reveal with more confidence than the previous ones herein whether the program had a causal influence on client outcomes. The most important weakness of the design, though, is that the clients selected to be in the program and those selected for the comparison groups are likely to have many differences that the design does not control for. Such differences are likely to have a considerable influence over the measure of the client outcome. This design also creates a potential ethical problem that needs to be addressed, as one could convincingly argue that the clients in the comparison group should receive the program intervention as well. They may, for example, have as great a need for the intervention as does the group receiving the intervention.

A comparison group should be as similar as possible to the intervention group, particularly with variables or characteristics important to a study. For example, both groups should have similar demographic characteristics (e.g., age, gender, ethnicity), and both groups should be similar in terms of the important variables of the evaluation, such as their mental illness diagnosis or the problems that the program addresses. Comparison group studies should report on these characteristics and indicate when the two groups are significantly different according to specific characteristics. This reporting helps the reader take into account whether any of the differences in characteristics could have influenced their respective client outcome scores.

Example of Determining Similarity between Treatment and Comparison Groups

Waites (2000) assessed the generalist problem-solving skills of two groups of students, those beginning and those graduating from a BSW program. This can be thought of as a pretest-posttest comparison group design, with the graduates as the group receiving the intervention (successful completion of the BSW program) and the beginning students as a comparison group. Waites wanted to find out whether the comparison group was similar to the graduating group given several important characteristics: gender, ethnicity, age, grade point average, extent of volunteer experience, and number of social work courses completed. She found that the two groups were not significantly different on the basis of gender, ethnicity, age, or grade point average. They were different on the basis of volunteer experience and number of social work courses taken; these differences were expected given the group members' different status in the BSW program.

Time-Series Design

A time-series design is another type of quasi-experimental design. This design has many of the features of the previous designs and is also different from the other designs in that it has *several* pretest and posttest outcome measures, not one. The design involves obtaining several client outcome measures before the introduction of an intervention and several additional measures after the intervention has been implemented. Table 9.1 diagrams a time-series design.

A major advantage of a time-series design is that it overcomes some of the ethical problems of the designs that use comparison and control groups, as it has neither. An important feature of the multiple pretest and posttest measures of this design are the data trends that can help determine the extent to which the intervention, as opposed to other factors external to it, are the causal agent. Stated another way, its multiple measures of client outcomes provide more opportunities to determine whether extraneous influences exist.

Pretest-Posttest Design with a Control Group

The fifth design, a pretest-posttest design with a control group, is the classical experimental design. It is the most powerful design for determining causality. It is similar to the pretest-posttest design with a comparison group with one exception. Clients are first randomly selected from a larger pool of prospective clients and then randomly assigned to either the intervention or the control group. Because of the two steps of random selection and assignment, the two groups of clients can be treated as statistically identical because the random selection and assignment tend to balance out the extraneous differences between the two groups. With this design, pretest and posttest measures are obtained from both groups before and after the intervention group receives the intervention.

This design is diagrammed in table 9.1 Prior to time 1, clients are randomly selected and assigned to either receive the services of the program or to a control group. During time 1 a pretest score of the outcome variable is measured for both groups. During time 2 the intervention is introduced for the group assigned to receive it and either nothing happens for the control group or it could continue to receive existing agency services. During time 3 a posttest measure of the client outcome variable is obtained for both groups.

Example of a Pretest-Posttest Control Group Design

Ciffone (2007) evaluated whether a curriculum-based suicide prevention program was instrumental in changing unwanted attitudes and in reducing students' reluctance to seek mental health treatment among groups of students in two demographically diverse high schools. He used a pretest-posttest control group design. Students were randomly assigned to treatment and control groups by the classes that they were assigned. Those in the treatment group were provided a three-day presentation by the school social workers who spoke in their health classes. Those in the control classes had no outside speakers in their health classes during the same period. The pretest and posttest instrument consisted of eight questions. The attitudes toward suicide were measured partially by the item, "Most teens who killed themselves were probably suffering from mental illness." Students' responses to the item in the intervention group changed from "no" to "yes" when their attitudes improved. Two other items measured help-seeking attitudes or reluctance to seek mental health treatment: "If suicidal thoughts crossed my mind regularly, I would seek out and talk to a friend about these thoughts," and "If I was very upset and suicidal thoughts crossed my mind, I would be willing to talk with a professional counselor about these thoughts." Higher percentages of students in the intervention group were favorable to these statements in the posttest than in the pretest.

This design is quite powerful in determining whether the program intervention influences the outcome measure for the client group in the program because it controls for all extraneous influences. Nevertheless, the design poses even more serious ethical challenges than any of the other designs. It can be viewed as unethical to randomly select and assign clients to receive or not receive an intervention, particularly without their consent. Most likely, if agency resources are able to provide a program intervention for all clients, the decision to select some clients should be made on the basis of professional criteria, not mathematical probability. This dilemma could be worked out by randomly selecting clients from a waiting list and then randomly assigning one group to receive the intervention and the other group to continue to wait for services offered at a later time. However, it would be important to explain this arrangement to clients in an informed consent protocol. Also, other unanticipated consequences must be considered, such as exposing the vulnerabilities of clients in the control group to life-threatening crises during a waiting period.

Posttest-Only Control-Group Design

The sixth design, a posttest-only design with a control group, is the same as the experimental design except that it does not have a pretest for either group. The design depends completely on the initial random selection and assignment steps to ensure that participants in the two groups are identical, which is particularly important because there are no pretest measures to determine whether the two groups begin essentially at the same point in their outcome measures.

This design is preferred over the pretest-posttest design with a control group if there is concern that administering a pretest measure could influence the outcome. For example, a test about a knowledge area used as a pretest measure may also be used as a posttest measure to determine how much the clients learned during the intervention phase. An intervention could be safe-sex training and the outcome measure could be a test that measures how well clients understand safe sexual practices. The problem here is that the test could be discussed informally among clients during the intervention phase to determine the correct answers and the clients could then report these answers in the posttest phase. In this case, testing factors rather than actual learning from the intervention could be responsible for any improvement in the test from pretest to posttest.

In other instances, this design could also be preferred over the pretest-posttest design with a control group if the pretest seemed unnecessary or undesirable. It may be undesirable or not logistically possible to implement, or an evaluator may find it too costly to administer a pretest measure because it would involve time and effort of the staff members to interview clients or administer a questionnaire as a pretest.

Table 9.1 diagrams the posttest-only control-group design. Prior to time 1, clients are randomly selected and are either assigned to receive the program's services or assigned to a control group. During time 1 a pretest score of the outcome variable is not measured for either group. During time 2 the intervention is introduced for the group assigned to receive it and either nothing happens for the control group or it continues to receive existing agency services. During time 3 a posttest measure of the client outcome variable is obtained for both groups.

This design, like the classic experimental design, is quite powerful in determining whether the program intervention influences the outcome measure for the client group in the program because it controls for all extraneous influences. However, this design also poses serious ethical challenges for the same reasons that it does for the classic experimental design. The clients could be randomly selected from a large waiting list and then randomly assigned either to receive the intervention or to wait for services to be offered later. However, it would be important to explain this arrangement to clients in an informed consent protocol, and a plan to address unanticipated consequences must be considered, such as the control-group clients' vulnerability to a life-threatening crisis during the waiting period.

It is important to note that all group designs have another major limitation if they only measure client outcomes immediately after clients complete a program. Such outcome measures, as mentioned earlier, are usually only short-term outcomes. Therefore, programs are encouraged to consider one or more additional outcome measures at later points in time (e.g., three and six months later) to determine whether clients' progress from participating in a program is sustained over time.

Outcome Evaluations for Practice

The outcome evaluations described previously are generally available for practice evaluations as well. Some of the variations in how outcome evaluations for practice and programs may differ are presented next, with an emphasis on how to implement outcome evaluations in an individual worker's practice.

Client Satisfaction and Effectiveness

It is important that practitioners hold themselves accountable for the effectiveness of interventions even when others may not do so. This is an ethical obligation mandated by the NASW's Code of Ethics (see chapter 3). The code points out that practitioners are to "monitor and evaluate policies, the implementation of programs, and our practice interventions" (NASW 1999, section 5.02[a]).

There are some basic questions that practitioners can periodically ask clients, such as the following:

- Are my interventions helping you? In what ways?
- Are my interventions helping you in the areas in which you are seeking help (e.g., related to presenting problems, identified needs, solutions desired, expressed hopes)?
- Are my interventions helping you meet your goals identified in our initial work together?
- How would you describe your progress so far in achieving your goals? How have my interventions played a part in helping you or in hindering you?

The specifics of how clients communicate that the practitioner's interventions have helped (or have not helped) can be especially important. For example, did they respond to the practitioner's questions or did they spontaneously offer comments? Spontaneous comments may be more authentic and more likely to be valid indicators of their views.

These and similar questions are considered client satisfaction questions to most people, but they are also quite relevant to the question of effectiveness. These types of questions focus on client outcomes and their connection to our intervention. They ask, in essence, did the intervention have a role in bringing about any positive changes to clients' goals or outcomes? In some instances, clients' responses to the previous questions may be the only available information. In this regard, they have limitations, especially because they are subjective and not necessarily reflective of actual outcomes. For example, clients could report accomplishments that did not actually happen (e.g., discontinued drug use) or overestimate what actually happened (e.g., reporting completion of homework every day, when it may be sporadic). That is why objective measures of outcomes are also extremely important to obtain, such as checking whether drug use is evident in a client's urine or obtaining an independent report of the client's drug use from a spouse or another reliable source.

As discussed in chapter 8, however, it could be argued that clients' reports on their outcomes and how the interventions have affected them are a necessary but not sufficient indication of intervention effectiveness. Conversely, obtaining an objective measure of a client's outcomes without some verification or concurrence from the client can be viewed as overlooking clients' role in having some awareness and control over their change.

Single-System Designs

Practice evaluations of outcomes can be conducted in several ways and many of them revolve around variations in a single-system design. A single-system design is a variation of a time-series design on a practice level in that it involves several measures of the outcome variable both before and after an intervention has been introduced. A single-system design (SSD) is a practice evaluation tool that measures whether there is a causal relationship between the practitioner's intervention and a client's outcome measure. This design is typically used with one client system at a time whether it is an individual, family, or group. The SSD uses a graph as a tool to visualize the clients' progress, and it is intended to be used by both the client and the social worker in determining whether any progress has been made. The graph helps simplify the explanation for how much progress has been made and it does not require a statistical test for explanation, although one can be used.

An SSD graph consists of two or more phases. A baseline phase (phase A) is always needed as well as one or more intervention phases (e.g., phases B, C, and D). The client outcome measure is plotted along the vertical axis, and a timeline for recording measures of the outcome measure is identified along the horizontal axis (e.g., daily, weekly). Figure 9.2 illustrates an ABC design with three phases: a baseline phase, a phase when the first intervention is introduced, and a phase when the second intervention is introduced.

An SSD can be conducted using a variety of designs, including AB, ABC, ABAB, and BAB. The simplest design is an AB design, which consists of a baseline phase and one intervention phase. In this case, the client outcome measure is obtained along a standardized timeline, such as weekly or daily intervals during both phase A (baseline) and phase B (intervention phase). For example, a woman with clinical depression wants to develop new friendships but is resistant to getting out and meeting people. The social worker attempts to help her by providing supportive services, as support has been missing in the client's life and is thought to be what she needs to begin attending social occasions in her church and local community center. The fre-

FIGURE 9.2   An ABC Design

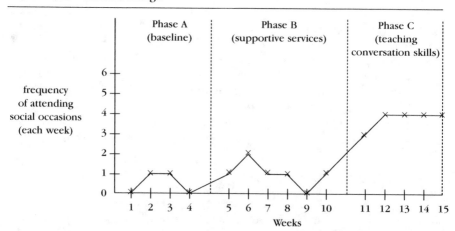

quency of attending these social occasions each week was the client outcome indicator, measured every week while the client was in contact with the social worker's agency. The social worker's intervention, introduced during phase B, is the support service. This AB design requires measurement of the frequency of the client's attendance each week for a few weeks to obtain a baseline measure that is stable or does not fluctuate highly. This outcome indicator continues to be measured weekly during phase B, when the social worker's intervention is introduced. The intent of the AB design is to discover whether the client attends more social occasions after the intervention is introduced than she did before.

Another single-system design is the ABC design, illustrated in figure 9.2. This design begins with a baseline phase (phase A) followed by the first intervention phase (phase B), and then followed by another intervention phase (phase C). The ABC design is particularly useful when the first intervention does not have sufficient impact by itself. A second intervention can then be introduced in phase C to either replace or supplement the first intervention. Often the combination of the two interventions can have a significant impact when neither intervention can have an impact by itself.

Using the same example of the woman with severe depression, providing support services weekly could be the first intervention to encourage more social contacts (phase B). If this intervention does not succeed, teaching the client conversation skills could be added as a second intervention (phase C). The ABC design can plot the client's attendance at social occasions during phases A, B, and C to determine whether attendance increases during implementation of both the first and the second intervention. In figure 9.2, combining the two interventions, support services and teaching conversation skills, visibly documents greater social contact for this client.

Another variation is the ABAB design, which consists of a baseline phase followed by an intervention phase, then another baseline phase when the intervention is removed, and finally the reintroduction of the intervention phase (figure 9.3). This design has a special additional feature

FIGURE 9.3   An ABAB Design

Phase A	Phase B	Phase A	Phase B

of withdrawing the intervention after phase B to find out whether other factors (e.g., a self-help group, a new friend, joining a new church or synagogue) may be responsible for any continuation of client progress evident in phase B. If progress on the client goal declines during the reintroduction of phase A, this provides further evidence that the intervention and improvement are linked. Finally, the intervention can be reintroduced in the second phase B to find out whether progress reappears.

Although the ABAB design can, in some ways, be an alternative to having a comparison or control group, it can also pose ethical problems if the intervention is withdrawn while the client still needs it. Similarly, it would also be unethical to withdraw the intervention if a client wishes to continue it or if withdrawal could cause harm. However, temporary withdrawal of the intervention may be less of an ethical concern if the social worker or client became unavailable because of a vacation or a visit to a sick relative. Withdrawal may also be less of a concern if the intervention is mandated and if the client wants a temporary break from services.

An ABAB design has another limitation in that it works only when the outcome measure can be reversed. If a client is taught a new set of behaviors, once he or she has learned the behaviors, they may not be reversed in many cases. For example, if a parent is taught new assertiveness skills in phase B, withdrawal of the intervention is not likely to lead to an immediate reversal of the newly developed skills.

Sometimes a BAB design is relevant if the social worker cannot begin with a baseline phase. This may be the case particularly when it is urgent to introduce the intervention during the first contact with the client. With this design, the baseline phase can be introduced after the intervention has been implemented for a while, and the intervention can be reintroduced in a third phase. However, like the ABAB design, withdrawal of the intervention could pose ethical problems and may not work with irreversible outcome measures.

Goal Attainment Scale

A goal attainment scale (GAS) is a versatile evaluation tool that can be used to measure client outcomes. It is quite useful in evaluating the extent to which the worker's interventions affect clients' goals or outcomes in a favorable way. The GAS works well as an outcome measure with any of the SSDs described previously. As table 9.2 indicates, a GAS is a five-point scale ranging from the most unfavorable to the most favorable outcome thought likely at a future follow-up time. The middle point on the scale is considered the expected level of success. The client and social worker use the right-hand column to fill in qualitative descriptors of each of the five points on the scale, with the expected level of success usually determined first.

A GAS has many advantages as an outcome tool. It is an incremental scale that can be used to measure degrees of progress. It can be individual-

TABLE 9.2   Goal Attainment Scale

Levels of predicted attainment	Scale
Most unfavorable outcome thought likely (−2)	
Less success than expected (−1)	
Expected level of success (0)	
More success than expected (+1)	
Most favorable outcome (unlikely but still plausible) (+2)	

ized to a client's particular or unique circumstances. And it is used most effectively when the client and worker collaborate in the development and use of the scale. When the tool is used in this way, it can be a great motivator in getting clients to work on their goals. The scale can also become a useful discussion topic when discrepancies become evident between what the worker and client perceive as the client's level of success. It can also become the focal point of an informal or formal contract between the worker and client.

Table 9.3 illustrates the use of a GAS in a parent-training program in which several parenting skills were introduced and practiced in small groups for parents who had been abusing their children. This is a building-block approach that begins with reading; learning comes next, followed by using or applying a parenting skill. Note that the scale reflects a decision to set an expected level of success for these parents after three months of simply learning one parenting skill. Although this may not seem like a far-reaching level of success, this program documented evidence that learning one skill would realistically take this long to internalize.

Cox and Amsters (2001) effectively used the GAS as a multidisciplinary measure of client outcomes for rural and remote health services. They found several principles to be important in using a GAS. The goals need to remain realistic and relevant to both the clients' capacity or potential and

TABLE 9.3   Goal Attainment Scale with Goal of Improving Parenting Skills

Levels of predicted attainment	Scale
Most unfavorable outcome thought likely (−2)	Ignore parenting skills altogether
Less success than expected (−1)	Read a book on parenting skills
Expected level of success (0)	Learn one new parenting skill
More success than expected (+1)	Use one new parenting skill with children
Most favorable outcome (unlikely but still plausible) (+2)	Use two new parenting skills with children

Notes: Date and rating at construction: January 5; Date and rating at follow-up or evaluation time: April 5.

the agencies' resources. In addition, the levels must be mutually exclusive and measurable. They found that the GAS had limitations as well; most important, it was not effective if staff were not fully trained in its use.

A GAS can be developed as either a qualitative or quantitative measure or a combination of the two. The scale in table 9.3 uses both types of measures; for example, it measures the number of parenting skills learned and takes into account four different behaviors that overlap: ignoring, reading, learning, and using. The scale can also include more than one variable at each level.

A GAS can be implemented with the following principles and sequential steps kept in mind (Dudley, 2005):

1. Consider whether the GAS is the most appropriate design to use with a particular client. Among other considerations, a GAS depends on clients meeting with a worker for more than one session and having measurable goals.
2. Make sure that you cover and that the client understands all the pertinent issues of informed consent, including the purpose of the selected tool, how it works, how the client can benefit, and the other aspects of informed consent.
3. Help the client identify the problem.
4. Identify a goal that can resolve this problem agreeable to the worker and client.
5. Set a realistic date for the goal to be achieved, referred to as a evaluation time.
6. Then work together to construct specific predictions for a series of five levels of reaching the goal (most unfavorable, less than expected, expected level of success, more than expected, and best anticipated success) by recording them on the scale. Usually the easiest way to do this is to first identify the expected level of success, followed by the outer limits of the most unfavorable and most favorable outcome. Finally, identify the less-than-expected and more-than-expected levels.
7. Now the GAS is ready to be used by measuring the client's actual level of attainment in reaching the goal during the first session as a baseline measure.
8. Finally, the client's actual level of attainment in reaching the goal can be measured during an evaluation session or during the last session. At this time, discuss the progress that has been made and how the GAS was helpful in measuring this progress.

Target Problem Scale

The GAS has limitations. For example, some problems may not easily translate into goals, or clients may not be either willing or able to identify goals to work on. Also, a GAS does not work well if a client is seen for only one session. An alternative outcome scale that can be used is a target problem scale (TPS). In brief, a TPS helps clients identify their problem(s), apply an intervention to overcome or cope with them, and then periodically rate the problem to measure any deteriorations or improvements. A TPS is helpful, for example, if the client remains preoccupied or overwhelmed with multiple problems and is not prepared to immediately pursue goals to overcome the problems.

Like a GAS, the TPS is an incremental scale. It measures the degree of severity of the problem, and the scale is individualized to a client's particular circumstances. Figure 9.4 describes a TPS (Marlow, 2005). In this scale, target problems are identified in the far-left column. This form provides space for up to five problems. Each problem is then assessed in terms of its degree of severity for each of six sessions. The five-point severity scale measures problems from "no problem" to "extremely severe." The next column to the right is the improvement scale used to calculate the degree to which a problem has changed for better or worse. Finally, an overall improvement scale can be used to determine the extent to which improvement has occurred.

The overall improvement rating is obtained by totaling the degree of change scores and dividing by the number of target problems. This results in a number that reflects clients' overall improvement on all problems.

FIGURE 9.4   Target Problem Rating (TPR)

<u>Target Problems</u>									<u>Overall Improvement</u>*
				<u>Degree of Severity</u> Session #				<u>Degree of Change</u>	
		1	2	3	4	5	6	(1 to 5 scale)	
1.									
2.									
3.									
4.									
5.									

<u>Severity Scale</u>	**<u>Improvement Scale</u>**
NP = no problem	1 = Worse
NVS = not very severe	2 = No change
S = severe	3 = A little better
VS = very severe	4 = Somewhat better
ES = extremely severe	5 = A lot better

*The Overall Improvement Rating is the total of the degree of change, divided by number of target problems, which results in a number that reflects the client's overall improvement on all problems.

An example of a TPS used with parents who were lacking strong parenting skills is described in figure 9.5. As the figure indicates, the parents had multiple problems, including overlooking parental neglect, getting to appointments late, spending too little time with their child, getting the child to bed late, and yelling at each other. Figure 9.5 summarizes the clients' progress or lack of it after six sessions. In brief, the TPS indicates that their difficulty in facing parental neglect improved from "extremely severe" in the first two sessions to somewhat better or "not very severe" by the sixth session. Overall, most of their progress on other problems over six sessions was in getting to counseling sessions on time and in spending more time with their child. A little improvement was evident in not yelling at each other so often.

Sequencing Blocks

Other means of evaluating a client's outcomes, positive or negative, are also available, even though they may not be readily known or used. For example, sequencing blocks are a qualitative exercise that helps clients explore

FIGURE 9.5 Target Problem Rating (TPR)

Target Problems							Degree of Change	Overall Improvement*
		Degree of Severity Session #					(1 to 5 scale)	
	1	2	3	4	5	6		
(Examples)								
1. Overlook parental neglect as a problem	ES	ES	S	S	NVS	NVS	4	
2. Come late to appointments	S	S	S	NP	NP	NP	5	
3. Ignore their child's need to spend time with parents	ES	NVS	NVS	NVS	NVS	NVS	4	
4. Get child to bed late	ES	ES	ES	VS	ES	ES	2	
5. Parents yell at each other	S	S	S	S	S	NVS	3	
								18/5 = 3.6

Severity Scale	Improvement Scale
NP = no problem	1 = Worse
NVS = not very severe	2 = No change
S = severe	3 = A little better
VS = very severe	4 = Somewhat better
ES = extremely severe	5 = A lot better

*The Overall Improvement Rating is the total of the degree-of-change scores, divided by the number of target problems, which results in a number that reflects the client's overall improvement on all problems.

the causal relationships among prior behaviors that resulted in a positive or negative outcome. In this case, the outcome behavior is known and the behavior that caused it is to be discovered.

Sequencing blocks can be used to help clients gain insight into prior behaviors and interactions that could trigger a current problem behavior that is being addressed (Laura Kroll, graduate student placed at Alexander Youth Network, Charlotte, NC, personal communication, April 15, 2006). This is an exercise that can use narrative from the discussions between a worker and client about a problem behavior, such as cursing out a teacher or getting angry and walking off a job. The discussion typically begins with the current problem behavior and its larger context. Then the discussion can work its way in reverse, going back to what happened just before the problem behavior occurred, and then what happened before that. The conversation eventually can get back to the initial set of behaviors or incidents in the overall episode. Figure 9.6 portrays typical sequencing blocks. As the discussion between the social worker and client proceed, individual behaviors and interactions are written into the blocks in the order that they occurred.

FIGURE 9.6   Sequencing Blocks

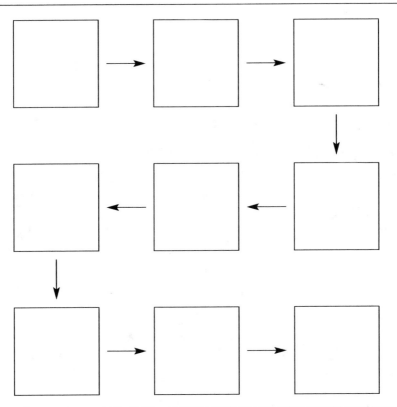

Figure 9.7 describes an example of a teenager who was expelled from school for cursing out his teacher. In this case, the teenager, John, was meeting with a school social worker about the incident upon returning to school from a suspension. The sequencing blocks were used to help him gain insight into the earlier triggers and the precipitating factors contributing to the problem. The discussion began with the problem behavior and worked its way back one behavior and interaction at a time. It eventually got back to a trigger in which the teacher perceived, incorrectly, that John had initiated

FIGURE 9.7   Example of Sequencing Blocks

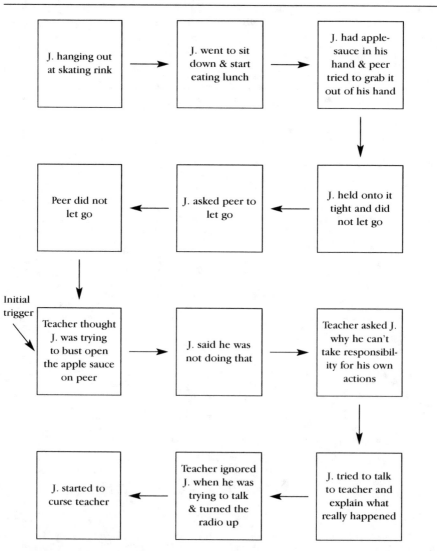

a conflict with a peer around opening a container of applesauce at lunch on a field trip. The sequencing block exercise helped John understand not only that his teacher had misperceived the cause of the conflict but also how he could have avoided the interchange with the teacher until after calming down and how he may have been able to avoid the incident in the first place, by avoiding sitting with the peer who got him into trouble.

Sequencing blocks can also be used to identify prior behaviors or decisions that result in positive outcomes for a client. For example, consider a client with a disability who has difficulty meeting women but who is interested in a friendship and had an unusually positive experience one night in meeting a new acquaintance. The client initially explained this discovery as a "miracle." The worker and client used this positive outcome to look back at prior behaviors and decisions made by the client that may have been positive triggers that could be tried again.

Key Terms

Clinical significance
Experimental designs
Goal attainment scale
Longitudinal study
Measurable client goal
Posttest
Pre-experimental designs
Pretest
Quasi-experimental designs
Sequence blocks
Single-system design
Statistical significance
Target problem scale

Discussion Questions and Assignments

1. Review the six group designs summarized in this chapter and then answer the following questions: (Appendix C has answers)

- Which design seems ideal? Why do you think so?
- Which design is the easiest and least expensive? What can be concluded from this design?
- Why are *multiple* measures of the client outcome variable obtained when conducting a time-series design? What are the benefits of the multiple measures?
- Which design may be the most practical for determining whether the program intervention was responsible for positive changes in the outcome variables? Why?
- What is useful about a pretest/posttest design?
- Under what circumstances would you consider a posttest-only control-group design?

2. This is an assignment that can be completed in class or as an assignment to tape and bring to class.

   A. Role-play a worker/client relationship using a goal attainment scale (GAS). Conduct a first session when the GAS is introduced. Identify a goal that you and your client want to work on. Make sure that you both mutually agree on the goal. Also identify a goal that both you and your client agree is measurable. Explain the GAS to the client so that it can be readily understood. Consider using a simpler version that fits your particular client: maybe a three-point scale, simpler words, modified wording (e.g., vision of the future or dreams rather than goals).

   B. Later, conduct a session in which the worker and client assess how well the client did in reaching the defined goal. Have your client rate her or his progress along with your rating, and then discuss why your ratings may be different. Finally, explore what the specific benefits of the evaluation tool are to the client.

3. Design a program or practice intervention and a set of outcome measures for a group of clients by following three steps:

   A. Select a group to focus on (e.g., teen fathers, teen mothers, teens who are not parents).
   B. Identify two outcome measures for the group.
   C. Design a program or practice intervention to help the group reach the outcomes.

4. Critique White's choices of outcome indicators (p. 203). Which ones do you think are most useful to use and why?

5. Assume that you are working in an agency serving people with a dual diagnosis of depression and alcohol abuse. Identify three outcome indicators for clients that could be used to measure the impact of a program on depression, and then identify three outcome indicators indicating that the alcohol abuse problem is reduced.

6. This a policy-related assignment. Set up two teams of students: one assigned the task of identifying and arguing for the advantages of keeping welfare recipients on the welfare rolls and the other on removing them from the welfare rolls. Each team should begin by identifying three to four desired outcomes of maintaining or reducing, respectively, the number of welfare recipients. For example, a possible outcome for reducing the rolls could be savings to the taxpayer, while an outcome for maintaining recipients on welfare could be to provide skilled job training or to provide medical assistance to families.

7. This is a major class assignment. Carry out the following steps in completing this assignment.

A. Identify a need for a practice evaluation in your field agency and a client system that can benefit from an evaluation. Inform the client system about the evaluation and encourage them to participate.

B. Select the type of evaluation and specific tool that most readily fits your client situation. Feasibility is one important consideration in your selection. For example, consider the number of sessions that you will likely see your client, the overall amount of time that your agency will serve the client, and any difficulty you may have in identifying a measurable goal(s) for the client. Choose a tool from the following: a single-system design, a goal attainment scale, a target problem scale, or sequencing blocks.

C. Discuss the assignment thoroughly with your field instructor to make sure that she or he understands the assignment and the evaluation tool that you will use.

D. Obtain informed consent either in written or oral form. Make sure that all of the pertinent issues of informed consent are covered and understood by the client (e.g., purpose of the selected tool; how it works; how the client, worker, and agency can benefit; expectations that you have for the client's participation; informing the client that this is a class assignment to be turned in; ensuring confidentiality; reminding the client of the option to say no or withdraw after the evaluation begins). Whenever your field agency has a protocol for obtaining informed consent, use it to complete this assignment.

E. Formulate and implement your practice evaluation.

F. Finally, describe what you have learned about evaluating your practice from doing this assignment and what advantages and limitations you see in using this tool.

G. Turn in or give a presentation that includes a description of how you implemented each of the above steps. Also, include the instruments that you used.

References

Babbie, E. (2001). *The practice of social research* (9th ed.). Belmont, CA: Wadsworth/ Thomson Learning.

Beck, A. T., Steer, R. A., & Brown, G. K. (1996). *Manual for the Beck Depression Inventory* (2nd ed.). San Antonio, TX: Psychological Corporation.

Cabarrus County. (2007). Performance report 2006. Concord, NC: Author.

Campbell, D., & Stanley, J. (1963). *Experimental and quasi-experimental designs for research*. Chicago: Rand McNally.

Ciffone, J. (2007). Suicide prevention: An analysis and replication of a curriculum-based high school program. *Social Work, 52*(1), 41–49.

Comfort, M., Loverro, J., & Kaltenbach, K. (2000). A search for strategies to engage women in substance abuse treatment. *Social Work in Health Care, 31*(4), 59–70.

Community Choices Inc. (2006). Helping mothers have healthy babies and families. Charlotte, NC: Author.

Cook, T. D., & Campbell, D. T. (1979). *Quasi-experimentation: Design and analysis issues for field settings.* Skokie, IL: Rand McNally.

Cox, R., & Amsters, D. (2001). Goal attainment scaling: An effective outcome measure for rural and remote health services. *Australian Journal of Rural Health, 10,* 256–261.

Dudley, J. R. (2005). *Research methods for social work: Becoming consumers and producers of research.* Boston: Allyn & Bacon.

Gambrill, E. (1999). Evidence-based practice: An alternative to authority-based practice. *Families in Society, 80,* 341–350.

Gibbs, L., & Gambrill, E. (1996). *Critical thinking for social workers: A workbook.* Thousand Oaks, CA: Pine Forge Press.

Harding, R., & Higginson, I. J. (2003). What is the best way to help caregivers in cancer and palliative care? A systematic literature review of interventions and their effectiveness. *Palliative Medicine, 17,* 63–74.

Litzelfelner, P. (2001). Demystifying client outcomes. *Professional Development, 4*(2), 25–31.

Lynch, C. J. (2007). *Exploring the implementation of a transitional services program for adolescents in the Texas Foster Care System.* Unpublished doctoral dissertation, University of Texas at Austin.

Marlow, C. (2005). Research methods for generalist social work (4th ed.). Belmont, CA: Thomson.

Martin, L. L., & Kettner, P. M. (1996). *Measuring performance of human service programs.* Thousand Oaks, CA: Sage.

McLean, T. (2007). *Evaluating progress on personal goals of a children's group using journaling: Proposal for the formation of a new group.* Unpublished manuscript. University of North Carolina at Charlotte.

National Association of Social Workers. (1999). Code of ethics of the National Association of Social Workers. Washington, DC: Author.

O'Hare, T. (2005). *Evidence-based practice for social workers: An interdisciplinary approach.* Chicago: Lyceum Books.

Thyer, B., & Meyers, L. (2003). Linking assessment to outcome evaluation using single system and group research design. In C. Jordan & C. Franklin (Eds.), *Clinical assessment for social workers: Quantitative and qualitative methods* (2nd ed., pp. 385–405). Chicago: Lyceum Books.

Waites, C. (2000). Assessing generalist problem-solving skills: An outcome measure. *The Journal of Baccalaureate Social Work, 6*(1), 67–79.

White, M. (2005, March 16). *A demonstration of evaluation as a central aspect of social work practice at the Women's Commission.* Presentation to a social work research class, University of North Carolina, Charlotte.

Part VI

Final Steps in Completing an Evaluation

Chapter 10

Analyzing Evaluation Data

Jeffrey Shears and James R. Dudley

How do we turn the data into useful information?

The analysis of evaluation data is another important step to address in the evaluation process. Although the basic principles of data analysis are virtually the same for evaluations and other kinds of research, differences are evident in emphasis and use. Such differences are the primary focus of this chapter. Data analysis is closely linked to the topic of the next chapter, writing a report and disseminating the results. In actuality, the choice of which data analysis tools to use depends on the kind of report and dissemination strategy that are most helpful to the stakeholders and others.

Formative or Summative Evaluations

Evaluations depend on both quantitative and qualitative data research methods as well as mixed methods. As discussed frequently in previous chapters, the methods used depend on the evaluation's purpose and the stage of program or practice development in which they occur. One way to decide whether to use quantitative or qualitative data analysis is to ask whether the evaluation is formative or summative.

Formative Evaluations

As mentioned in chapter 2, formative evaluations mostly focus on planning for a program or improving the implementation or delivery of services. The evaluations tend to be exploratory in nature and may need either qualitative or quantitative methods, or both, depending on their purposes. Formative evaluations are typically conducted by the agency administering the intervention, which allows for considerable flexibility in choosing the methods of data collection and analysis. Formative evaluations do not require one particular type of procedure, as they can be conducted to identify small glitches in programs, breakdowns in delivering services, or an unanticipated drifting away from the original program design. These evaluations can take on many different forms. Examples include a needs assessment questionnaire with forced-response and open-ended questions, a standardized scale, an open-ended journal format, or observations that are either unstructured or structured.

Formative evaluations may examine the interactions between clients and practitioners, management strategies, practice philosophies, or costs associated with a program. For example, an agency wants to understand why a program for eating disorders for teenage girls has not been successful in having participants complete the twelve-week program; only one-fourth of participants participated long enough to complete the treatment. A formative evaluation could provide some meaningful information to fine-tune the program. Here exploring questions that are critical of the program could be beneficial in identifying glitches in the delivery of services. Conducting a more in-depth evaluation of the clients and their needs or obtaining a profile of those who are successful and those who fail to complete the program are also important examples of a formative evaluation.

Summative Evaluations

Summative evaluations focus on the outcomes of programs and practice areas and attempt to answer the ultimate question: did the intervention reach its goals? These evaluations have a finality to them because they attempt to measure whether an intervention was effective. Summative evaluations are also typically conducted by an external agent, such as an independent evaluator or a governmental agency, to ensure that they are objective. Further, they primarily depend on choosing from a more limited set of research design options, such as a quasi-experimental or experimental design. These designs work best when they use quantitative measurement instruments with strong psychometric qualities.

If an evaluator's question is to determine whether an intervention is effective, then this is considered a summative evaluation and thus draws from quantitative research methods. Summative evaluations seek to explain how the independent variable, a program intervention, affects the dependent variables, or the desired client outcomes; for example, Does program participation influence parental attitudes? Does group therapy improve marital stability? Do parental education classes significantly improve parents' ability to support early infant development?

Stages of Program and Practice Development and Data Analysis

The stage of development of a program or practice area, whether planning, implementation, or outcome, also provides some clarity about what data collection and analysis methods are used and whether quantitative and/or qualitative data analyses are preferred.

The Planning or Input Stage

One area in which data analysis is needed is the input or needs assessment stage of a program. Needs assessments, as discussed in chapter 6, are usually proposed when there is a concern that a new intervention may be important to consider for a specific target population. During this stage, various evaluation strategies, such as giving out questionnaires or analyzing secondary data, might be used to examine the specific needs of a community. Evaluators could also conduct focus groups or individual interviews with community members, or consult other local experts to clarify where services are needed and how to better allocate resources. For example, a needs assessment of a new target population to be served by a county's mental health system might involve interviewing prospective clients, giving out questionnaires to staff members who work with mental health clients, or conducting focus groups with other stakeholders who have a vested interest in an issue. These strategies can be qualitative or quantitative in nature. In general, it is wise to combine different strategies. Royse, Thyer, Padgett, and Logan (2006) discuss the importance of triangulation, or seeking multiple sources and comparing them. For example, interviews with people who are homeless, those who work with the homeless, and other key informants could all be initiated and compared to discover their similarities and differences.

Because of the varied nature of needs assessments, there are a number of types of data analyses that can be used to answer questions about the perceived needs of a community. Using focus groups with stakeholders, for example, could involve tape recording their responses to a few open-ended questions and analyzing the responses through a content analysis of the words that are used. Another possibility is to organize their responses into themes at a more abstract level to discover possible links among these themes. Berg (2004) and others present other impressionistic approaches that can be used to evaluate qualitative data collected from evaluations.

In other instances, strategies for assessing the needs in a community can be quantitative in nature. The data resulting from a questionnaire with forced-response questions or existing secondary data collected from a previous evaluation are examples. Let's assume that there is a concern that more public housing is needed for homeless people in a local area and that existing shelters keep detailed records on these people. An evaluator might be able to complete a needs assessment by developing a descriptive account or profile of the homeless population. The descriptive analysis could give some insight into the severity of the issue. The descriptive statistics could include simply calculating mean (average) scores along with standard deviations and ranges; or frequency distributions of such variables as age, gender, income, family structure, and length of time being homeless. This information would be informative to stakeholders, as it provides concrete data for making informed decisions about the needs of homeless people in the community.

Another possibility for data analysis is to compare the quantitative responses of two different groups of interviewed people. In this case, bivariate analysis would be used to help determine whether the responses of the two groups are significantly different and the amount of difference that is evident. Given the previous example of a needs assessment of prospective mental health clients, you may find that groups of prospective clients and mental health workers agree that particular types of services are needed in a satellite office somewhere in the county, but they may disagree about where the location should be. Using this information, the evaluator can report on how much consensus and difference exists in the responses of the two stakeholder groups.

Implementation Stage

Another point in time in which data analysis is needed is the implementation stage of an intervention. This is the stage in which the most varied types of evaluations can occur, as described in chapter 8. A range of evaluation activities can be considered that are similar in some ways to those mentioned for the input stage. Evaluators could conduct focus groups, interviews, administer questionnaires, conduct observations, or undertake a combination of these activities. However, the intent of these evaluations is very different from those conducted during the input stage. Evaluations during the implementation stage are intended to find out whether an intervention works as planned; how well it works; and whether some components, such as a staffing issue, an intake glitch, or ambiguity in how a particular service is delivered, need to be changed or at least fine-tuned.

For example, an intake unit responsible for assessing and diagnosing clients' problems or needs in a mental health outpatient clinic may refer clients to various staff members and recommend different kinds of services, but the staff members may treat the recommendations differently. Some may ignore them, others interpret them one way, and still others interpret them another way. It appears that clarity and consistency are needed in how the intake referrals are prepared, received, and used.

Because of the varied nature of evaluations that occur during the implementation stage, there are several types of data analyses that can be used to answer questions about the intervention's implementation. In the example of intake services at a mental health clinic, interviews with intake workers and staff could include a set of open-ended questions to determine whether there are differences in their perspectives and/or understandings of procedures.

For example, an open-ended question is, "What do you see as the relationship between the recommendations provided by the intake workers and the decisions made by the treatment staff on how services are to be implemented?" Because these would be open-ended questions and qualitative responses, a content analysis could be conducted to categorize comments by key words. The categories could then be cross-tabulated by whether they were made by intake or treatment workers. If an examination of specific words failed to reveal important distinctions in comments, then themes could be teased out of the comments at a more abstract level of analysis and cross-tabulated.

Another possibility for data analysis is to compare the quantitative responses of two different groups of interviewed people. In the example of intake issues at a mental health clinic, a set of forced-response statements is possible. For example, "The intake workers' recommendations are optional to implement," and "The recommendations of intake workers are usually not feasible." Response categories for such statements could include: strongly agree, agree, disagree, and strongly disagree. In this case, bivariate analysis would help determine whether the responses of the two groups are different and, if so, by how much. Using this information, the evaluator can report on how much consensus or difference exists in the responses of the two stakeholder groups on the intake workers' recommendations.

Outcome Stage

Outcome evaluations emphasize different kinds of data analysis than those used during the planning and implementation stages. Outcome studies focus on the relationships between the intervention and the desired client outcomes. This focus is used not only to determine whether there is an association between the intervention and outcome but also to go a step further and determine whether the intervention caused the outcome measure to change favorably.

For example, in a substance abuse agency, interventions might be group treatment. The evaluator wants to conduct an outcome evaluation to find out whether the intervention is responsible for any progress in clients' short- and long-term decreased substance use. An association will need to be found between the two entities, as well as an evident causal relationship. Several types of controls are needed to determine whether there is a causal relationship between group treatment and progress made to discontinue substance use. This could include being able to rule out other environmental events in clients' lives and other changes beyond external events. As was discussed in chapter 9, a quasi-experimental or experimental group design would need to be used to take into account extraneous influences.

Data analysis strategies used in the outcome stage are the most complex, and several are reviewed subsequently to highlight when to use each strategy and what each strategy can accomplish. Each strategy has limitations; thus, the limitations are also described. For example, some statistical strategies can be used to find out whether there is an association between an intervention and client outcome. Other strategies can be used to determine whether a causal relationship exists and to what extent a causal relationship is evident.

Summary of Pertinent Tools for Qualitative Data Analysis

As reported earlier in this chapter, many evaluations are qualitative in nature or at least have qualitative components. They may collect data using open-ended questions, in-depth interviews, focus groups, unstructured observations, or existing data sources. Three qualitative data analysis strategies are especially relevant for such evaluations, including case studies, condensed responses to general categories, and theme analysis.

Case Studies

Case studies involve one or a few people, but they are intended to provide stakeholders with insights into an entire group of people that the case example represents. Case studies are detailed portrayals of an individual that can illuminate how a larger group of people that the individual represents is functioning. Case studies are also possible with other social units such as a cultural group, a family, or neighborhood (Dudley, 2005). Case studies can be prepared using many different research strategies, such as in-depth interviews, participant observation, and existing documents. Case studies typically do not go beyond a descriptive state. A few examples of case studies follow.

A Mexican boy recently immigrated to the United States with his mother, who was an undocumented worker. The boy was having extreme difficulty adapting to his peers and teachers in the public school in his new community. He was finally suspended. He ended up in the juvenile court system after torturing and killing stray animals. A case study describing his difficulties in adapting to a U.S. school could provide valuable insights into the struggles that many immigrant children face as they attempt to adapt to a new environment in the United States.

A teenager living secretly with HIV was experiencing severe depression because she did not know what to do. She did not want to seek treatment from a health clinic because she was uninformed about the treatments that could be made available to her, and she did not want to disclose her condition to her family for fear of being disowned. To make things even worse, she had no one she could trust to talk to about what she was going through. She began to have suicidal thoughts and contemplated running away. A case study describing the challenges that this teenager faced and the obstacles associated with attempting to get help could provide valuable insights into how teenagers with HIV or AIDS could be helped in the early stages of this disease.

Case studies can be an important approach to consider because they offer insights about what might be typical, challenging, or possibly misunderstood about particular types of clients who participate in a specific program. A case study could also illustrate how a client was especially successful in participating in and using the specific services of a program. Quality assurance evaluations use the case study approach to explore how a few randomly selected clients function in a program and interact with providers.

The studies also can be used in a needs assessment to gain a fuller understanding of the social circumstances of prospective clients. Case studies used to conduct a needs assessment are described in chapter 6.

The data analysis involved in preparing a case study begins with careful planning. A case or cases needs to be selected and specific topics for exploration chosen. Such decisions are determined by carefully considering what the evaluator wants to accomplish and what is practically possible. Other issues are important once data has been collected. A case description should be prepared and organized to tell the story about an individual (or a family, a group, a neighborhood) in the most effective way. Constructing an outline of the story can help identify the most important topics and further questions to ask. Another task is to determine when enough data has been collected on each chosen topic or when additional data is needed to fill out the story. As a case study is prepared and all the data on topics are assembled, another consideration is to discover and describe how the topics may be related so that the story can reflect a more holistic account and perspective. It should be kept in mind that preparing a case study is an effort in creativity and art as well as science. The important thing to remember is to tell the story that needs to be told in the most creative, accurate, compelling, and comprehensive way.

Condense Responses into General Categories

Another strategy for analyzing qualitative data is to create a set of general categories (usually no more than ten) and assign responses to the categories. This option is mostly used with data collection strategies that elicit brief qualitative answers. Qualitative methods that lend themselves to brief answers include open-ended questions in interviews and questionnaires, some questions asked in focus groups, and some semistructured observations. Condensing a large number of short responses into fewer general categories is useful for succinctly summarizing and organizing responses together that have similar meaning. For example, a client satisfaction study could have the question, What do you like about living here? asked of residents of a group home for people with developmental disabilities. The responses of a large sample would be too numerous to meaningfully grasp in their original form, so a smaller number of general categories can be used, such as "types of food or beverages," "social activities," and "hygiene activities."

In some ways, this strategy is similar to the manner in which a frequency distribution summarizes the quantitative responses to a forced-response question. The only difference is that the quantitative responses are already in categorical form, whereas the qualitative responses are assigned to general categories on the basis of their similarities (e.g., taking baths and brushing teeth fit into the "hygiene activities" category). The general categories created from this qualitative strategy are usually at the prenominal level of measurement and could be used as a set of response categories for a forced-response question in a later study.

The steps involved in condensing qualitative responses of an open-ended question into fewer general categories are as follows (Dudley, 2005):

1. Prepare the brief responses for analysis by listing them all together with other responses to the same question.
2. Review and become familiar with all responses to the question.
3. Code responses using the same code for all similar responses (e.g., symbols, such as a letter in the left margin, or different colors).
4. Group similar responses together into categories and give each category a label, which should clearly describe the category of responses (e.g., "hygiene activities" includes taking a bath, washing in warm water, brushing my teeth).
5. Assign each of the brief responses to the category that fits best and count the number of responses that fall into each category.
6. Report the results in quantitative form (e.g., hygiene activities: 27; food or beverages: 22; social activities: 19).
7. Although general categories provide a useful summary of the responses, it may be helpful to include some specific responses for a category in parentheses as examples, which help emphasize the human side of data.

It is important to involve two evaluators who work independently in selecting the general categories and assigning responses to the categories. Two reviewers are used to ensure that there is interrater reliability.

Theme Analysis

A third qualitative data analysis strategy is to identify common themes or patterns that are prevalent in narrative data. Theme analysis is useful in analyzing lengthy narrative material from data collection strategies such as participant-observation, in-depth interviews, focus groups, and unstructured observations. This strategy can also be used to analyze existing data from sources such as journal articles, case records, and other agency material.

Example of a Theme Deriving from Focus Group Responses

A social work student (Leary, 2003) conducted a focus group study of volunteers of several churches that had been sponsoring shelters for homeless people in their churches on a weekly basis during the winter months. A theme resulting from the sessions was identified as a perceived need of homeless people to talk to someone at the church. When the volunteers began discussing the needs they witnessed from the homeless people, they identified the homeless people's need to talk to someone who could listen to them and provide compassion. An abbreviated version of four of the comments found in the narrative that reflected that theme were as follows:

- I think one of the big needs is just to listen to them, be compassionate, and be there for them. I remember one evaluation meeting . . . when you have the homeless at the meeting with you, and I remember one of the fellows saying, "Just don't feed us and leave us."
- I would have loved to have one of the clergy members, deacons, priests, whatever, come and say an opening prayer with our people as it can be a show of force that this whole congregation is behind this program. . . . I think that is a really important part, to have a show of force, that clergy and staff support the program 100 percent. I think the guests actually get a sense of being special when we are all present.
- During Lenten season, when we would have community meals on the same night as the shelter program, one of the things that was very interesting was that . . . they were much more likely to sit down with [one of the pastors]. Some of the issues that were shared . . . [included] offering the possibility of some counseling services and providing that there. I see that as caring, a very crucial kind of caring, to their situation, and also it's definitely a help.
- A lot of them have a lack of self-confidence; they don't believe in themselves anymore. Mainly they need someone to talk to, to reassure them they are still a human being and worth something.

Conducting a theme analysis usually takes more time, covers more data, and can be more intellectually demanding than the previous two strategies. Like the strategy of reducing responses to fewer general categories, it is important to involve two independent evaluators in coding themes to insure interrater reliability. If the two people disagree on a particular theme or how it is reflected in narrative, a third person can be involved to help reach a consensus.

The major stages involved in conducting a theme analysis include the following (Dudley, 2005):

1. Prepare narrative data for analysis by typing it into electronic files.
2. Carefully review and become familiar with all narrative data.
3. Assign a code (e.g., using symbols or magic markers) to each point in the narrative that reflects a specific theme.
4. Group the coded narrative reflecting each theme on one page (e.g., copy and paste to move data around the file).

5. After carefully reviewing the narrative for each theme, give the theme an accurate label (e.g., a few words, a phrase, a sentence).

Theme analysis can involve additional steps, such as examining how the coded narrative of each theme might vary. For example, some of the narratives illustrating a theme may describe it in a positive way, while others describe it in negative terms. Identifying variations in how a theme is depicted can help further delineate what the theme actually means.

Example of Identifying Variations in a Theme

In one student's evaluation (Grantham, 2001) of the needs of patients in a hospice setting, several people identified the theme of legal issues related to finances, end-of-life care, or insurance. On further examination, she found that variations in the comments about legal issues seemed to refer to one of three things: financial problems, a legal will, or advanced directives.

Another step that can be taken in a theme analysis involves capturing how different themes may be related to one another according to what the narrative suggests for each respondent. Relationships among themes can be explored further in later evaluations as hypotheses.

Summary of Pertinent Tools of Quantitative Data Analysis

Descriptive Analyses

It is important for evaluators to ask descriptive questions to understand more about the clients participating in a program, such as, How old are the clients in the program? What is the education level of those who complete the program? and What is the demographic profile of those who drop out of the program? Other descriptive questions might be, What is the level of stress of the clients? How many children attended the program? What is the educational level of participants who do not complete the program? and, How many sessions did both the fathers and mothers participate in together?

Descriptive analysis, or univariate analyses, is used to answer descriptive questions. The analyses are considered univariate because the descriptive question focuses on only one variable at a time. Univariate questions provide a way to describe something about the sample, such as its variability or range. The level of measurement of the variables in descriptive research will inform you about which univariate analyses to use. If the level of measurement of the variable is ordinal or nominal, for example, then percentages and frequency distributions are appropriate. If variables are at the interval/ratio level, then you can report the mean, range, and standard deviation.

TABLE 10.1   Review of Levels of Measurement

Levels	Examples	Measurement procedures	Mathematical operations permitted
Nominal	Gender, ethnicity, political affiliation	Categories	Counting the number in each category and comparing sizes of categories
Ordinal	Likert scales, social class, military rank	Categories and ranking with respect to one another	All of the above plus statements of *greater than* and *less than*
Interval/ratio	Age, years of education, household income	All of the above plus description of numerical distances between scores	All of the above plus all other mathematical operations

Levels of Measurement.   Nominal-level data are the simplest form in which numerical labels are used. Nominal data are categorical, and categories are distinct, mutually exclusive, and exhaustive of all possible circumstances (e.g., gender, race). The categories or scores in nominal level data cannot be ranked, ordered, or manipulated mathematically (e.g., addition, division, multiplication).

A higher, more sophisticated level of measurement is ordinal-level data. Ordinal data are ranked or ordered from lowest to highest, such as Likert scales that range from strongly disagree to strongly agree, which are ordinal-level measures. The limitation with ordinal-level data is that there is no way to determine the distance between the various levels. For example, it is not possible to calculate a numeric distance between strongly disagree and disagree.

Although there are four levels of measurement, we do not usually differentiate between interval and ratio data. As a result, interval and ratio data are combined and presented together. Unlike nominal and ordinal measures, interval/ratio data permit classification, ranking, and signifying the exact distance between scores to be defined. Measures such as age in years, number of days on a job, or annual income are interval/ratio data.

Frequency Distributions.   A frequency distribution is a statistic that describes the number of times that each value of a variable is observed in a sample. For example, in a question using a Likert scale, a frequency distribution describes how many participants selected "very satisfied," "satisfied," "dissatisfied," and so on. Frequency distributions can be presented as actual frequencies or as percentages. Usually percentages are easier to grasp with the large samples. Often, however, frequency distributions list both frequencies and percentages. Frequency distributions are an appropriate statistic for use with categorical variables, including both nominal and ordinal variables. A frequency distribution could also be used with an interval/ratio variable if the responses are reduced to categories.

Measures of Central Tendency.   Three types of measures of central tendency are possible to use in evaluations: mean, median, and mode. The mode is the easiest measure to use, as it is the most common or frequently occurring number. In addition, the mode can be used regardless of the level of data measurement. The median is the middle point, or the fiftieth percentile of the data, and can be used with ordinal, interval, or ratio data.

The most commonly reported measure of central tendency in research is the mean. Keep in mind that the mean score is an average and that its interpretation is limited, as it can be extremely sensitive to outliers. As a result, the mean score might not be very close to most scores in a sample. This can be problematic when the mean is reported by itself; for example, we often see the mean score reported for a standardized test, income, or housing prices. As a result, we should be mindful that stakeholders may need to be given an explanation of a mean score and its limitations. When using analyses on interval/ratio data, we should report not only the mean but also the range and standard deviation. This will give stakeholders an idea of how the data are distributed and will make the mean score more meaningful.

Measures of Variability.   The range of scores is important when presenting interval/ratio data, as the mean can be sensitive to extremes in scores. As a result, knowing the range of scores can indicate the distribution and help determine whether the mean actually reflects most people in the sample. For example, if the mean age of mothers in a support group is thirty years, but the range is from nineteen to sixty-five years, the mean score may not indicate most women's age in the group, as a few sixty-five-year-old women can greatly increase the mean age of the sample.

When you add the standard deviation to the mix it gives a clearer picture of the sample distribution. The standard deviation is the measure of variability that informs how scores relate to one another and to the mean. The standard deviation is useful in interpreting the percentage of scores that are close to the mean. Let's get theoretical here! In normally distributed data, 68 percent of scores fall within plus or minus 1 standard deviation from the mean. Further, 95 percent fall within two standard deviations of the mean, and 99 percent fall within three standard deviations. Returning to the age of mothers, if the data are normally distributed and the mean age is thirty and the standard deviation is 3, then you would expect that 68 percent of mothers are between the ages of twenty-seven and thirty-three (30±3, where 3 is 1 standard deviation). Similarly, 95 percent of mothers in the study are between twenty-four and thirty-six years old (30±6, where 6 is 2 standard deviations). Further, you could conclude that 99 percent of mothers are be-tween twenty-one and thirty-nine years old. This interpretation could be trusted if data are normally distributed; in reality, though, much of the data are skewed and not normally distributed. In other words, if there are a few sixty-five-year-old mothers in the sample, they do not indicate a normally dis-tributed age of participants, with a standard deviation of 3.

Testing Hypotheses

Often program and practice evaluations are designed to test the hy-pothesized relationship between the intervention and progress on client outcomes. The intervention is considered the independent variable and the client outcome is the dependent variable.

Research Terms

A *hypothesis* is a hypothetical explanation describing the rela-tionship between two variables.

An *independent variable* is the variable presumed to cause a change to occur in the dependent variable.

The *dependent variable* is the effect variable, or the variable changed by the independent variable.

Several different types of hypothesis testing are possible to determine whether there is a relationship between the intervention and client out-come. Each type of testing is determined by the type of quasi-experimental or experimental design used (see chapter 9). Table 10.2 summarizes the types of hypotheses that are possible, the level of measurement required for independent and dependent variables, and the statistical tests to be used.

Questions of Association.   Many times hypothesis testing occurs only to explore an association between the intervention and outcome. When the in-tervention is introduced, the client outcome is expected to change. With questions of association, nothing more can be determined, such as whether the intervention had a causal influence or was responsible for the change in client outcome. Questions of association are explored in a one-group pretest-posttest design. This design is a pre-experimental design (see chapter 9).

Questions of association between the intervention and client outcome can be determined by applying a statistical test. The two most common sta-tistical tests are chi-square and correlation. A chi-square test is used to de-termine whether the values of one variable are associated with the values of another variable. This test is also sometimes referred to as a cross-tabulation of variables. The chi-square test is used only when both the intervention and

TABLE 10.2   Types of Hypotheses

Type of hypotheses	Level of measurement of variables	An appropriate statistical test to use
Questions of association	Independent variable and dependent variable are nominal	Chi square
Questions of association	Independent variable and dependent variable are interval/ratio	Pearson correlation
Questions of difference between two groups	Independent variable is nominal; dependent variable is interval/ratio	*t*-test
Questions of difference between three or more groups	Independent variable is nominal; dependent variable is interval/ratio	ANOVA
Questions of prediction	Independent and dependent variables are interval/ratio	Linear regression
Questions of prediction	Independent variables are interval/ratio; dependent variables are nominal	Logistic regression

the outcome are measured at the nominal or ordinal level. In other words, both variables must be categorical. For example, the evaluation question could be, Does attending a psycho-educational group session about the high risk factors associated with contracting AIDS result in more correct answers (to true/false questions on a test) after the session than before it?

A correlation test is the other statistical test frequently used to explore questions of association. It is also sometimes referred to as a Pearson correlation. This test not only answers the question of whether there is an association between the intervention and client outcome but also indicates how strong the association is. For example, the evaluation question might be, Is there a relationship between the number of group sessions attended and the number of fathering activities carried out? The assumption in a correlation test is that both variables are at the interval/ratio level. In this example, the intervention measured at the interval/ratio level could be how many group sessions members attended or for how many hours they attended group sessions. The client outcome variable is also at the interval/ratio level and can be how often a father participates in specific activities with his child over the duration of a week. The results of the correlation test may indicate that the variables are positively associated, negatively associated, or not associated.

The correlation test indicates the strength of the relationship between the intervention and client outcome and can range from –1.0 to 1.0 with a score of 1 or –1 indicating a perfect association, positive or negative, respectively. Evaluators are much more likely to find correlations between the intervention and client outcome to be less than ±0.6.

For example, we might say that a correlation score of 0.3 is a weak correlation, but we have to keep in mind that most correlation scores in evaluations are rarely greater than 0.6. A positive correlation generally occurs when large numbers for one variable are associated with large numbers of another variable, and a negative correlation generally occurs when large numbers of one variable are associated with small numbers of the other variable. For example, an evaluation that finds a negative association between family therapy and reduced marital stress could find that the number of counseling sessions increases as the level of marital stress decreases.

Questions of Differences between Groups.   A second type of hypothesis testing explores whether there is a difference between two or more groups, such as the group receiving the intervention and a comparison group that is not. A group design that is likely to rely on this type of analysis is the one-group pretest-posttest design with a comparison group. Two commonly used tests of differences between groups are the *t*-test and analysis of variance (ANOVA). *T*-tests examine differences across two groups, whereas ANOVA examines differences across three or more groups.

The requirements for using a *t*-test are that the independent variable (whether or not an intervention is introduced) must be dichotomous and nominal. The dependent variable (e.g., the client outcome) must be measurable at the interval/ratio level. The requirements for using an ANOVA are the same as for a *t*-test, except the independent variable is nominal and includes three or more categories. In an evaluation, this could mean comparing three different groups of participants (e.g., intervention group, group receiving traditional services, and group receiving no services).

There are some basic questions that the *t*-test can answer in evaluations. For example, a program evaluation question may ask whether there is a difference in parenting attitudes (the client outcome) between those who have completed a nine-week intervention on parenting and those who have had no intervention. In brief, a *t*-test can be used to determine whether the two groups are significantly different on the basis of their parenting-attitudes scores. What we attempt to determine is whether the mean score for one group differs significantly from the mean score for the other group, or whether the observed differences are attributable to either sampling error or chance factors. If we cannot determine that the mean scores are significantly different, then we can conclude that the groups are the same.

There are two types of *t*-tests that are often used in evaluations: paired samples and independent samples. The requirements for both tests are that the independent variable is nominal and the dependent variable is interval. The decision on which type of t-test to use in an evaluation is based solely on the makeup of the groups in an evaluation.

A paired-samples t-test is used if there is an interest in comparing a pretest score and a posttest score of the same group. This test is often used with a one-group pretest-posttest design. For example, the evaluation question may aim to determine whether a ten-week community center enrichment program decreased classroom disruptions in adolescent boys. The pretest measures indicate how many disruptions the teacher reported over the first semester of school before implementation of the program. During the second semester of the school year, the adolescents complete the program and the teacher records the number of classroom disruptions again. Let's presume that the pretest scores for the group were 11.5 disruptions per week during the first semester. The posttest scores indicate a drop to 9.2 disruptions after the program is completed. The question is, Was there a significant difference in scores or are the differences attributable to chance or error. The t-test informs us whether the scores are statistically significantly different from one another, in which case we could reasonably say that the program effectively reduced classroom disruptions. If the scores are not found to be significantly different, then the pretest and posttest scores are basically the same, and the intervention did not significantly decrease classroom disruptions.

An independent-samples t-test is used to compare two different groups. This test is often used with a one-group pretest-posttest design with a comparison group. An example would be to compare the self-esteem scores of two groups of clients after the first group completed a special program and the comparison group received no intervention. We could compare the self-esteem posttest mean score of the first group with the posttest mean score of the second group.

ANOVA allows for expansion of the principles of the t-test to a statistical test that examines whether there are differences across three or more groups. The ANOVA and t-test assume that the independent variable is nominal and that the dependent variable is interval/ratio. In an ANOVA evaluation, for example, this could mean comparing three different groups of participants (e.g., an intervention group, a client group receiving traditional services, and a client group receiving no services). We would compare the mean posttest scores of the three groups to determine whether one made significantly more progress on the client outcome measure than the other two groups.

An ANOVA can also be used to determine whether there are significant differences in the interventions of three different groups. An ANOVA can be used if, for example, there are concerns that clients received different numbers of therapy sessions because of their geographic location. The research question might be, Is there a difference in the number of therapy sessions because of clients' geographic location? In this case, location could be measured as urban, suburban, and rural. The independent variable is the three geographic locations (nominal) and the dependent variable is the number of therapy sessions (interval/ratio). Let's say that you conduct an evaluation and find out that urban clients received an average of twelve sessions per week, suburban clients received an average of sixteen sessions a week, and rural clients received an average of seventeen sessions a week. Your initial thought may be that urban clients receive significantly fewer therapy sessions than do suburban and rural clients. However, the ANOVA findings indicate that the there is not a statistically significant difference in the number of therapy sessions among these groups; thus, you conclude that the difference in number of therapy sessions is simply due to chance and there is really no difference in the number of therapy sessions in each group.

Questions of Prediction. Regression models are another statistical test that can be used in program evaluations. Several regression models or tests are available to predict a client outcome (dependent variable) from more than one intervention (independent variables). A regression model can investigate whether an intervention is more effective with men or women or with some age groups more than others. If participants have experienced a variety of interventions, then a regression model can show how the interventions, working together, predict the dependent variable. Consider an agency that serves families after a child dies. If the family members participate in group therapy, individual grief counseling, and a support group, then the regression can show how much variance or change in the client outcome (e.g., recovery from grief) is accounted for by the combination of all three interventions. In addition, the regression can show whether specific interventions, such as group therapy, are more effective than other interventions in improving the client outcome. If one intervention is found not to be a significant predictor of client outcome, then this is scientific evidence that this intervention may not be effective.

Two regression models that can be used in evaluations are linear regression and logistic regression. Both allow the research question to predict a dependent variable from a number of independent variables. The difference between the models is that the dependent variable is at the interval/ratio level in linear regression and at the nominal level in logistic regression (for more information on regression analysis, see Weinbach & Grinnell, 2007).

Mixed Methods and Data Analysis

Qualitative and quantitative data analysis have been described separately so far. This is not intended to mislead readers into thinking that the methods are not connected, which is certainly not the case. Often evaluations use mixed methods, quantitative and qualitative, that complement each other. The combination of qualitative and quantitative methods offers several advantages to evaluations, including complementarity, triangulation, and accountability.

Complementary Data

Quantitative and qualitative methods each provide distinct kinds of data that can be complementary to each other and useful in evaluations. Quantitative data are useful for purposes such as providing numeric measures of client satisfaction, client outcomes, and profiles of prospective clients. The numeric measures can also be used to make decisions about program effectiveness. In contrast, qualitative data provide a human side to quantitative measures, showing why quantitative measures are important and how they affect real people. These naturalistic data can provide a fuller picture of the concerns and encounters of people and bring greater identification with them, their plight, and the need to take action.

Triangulation

Qualitative and quantitative findings on the same topic can be helpful in triangulation of the findings. Use of both methods can provide two types of information sources on the same topic. For example, in one evaluation, clients with a dual diagnosis of developmental disability and mental illness were ask forced-response questions such as, "Do you like living here?" (Dudley, Calhoun, Ahlgrim-Delzell, & Conroy, 1998). They were also asked open-ended questions on the same topics to learn more about the meaning of their responses. Open-ended questions included, "What do you like about living here?" and "What do you not like about living here?" Sometimes there were inconsistencies in responses. For example, a few responded that they liked living where they were but then they focused on a long list of things that they did not like in responses to the open-ended questions. So, the combinations of questions provided the evaluator with an opportunity to ask for clarification about any discrepancies between responses to both types of questions. In other cases, open-ended questions clarified why many clients said that they liked where they lived, as several qualitative comments confirmed their positive responses (e.g., they liked having their own bedroom, being treated with respect, having more freedom than in the past).

Accountability in Giving Answers

A third advantage of using mixed methods in evaluation is that it holds participants accountable for their answers. When forced-response questions are asked, it is relatively easy for participants to answer them without revealing much, if any, information about their views or motives. In the previous example of clients with a dual diagnosis, a "yes" response to the question about whether they like where they live tells little about what they like. They may answer affirmatively because that is the normative response to give and they think a negative response could get them into trouble with providers. Therefore, qualitative responses on the same topic can hold participants accountable for their answers. If they do not like where they live, it will be more difficult for them to cover up their negative feelings in responses to open-ended questions. Further, qualitative responses provide useful information that can be addressed directly. Accountability in this case addresses validity and accuracy issues as well, for when a question is asked in two different ways, responses are likely to be closer to the truth or reality.

The chapter has highlighted many of the data analysis tools and strategies that can be used to analyze evaluation data. Quantitative, qualitative, and mixed methods strategies have been offered. This information can be supplemented by several specialized qualitative and quantitative data analysis texts that provide more detail on how to conduct an analysis. Some of these texts are identified in the chapter and listed as references. The next chapter addresses the last steps in an evaluation, preparing a presentation of the findings and disseminating them to stakeholders and other interested parties. The findings incorporated into a presentation are determined, to a large extent, by the choices made in data analysis, so this chapter is an important resource to use in the final steps of preparing and disseminating a report of the findings.

Key Terms
ANOVA
Case studies
Chi-square
Correlation
Creating general categories
Descriptive statistics
Frequency distributions
Independent samples *t*-test
Measures of central tendency
Measures of variability
Mixed methods
Paired-samples *t*-test
Questions of association
Questions of differences in groups
Questions of prediction
Regression models
Theme analysis
t-test

Discussion Questions and Assignments

1. Select an evaluation report from a social work or evaluation journal. Critique the methods section of the evaluation by answering the following questions:

   - What data collection methods were used? Were the methods distinctly quantitative and/or qualitative?
   - How were the data analyzed? Which qualitative and quantitative data analysis tools described in the chapter were used?

2. Find and review an evaluation study that used mixed methods. Did the authors refer to the evaluation as a mixed-methods evaluation? How did the data analysis procedures connect the two different quantitative and qualitative data analyses? Describe the findings that made connections between the quantitative and qualitative findings. Explain whether you think such findings were helpful to the overall findings section. If you think these combined findings were not helpful, explain why not.

References

Berg, B. (2004). *Qualitative research methods for the social sciences*. Boston: Pearson.

Dudley, J. R. (2005). *Research methods for social work: Becoming consumers and producers of research*. Boston: Pearson.

Dudley, J., Calhoun, M., Ahlgrim-Delzell, L., & Conroy, J. (1998). Measuring the consumer satisfaction of class members of a law suit. *Journal of Intellectual Disability Research, 42*(3), 199–207.

Grantham, V. (2001). *Theme analysis of client records*. Unpublished student assignment, University of North Carolina at Charlotte.

Leary, A. (2003). *Room in the inn: Exploring church involvement in serving the homeless*. Unpublished student research project, University of North Carolina at Charlotte.

Royse, D., Thyer, B., Padgett, D., & Logan, T. (2006). *Program evaluation: An introduction* (4th ed.). Belmont CA: Brooks/Cole.

Weinbach, R. W., & Grinnell, R. M. (2007). *Statistics for social workers* (7th ed.). Boston: Pearson.

Chapter 11

Preparing and Disseminating the Report of Findings

How do we prepare a report that will be useful?

This chapter explores the final steps in an evaluation: preparing a report of the findings and disseminating them to others. Once the data are gathered from an evaluation and analyzed, preparing a report naturally follows. Several different types of reports are possible, depending on the needs of various stakeholders. A report can be communicated orally, in written form, or both; comprehensively or in brief summary form; and the formatting options are almost unlimited. Reports can be technical, a formal presentation at a public meeting, a set of topics and questions covered at a staff workshop, a series of informal discussions, a brief written summary, a paragraph for state legislators, a manuscript, a press release, or other formats.

Once the report is completed, the findings are expected to be disseminated to all stakeholders and interested parties. This dissemination, of course, should occur in the most useful form possible. Ideally, findings are disseminated to several different types of stakeholders; some are obvious, such as funding agencies and agency administrators overseeing the program. Other important stakeholders can be easily overlooked or forgotten, such as clients and pertinent community groups, such as family members and community advisory committees.

Although different strategies are available to disseminate findings, they largely depend on the format chosen for the report. In other words, the two steps of preparing a report and disseminating findings are largely intertwined. The decision about a report's format influences how and even if it will be useful to some stakeholders. For example, a lengthy technical research report may be useful to a funding agency or a professional journal but not to other stakeholders, such as clients and their families. For this reason, it is best to begin by exploring the needs of each stakeholder, finding out what kinds of information and what format will be most helpful to them, and proceeding to select the most useful reports and means of distributing the findings.

Considering the Input of Stakeholders

Like all the previous steps of an evaluation, it is very important to spend an adequate amount of time thinking about and planning these final steps.

Unfortunately, a poorly thought-out and written report can easily negate all the hard work up to this point. Likewise, neglecting to give enough time and serious thought to how to disseminate findings could deter what an evaluation was intended to achieve.

The best way to begin these two final steps is to consider who the stakeholders and other potential readers of the report will be (e.g., funding agencies, board members, advisory committee members, administrators, program service providers, legislators, current or prospective clients, community groups, advocacy groups, professionals, the public). Some stakeholders may be designated as primary and others secondary, which can help prioritize where more of the time and energy should be devoted to dissemination (Morris, Fitz-Gibbon, & Freeman, 1987). The evaluation sponsor and others who requested the evaluation are examples of primary stakeholders, and others could include a funding agency, the agency's board of directors, a chief executive officer, program directors, other key staff members, and any other decision makers. Secondary stakeholders are more likely community groups, other staff members, clients, other organizations interested in the program, the public, and legislators. Although the latter groups may be considered secondary, they should not be overlooked.

Each group is likely to have different needs related to a report, and the differences are usually reflected in how easy it is to understand the material and how relevant and useful the information is. Timing may also be important for stakeholders, as timing may be crucial to a decision-making timetable. Therefore, it is likely that different types of reports and strategies for dissemination are needed, especially to address a diverse audience of stakeholders.

It is usually wise to ask stakeholders several types of questions before you begin to write a report. Morris et al. (1987) suggest the following questions:

- What do you want to know about the evaluation and why? What expectations do you have for a report?
- Will you answer any important questions or make any decisions about policies, programs, or practice on the basis of the report's findings? If so, what are these questions?
- Are there any acceptable criteria that you have adopted to claim success or lack of it? For example, do you expect a minimum amount of increase in client scores from pretest to posttest or a minimally acceptable percentage of clients who are satisfied with services?
- Are there any ethical or political considerations that need to be carefully thought out before preparing the report? For example, are there controversial issues that need to be addressed cautiously and in a delicately balanced way? Is there any potential resistance to some of the findings that could come from particular groups?
- Should the results of the study be made available to clients? If so, in what form?

- How can the clients benefit from the findings? What can be done to maximize client benefits?

Format of the Report

Several communication formats are possible for sharing evaluation results with stakeholders (Morris et al., 1987), including several written possibilities, such as a technical research report, an executive summary, a manuscript for a professional journal, a special report for clients, an agency brochure, a press release, or a one-page flyer or memo. Oral report options could include a curriculum for a staff workshop, a presentation before a public or community meeting, a poster session at a conference, personal discussions with some stakeholders, or a discussion that social workers can have with their clients in which they share some of the findings with them.

Technical Report

A technical report tends to be formal and lengthy. It is a comprehensive report that documents all steps in the evaluation process. It is the format that is most helpful for assessing whether the evaluation methods used reflect sound scientific principles, and it is the best format for demonstrating evidence-based research. A technical report uses a format similar to that of a formal research report. An outline of a typical technical report of a research study is likely to have all the following items:

- An abstract that summarizes the purpose of the study, the methods and sampling approach used, findings, and recommendations
- Background information on the research problem or topic, including a literature review, relevant viewpoints, and theories that help explain the topic
- The purposes of the study, including research questions and/or hypotheses
- A description of the sample characteristics and sampling approach used
- Description of the informed consent protocol
- Description of the data collection approach and specific measurement instruments
- A data analysis plan
- Findings, which can be an overall summary, highlights of the most important findings in tables and graphs, and results of data analysis
- Recommendations for how to use findings
- Limitations of the study (e.g., in the instrument, important questions that were not asked, poorly constructed questions, sample size, an availability sampling approach, no baseline data collected, uncontrolled important extraneous variables)

Technical reports are usually most appropriate for summative evaluations. This type of report is often what funding agencies, program administrators, and others inclined to review the scientific aspects of an evaluation need. A technical report can also become a master copy of the evaluation process that can be reduced and modified to fit the needs of other smaller reports.

Executive Summary

An executive summary is short, often no more than one page. It usually contains a summary of a sentence or two for each section of a larger report. For example, an executive summary developed for a technical research report would summarize background information on the program concern, the purpose of the study, the research design, the findings, recommendations, limitations, and other implications. The summary is sometimes referred to as an abstract, particularly for journal submissions.

Executive summaries usually precede a technical report and help readers determine the contents of the technical report and whether it is worthwhile to read the full report or only sections. Executive summaries are useful for any stakeholders who may be interested in reading the technical report that it summarizes.

Journal Publication

Many times, an evaluation contributes something new to a practice field and may be a breakthrough worthy of dissemination to a national or even international audience. Perhaps the program model that is evaluated is worth sharing with other providers because it addresses a common or especially challenging problem area, or findings from the evaluation may be new evidence-based knowledge that a particular program model or practice theory has been effective in helping a particular client population, or the methodology might be able to be replicated in other evaluations. There are several excellent evaluation journals that publish a manuscript addressing any such breakthrough (see chapter 6).

Reports to Clients

Seldom do clients hear about the results of an evaluation relevant to them. Many times such reports can be shared, but they must fit clients' particular needs and be presented in readily understandable language. A possibility is to share just one set of findings from an evaluation. For example, a university-conducted study on binge drinking to document the extent to which binge drinking was a problem among students found that more than 95 percent of student participants indicated that they did not binge drink.

The university sponsor thought that this finding could encourage students to avoid binge drinking, so signs stating this finding were posted at various locations on campus. The finding was part of a larger effort by the university's dean of student services to overcome early signs that binge drinking was becoming a pattern among students.

Similarly, a finding on the success rate of clients completing a program could be publicized openly in an agency. For example, an evaluation might highlight the high rate of success of graduates of a programs on key client outcome measures such as the following:

- Finding a job after participating in a job-training program
- Remaining in recovery after completing a residential program for substance abusers
- Lower divorce rate among graduates of a marital enrichment program than among nongraduates
- An increase in self-reported satisfaction of participants' parental role after attending a series of parent-training sessions

There are other creative ways to inform clients about findings. A simple flyer available at the front door of an agency or posted on a community bulletin board can highlight findings as well. These highlights should be prepared so that they are easily read and understood. Creativity is of utmost importance in preparing these reports, with graphics, photos, and personal testimonies among the resources to consider. It might be a good idea to attach a tear-off sheet to flyers for clients to give feedback or to make suggestions for follow-up actions.

Another way to share evaluation findings with clients is in the context of the worker-client relationship. In many instances, findings from an evaluation and the program or practice concerns that catalyzed the evaluation can be introduced into conversations with clients. Discrete findings that directly relate to what a client is working on can be quite helpful if timed well. Client satisfaction evaluations are a good illustration of this. The findings of a client satisfaction study can be introduced in a conversation between a social worker and client as follows:

Worker: We just completed our survey of client satisfaction. Do you remember filling it out?

Client: Yes, I did, but I am not expecting anything to come of it. These things are usually done to benefit the big people like the director of the agency.

Worker: Well, one finding revealed that a large percentage of the clients were not very satisfied with our group therapy program. They indicated that the topics that are covered and the discussions didn't really help clients solve the problems that they came here to solve in the first place.

Client: I could have told you that a long time ago. You didn't need a study to find that out. We [clients] often talk among ourselves about how we hate that group and wish we didn't have to attend it.

Worker: Do you want to know what we found were the reasons for dissatisfaction with the group therapy program. I have them here . . .

In these conversations, the findings should touch on issues of relevance to clients; in addition, an opportunity can be introduced for the client to react to the findings and to add his or her own interpretations and thoughts. Also, it is important to reassure clients that the agency is committed to doing something about client dissatisfaction because of the importance of their viewpoints. Some initial recommendations of the study could be mentioned in such conversations as well, with feedback sought from clients' perspectives. The feedback sessions should be documented and reported back to the evaluator and other stakeholders as a next step in resolving the identified problems.

Agency Public Relations Reports

The findings of a program evaluation can be a major news item for an agency when preparing its annual report or creating a brochure to inform other agencies and prospective clients about programs. Evaluations with positive findings are obvious materials for public relations promotions. A public child welfare program, for example, needed more positive press to highlight its success in finding adoptions for children. So, it used some key findings from an evaluation to do so and included them in its annual report. The presentation, however, was similar to newspaper headlines rather than a technical report: "There has been an INCREASE in the number of foster children *being adopted each year*. From 895 in 1998/99 to 1,379 in 00/01," and "In 2002, the number of children in foster care *has DROPPED for the FIRST TIME* since 1990 to below 10,000 children."

Staff Workshops

Staff workshops and other types of staff gatherings are excellent venues for discussing most evaluation findings. Staff workshops are mentioned here because they usually focus on training, skills development, and information sharing. Staff members are key stakeholders who have direct contact with clients and firsthand exposure to their problems; they may also be the most well-informed source on the functioning of programs and the conduct of practice.

Staff members are among the most important stakeholders of evaluations of programs and practice, whether they are recognized as stakeholders or not. When they are excluded from participating or from having a significant voice in an evaluation that affects them, it is quite possible that their exclusion will result in unnecessary complications, misunderstandings, and conflicts with agency administrators and the evaluators. Because staff cooperation is essential for most evaluations to occur optimally, evaluators will want these relationships to be cooperative and collaborative.

The findings of most evaluations are relevant for staff members to hear about and discuss. During the planning stage for a new program, the findings of a needs assessment can provide a range of information about prospective clients for the program. Staff members need this information for several reasons, such as to identify and recruit clients and assess their suitability for a program. During the implementation stage of a program, staff workshops could be used to discuss the findings of a staff morale study or a staff satisfaction study. It would also be useful for staff to become informed about findings on program accessibility, as they will need to implement many of the recommended strategies for reaching underserved groups.

Client satisfaction studies are directly relevant to staff and can provide helpful feedback on the interventions that need improvement. Program quality evaluations, as described in chapter 4, are designed to involve staff members as reviewers and peer evaluators. Evaluations that monitor their practice and involvement in programs are directly pertinent to them and can give them feedback on their interventions. Finally, outcome evaluations inform staff whether their interventions effectively help clients. One evaluation that attempted to articulate a new model of practice illustrates how teams of social workers can become involved by responding to the findings of an initial evaluation (Gardner, 2000).

Presentations to the Public

In many instances, the findings of an evaluation should be communicated to the general public and to those who cannot be easily identified for invitation. The community surrounding agencies in particular may have a special stake in an evaluation's findings. Community residents could be invited to hear about an agency's plans. An agency that serves people with mental retardation by sponsoring group homes in the community, or a Head Start program located in a local church or settlement house are examples.

Sometimes public meetings are open to all and advertised as such; other times the meetings can be by invitation and a range of people may be invited to attend, such as civic leaders, volunteers, staff representatives of other agencies, local officials, and other active citizens. The format of the meeting can range from a formal presentation to an open discussion, but it is most important that the report of findings be prepared in a form that is pertinent and understandable to participants. These meetings could be opportune times to seek feedback from participants on recommendations before they are actually implemented.

Testifying at public hearings is another outlet for sharing evaluation findings. Sometimes the findings of an evaluation can document the progress or lack of it for clients in the public spotlight. For example, evaluation findings may assist offenders in the criminal justice system who are on probation or parole and need verification of their progress or achievements. Data can be provided on the progress of individual clients as court testimony for their early release for good behavior. Evaluation findings can also be valuable for class action suits on behalf of groups of clients who need documentation that they are improving in their behavior from designated program interventions. An example of this kind of documentation is provided in a longitudinal evaluation by Dudley, Calhoun, and Ahlgrim-Delzell (2002).

Evaluation findings can also be publicized through a newspaper column or series, a radio talk show, or a television program. Stories of individual clients are the most effective way to portray to the public the plight of particular types of people and the possibilities of their overcoming such obstacles. A qualitative evaluation is typically a descriptive account of the lives of a group of clients and makes an excellent source for such a story. Such evaluations can illustrate how a group of clients learned to cope with their problems or were helped by a program to become more independent and satisfied with their lives. Informed consent procedures can be used to protect the identity of clients who are exposed in these stories by using fictitious names, making minor changes in their personal circumstances to prevent identification, and restricting access to narrative evaluation material.

Informal Exchanges of Information with Stakeholders

Another format for sharing findings with stakeholders is to arrange informal exchanges with particular stakeholders. In some instances, it may be important to provide handouts of findings as part of an informal oral report for special stakeholders such as board officers and advisory committees. These materials can be flexibly presented so that recipients can fully air their views and ideas for follow-up. Participants can also be consulted about the best venue for holding larger meetings of boards, advisory committees, and the community at large, as they may know best what aspects of the findings to share and how to do so most effectively.

Strategies for Preparing a Report

As was emphasized earlier in the chapter, reports can take many forms. They can be long or short, oral or written, and they can use many formats. Preparing the report may take considerable or little time, depending on its nature. Either way, however, it needs to be thoughtfully planned and executed. Four likely tasks to consider are highlighted next: clarifying the purpose of the report and its targeted audience, presenting helpful background information, organizing the findings, and making recommendations.

Clarifying the Purpose of the Report

The overall purpose of a report is to describe the findings and to offer recommendations to address the concerns about a program or practice area. However, as indicated earlier, a report can vary widely depending on who the stakeholders are. Before preparing the report, it is important to hold discussions with stakeholders to identify their needs. The specifics of the report can be determined from such discussions. Several specifics to consider are the specific findings to highlight and why. In addition, what recommendations are most important?

Equally important to selecting the specifics for the report are the strategies for disseminating them. An important question to ask about dissemination is, How can the report be presented to address the interest of the stakeholders and involve them in contributing to the implementation of the recommendations and any plans for follow-up?

Background Information

Most reports will need to include some background information on the evaluation before the findings. A technical report may do so in a lengthy and thorough way, whereas brief reports to other stakeholders may only mention helpful details in a few sentences, followed by questions. Most stakeholders will want to be reminded about the purpose of the evaluation, the evaluation questions, the types of people studied, and the methods. They may also want to be reminded of the concerns that led to initiation of the evaluation and the options currently available to address what to do about the program now.

Organizing the Findings

Next, the findings of the evaluation need to be organized and presented so that they are readable, relevant, and useful. Organizing the findings is a very important task, which entails focusing the findings, ensuring their accuracy and clarity, and using visual aids when appropriate. Focusing the findings depends on the needs of stakeholders and on the initial evaluation questions. The questions can provide a focus and an organizing framework for the report, as the findings are supposed to answer the questions.

Example of Preparation of a Report for a Qualitative Study

A study (Leary, 2003) was conducted of several volunteers of an ecumenical program that offers overnight shelter to small groups of homeless people once every week during the winter months. Initially, the researcher identified three research questions to focus the study: (1) What are the needs of the homeless guests? (2) What efforts have the churches made to try to meet these needs? and (3) What efforts might churches try in the future? Although the evaluator explored all three questions in focus groups, participants gave much more attention to the third question, and the sponsor organization and participants perceived it as the central set of findings. Therefore, it was decided that the major focus of the report would be on the third question.

It is also important to present findings accurately. Some of the questions to ask related to accuracy could be the following: Are the correct statistical tests used to analyze the data? Is there a balance of positive and negative findings when both exist? Are tables and graphs prepared accurately and are they easy to understand? Do the tables and graphs focus on the most important findings?

A report that includes only uninterrupted written or oral material can be boring and tedious. Therefore, in preparing a report, consider using tables, graphs, and other visual aids to creatively highlight and summarize important findings. The Statistical Package for the Social Sciences (SPSS), Microsoft Excel, and other computer programs can be used to prepare graphics. Tables are useful for consolidating several data points into a single visual presentation to highlight an important finding. For example, a table can highlight the characteristics of research participants, compare the outcomes of a treatment and comparison group, or compare the pretest and posttest measures of a one-group pretest-posttest design. Table 11.1 presents a summary of two

TABLE 11.1　Prevalence of Maltreatment in Female Teenagers, by Demographic Characteristics

Characteristics	Whether Maltreated (%)		
	Yes	No	n
Total sample	14	86	249
Welfare recipient*			
Yes	19	81	134
No	6	94	96
Parent education			
Not high school graduate	13	87	137
High school graduate	14	86	111
Family structure*			
Other	17	83	180
Both biological parents present	4	96	64
Race and ethnicity*			
White	33	67	16
Hispanic	5	95	33
African American	13	87	200

Source: Smith, 1996.
*$p < .05$, one-tailed.

subgroups of female teenage participants, those who were maltreated in childhood and those who were not, to highlight their differences. Note that the table reveals that the two subgroups were significantly different on the basis of family structure, race and ethnicity, and welfare status. Pie and bar charts are other ways to highlight findings. Bar charts can compare two or more groups of people on a particular measure. Pie charts are useful when a circular display communicates more effectively than a linear bar chart.

Qualitative findings can be presented in several different ways, as case studies to illustrate insightful issues or remarks about a pertinent topic, or organized into general categories or themes.

Making Recommendations

Next, the findings are to be interpreted; interpretations in evaluation studies often take the form of practical recommendations. The recommendations are an important section of a report; which needs to be developed carefully. Morris et al. (1987) suggest that recommendations are the most important part of the report because stakeholders tend to turn to this section for guidance. Several guidelines can be helpful when preparing recommendations for a research report:

- Attempt to draw some general conclusions from the findings. What do they seem to say?
- List specific recommendations in such a way that they are relevant and useful to stakeholders.

Recommendations must be supported by the findings. Recommendations should not be a wish list or an excuse to promote a particular viewpoint unsupported by findings. A helpful exercise is to identify each recommendation in a report and then identify the specific findings of the evaluation, if any, that support each recommendation. When there are no findings to support a recommendation, it should be omitted. Recommendations are usually stated tentatively, especially in formative studies, to permit the stakeholders to offer their own thoughts. Recommendations should be practical and address such questions as whether the program should be continued, modified, expanded, or take another course. Good recommendations are stated in a way that is helpful to the agency and to clients.

Sometimes, the more recommendations that are offered, the more helpful they are. For example, the evaluator may find out in an evaluation on staff morale that staff morale is low for several reasons, not one, and they are all supported by findings. Examples of recommendations from a staff morale study could include raising salaries, improving supervision, and/or reducing caseloads or workloads.

The discussion of a study's recommendations should also mention any limitations that need to be considered in implementing them. For example, an evaluation about the school adjustment of children born and raised in the

United States may not have direct applicability for children who are recent immigrants. Examples of limitations that should be reported are a small sample, questions that were poorly formulated or not asked, a convenience sample or other nonprobability sampling approach, a low response rate for a questionnaire, no baseline data collected, and uncontrolled important external variables.

Strategies for Disseminating Reports

A proactive strategy is needed to inform the stakeholders about the results of an evaluation. The information that stakeholders receive should be clear, thorough, and relevant to their needs. Because stakeholders have diverse needs, the information they receive should take into consideration such things as what to emphasize, how much material to report, and useful recommendations. Numerous strategies are available that reflect various ways to communicate findings. Oral options include presentations, informal discussions, conversations between social workers and clients, staff workshops, and poster sessions in the community. Providing helpful written materials is equally important and can take the form of technical reports, summaries and sections of technical reports, published results in professional journals, memos and flyers, brochures and other educational materials, and more.

A report's preparation and dissemination are usually planned together. A dissemination strategy often naturally evolves from the format of a report. For example, a technical report is usually disseminated in written form and could be explained in a presentation. In contrast, findings of interest to clients are likely to be focused and shared informally through discussions and question-and-answer formats. Identification of a strategy begins with discussions with stakeholders about what they need and find useful. From there, an oral or written report is planned, as well as a strategy to share the report in meaningful ways with stakeholders.

Table 11.2 summarizes the many options available for the range of stakeholders. Some types of stakeholders, such as funding agencies and agency board members, are likely to want to receive lengthy technical reports and summaries. These reports can be disseminated through informal discussions and more formal presentations with question-and-answer formats. Other types of stakeholders (e.g., neighbors, representatives of other civic organizations and agencies, the public) may prefer special reports or brief summaries that can be presented and discussed in a more informal and spontaneous manner.

Why Invest in Dissemination?

There are several reasons to devote time, money, and energy into disseminating evaluation findings. The most practical reason is to involve stake-

TABLE 11.2 Options for Preparing and Disseminating Reports

Stakeholders	Primary Formats for Report	Possible dissemination strategies
Funding agencies	Technical report	Presentation at a meeting Giving out report
Board members	Technical report Executive summary	Presentation at a meeting Giving out report
Advisory committee members	Technical report Executive summary	Informal discussions Presentation at a meeting Giving out report
Administrators of program	Technical report	Informal discussions Giving out report
Legislators	Brief memo or executive summary	Mailing or e-mailing memo to all relevant legislators and providing access to more information
Current or prospective clients	One-page flyer Agency brochure	Informal discussions Conversation within worker/client relationships Giving helpful written material Radio announcements
Staff members and volunteers	Special reports	Staff workshop Presentation at other staff gatherings
Community groups	Special report One-page flyer Using helpful visual aids	Informal discussions Presentations at a community meeting
Public at large	Special report Press release One-page flyer or memo Using helpful visual aids	Presentation at a community meeting Personal discussions
Professional community	Manuscript for a journal Press release	Presentations at professional or community meetings Poster sessions at conferences Informal networking

holders in any follow-up action for addressing a program or practice concern. Usually, evaluation reports include a list of recommendations to be considered, such as whether a program should be continued, expanded, changed, or discontinued after an evaluation is completed. One could easily reason that the more that stakeholders are involved in the decision-making process, the better the decisions will be because they will be based on a wide range of relevant perspectives.

In addition, many stakeholders will expect to hear about the results of an evaluation, especially if they participated in the earlier planning and execution steps. Leaving some stakeholders out of the final step could lead them to feel that they are not important participants. Staff members, clients, and community groups are among the stakeholders most often left out of this final step, with negative consequences not only for them but for the intervention as well. Staff members and clients in particular should become more active participants in the decision-making process, especially in an advisory capacity, and involving them and their feedback can enhance the functioning of interventions.

Another reason to give special attention to disseminating findings is that agencies usually want stakeholders to be ongoing participants in programs and practice areas, and many stakeholders want this as well. Viewing the findings can provide them with new information and insights about an intervention and the agency. It can help them become more informed in their roles as stakeholders, and they can discover the important role that evaluations play in enhancing programs and practice.

Ultimately, evaluation is an accountability measure. It addresses important questions such as the following:

- Is the program or practice intervention focusing on the target population with the greatest need?
- Is the intervention meeting the specified short- and long-term needs of the target population?
- Is the intervention being implemented with high standards?
- Are clients satisfied with the program?
- Is the intervention achieving its goals and objectives?
- Is it cost-effective?

These are questions that should not be left solely to evaluators and program administrators. Involving an active team of stakeholders, as advocated throughout the book, can optimize the likelihood that accountability will be real and substantive.

Key Terms
Agency public relations reports
Disseminating a report
Executive summary
Findings
Informal exchanges
Journal manuscript
Presentations to the public

Recommendations
Reports to clients
Staff workshops
Strategies for disseminating a report
Strategies for preparing a report
Technical evaluation report

Discussion Questions and Assignments

1. Select an evaluation report from a social work or evaluation journal.
   Critique the findings section by answering the following questions:

   - What are the major findings?
   - Were the findings presented clearly? If not, what was unclear? How
     could they be presented more clearly?
   - Were the tables easy to understand? If not, why not?
   - How are the findings useful to you as a social worker?
   - Are the limitations of the study discussed? What are the limitations?

2. Using the same evaluation report used in Question 1, determine how
   well the recommendations are supported by the findings by answering the following questions:

   - Identify each recommendation.
   - Identify the specific findings, if any, that support each recommen-
     dation.
   - In your opinion, is each recommendation adequately supported
     by a specific finding. If not, why not?
   - What recommendations were useful to you as a social worker?

References

Dudley, J., Calhoun, M., & Ahlgrim-Delzell, L. (Eds.). (2002). *Lessons learned from a lawsuit: Creating services for people with mental illness and mental retardation.* Kingston, NY: National Association for the Dually Diagnosed Press.

Gardner, F. (2000). Design evaluation: Illuminating social work practice for better out-comes. *Social Work, 45*(2), 176–182.

Leary, A. (2003). *Room in the inn: Exploring church involvement in serving the homeless.* Unpublished student research project, University of North Carolina at Charlotte.

Morris, L. L., Fitz-Gibbon, C. T., & Freeman, M. (1987). *How to communicate evalua-tion findings.* Newbury Park, CA: Sage Publications.

Appendix A

The American Evaluation Association's Guiding Principles for Evaluators

A. **Systematic Inquiry:** Evaluators conduct systematic, data-based inquiries.
   1. To ensure the accuracy and credibility of the evaluative information they produce, evaluators should adhere to the highest technical standards appropriate to the methods they use.
   2. Evaluators should explore with the client the shortcomings and strengths both of the various evaluation questions and the various approaches that might be used for answering those questions.
   3. Evaluators should communicate their methods and approaches accurately and in sufficient detail to allow others to understand, interpret, and critique their work. They should make clear the limitations of an evaluation and its results. Evaluators should discuss in a contextually appropriate way those values, assumptions, theories, methods, results, and analyses significantly affecting the interpretation of the evaluative findings. These statements apply to all aspects of the evaluation, from its initial conceptualization to the eventual use of findings.

B. **Competence:** Evaluators provide competent performance to stakeholders.
   1. Evaluators should possess (or ensure that the evaluation team possesses) the education, abilities, skills, and experience appropriate to undertake the tasks proposed in the evaluation.
   2. To ensure recognition, accurate interpretation, and respect for diversity, evaluators should ensure that the members of the evaluation team collectively demonstrate cultural competence. Cultural competence would be reflected in evaluators seeking awareness of their own culturally based assumptions, their understanding of the worldviews of culturally different participants and stakeholders in the evaluation, and the use of appropriate evaluation strategies and skills in working with culturally different groups. Diversity may be in terms of race, ethnicity, gender, religion, socio-economics, or other factors pertinent to the evaluation context.

3. Evaluators should practice within the limits of their professional training and competence, and should decline to conduct evaluations that fall substantially outside those limits. When declining the commission or request is not feasible or appropriate, evaluators should make clear any significant limitations on the evaluation that might result. Evaluators should make every effort to gain the competence directly or through the assistance of others who possess the required expertise.

4. Evaluators should continually seek to maintain and improve their competencies, in order to provide the highest level of performance in their evaluations. This continuing professional development might include formal coursework and workshops, self-study, evaluations of one's own practice, and working with other evaluators to learn from their skills and expertise.

C. **Integrity/Honesty:** Evaluators display honesty and integrity in their own behavior, and attempt to ensure the honesty and integrity of the entire evaluation process.

1. Evaluators should negotiate honestly with clients and relevant stakeholders concerning the costs, tasks to be undertaken, limitations of methodology, scope of results likely to be obtained, and uses of data resulting from a specific evaluation. It is primarily the evaluator's responsibility to initiate discussion and clarification of these matters, not the client's.

2. Before accepting an evaluation assignment, evaluators should disclose any roles or relationships they have that might pose a conflict of interest (or appearance of a conflict) with their role as an evaluator. If they proceed with the evaluation, the conflict(s) should be clearly articulated in reports of the evaluation results.

3. Evaluators should record all changes made in the originally negotiated project plans, and the reasons why the changes were made. If those changes would significantly affect the scope and likely results of the evaluation, the evaluator should inform the client and other important stakeholders in a timely fashion (barring good reason to the contrary, before proceeding with further work) of the changes and their likely impact.

4. Evaluators should be explicit about their own, their clients', and other stakeholders' interests and values concerning the conduct and outcomes of an evaluation.

5. Evaluators should not misrepresent their procedures, data, or findings. Within reasonable limits, they should attempt to prevent or correct misuse of their work by others.

6. If evaluators determine that certain procedures or activities are likely to produce misleading evaluative information or conclu-

sions, they have the responsibility to communicate their concerns and the reasons for them. If discussions with the client do not resolve these concerns, the evaluator should decline to conduct the evaluation. If declining the assignment is unfeasible or inappropriate, the evaluator should consult colleagues or relevant stakeholders about other proper ways to proceed. (Options might include discussions at a higher level, a dissenting cover letter or appendix, or refusal to sign the final document.)

7. Evaluators should disclose all sources of financial support for an evaluation, and the source of the request for the evaluation.

D. **Respect for People:** Evaluators respect the security, dignity, and self-worth of respondents, program participants, clients, and other evaluation stakeholders.

1. Evaluators should seek a comprehensive understanding of the important contextual elements of the evaluation. Contextual factors that may influence the results of a study include geographic location, timing, political and social climate, economic conditions, and other relevant activities in progress at the same time.

2. Evaluators should abide by current professional ethics, standards, and regulations regarding risks, harms, and burdens that might befall those participating in the evaluation; regarding informed consent for participation in evaluation; and regarding informing participants and clients about the scope and limits of confidentiality.

3. Because justified negative or critical conclusions from an evaluation must be explicitly stated, evaluations sometimes produce results that harm client or stakeholder interests. Under this circumstance, evaluators should seek to maximize the benefits and reduce any unnecessary harms that might occur, provided this will not compromise the integrity of the evaluation findings. Evaluators should carefully judge when the benefits from doing the evaluation or in performing certain evaluation procedures should be foregone because of the risks or harms. To the extent possible, these issues should be anticipated during the negotiation of the evaluation.

4. Knowing that evaluations may negatively affect the interests of some stakeholders, evaluators should conduct the evaluation and communicate its results in a way that clearly respects the stakeholders' dignity and self-worth.

5. Where feasible, evaluators should attempt to foster social equity in evaluation, so that those who give to the evaluation may benefit in return. For example, evaluators should seek to ensure that those who bear the burdens of contributing data and incurring

any risks do so willingly, and that they have full knowledge of and opportunity to obtain any benefits of the evaluation. Program participants should be informed that their eligibility to receive services does not hinge on their participation in the evaluation.

6. Evaluators have the responsibility to understand and respect differences among participants, such as differences in their culture, religion, gender, disability, age, sexual orientation, and ethnicity, and to account for potential implications of these differences when planning, conducting, analyzing, and reporting evaluations.

E. **Responsibilities for General and Public Welfare:** Evaluators articulate and take into account the diversity of general and public interests and values that may be related to the evaluation.

1. When planning and reporting evaluations, evaluators should include relevant perspectives and interests of the full range of stakeholders.

2. Evaluators should consider not only the immediate operations and outcomes of whatever is being evaluated, but also its broad assumptions, implications, and potential side effects.

3. Freedom of information is essential in a democracy. Evaluators should allow all relevant stakeholders access to evaluative information in forms that respect people and honor promises of confidentiality. Evaluators should actively disseminate information to stakeholders as resources allow. Communications that are tailored to a given stakeholder should include all results that may bear on interests of that stakeholder and refer to any other tailored communications to other stakeholders. In all cases, evaluators should strive to present results clearly and simply so that clients and other stakeholders can easily understand the evaluation process and results.

4. Evaluators should maintain a balance between client needs and other needs. Evaluators necessarily have a special relationship with the client who funds or requests the evaluation. By virtue of that relationship, evaluators must strive to meet legitimate client needs whenever it is feasible and appropriate to do so. However, that relationship can also place evaluators in difficult dilemmas when client interests conflict with other interests, or when client interests conflict with the obligation of evaluators for systematic inquiry, competence, integrity, and respect for people. In these cases, evaluators should explicitly identify and discuss the conflicts with the client and relevant stakeholders, resolve them when possible, determine whether continued work on the evaluation is advisable if the conflicts cannot be resolved, and make clear any significant limitations on the evaluation that might result if the conflict is not resolved.

5. Evaluators have obligations that encompass the public interest and good. These obligations are especially important when evaluators are supported by publicly generated funds; but clear threats to the public good should never be ignored in any evaluation. Because the public interest and good are rarely the same as the interests of any particular group (including those of the client or funder), evaluators will usually have to go beyond analysis of particular stakeholder interests and consider the welfare of society as a whole.

Appendix B

Glossary

ANOVA ("one-way analysis of variance") is a bivariate statistical test that is used to determine whether three or more groups are significantly different from one another with respect to a particular characteristic.

Assessments of client strengths (and weaknesses) are assessment tools in practice that include questions to explore clients' strengths and weaknesses; the assessment of clients' strengths is often an area that is otherwise overlooked in assessments.

Best practices are the "best" or most effective programs or practices known to help people overcome their problems. Evidence-based practices, in many ways, are synonymous with "best practices."

Biopsychosocial assessment tools are assessment tools in practice that identify questions and topical areas to explore with clients in three areas of their lives: biological, psychological, and social. Sometimes these tools also include assessment questions about the spiritual, mental, and cultural dimensions of a client.

Case managers monitor the range of services provided to their clients to ensure their quality and continued appropriateness. Case managers typically find services for clients, negotiate or facilitate contracts with agencies that offer services, monitor services to ensure that the agency actually delivers the contracted services, and advocate when necessary on behalf of clients.

Central tendency measures are statistics that summarize an entire set of scores by calculating a single representative number. Three types of measures of central tendency are available for use in evaluations: mean, median, and mode.

Chi-square test is a bivariate statistic used to determine whether the values of one variable are associated with the values of another variable. This test is also sometimes referred to as a "cross-tab," or cross-tabulation, of these variables.

Clinical significance is a way to determine whether enough improvement occurred in the client's outcome variable after implementation of the intervention. Clinical significance is based on clinical criteria established by a professional group or agency. In this case, the amount of improvement in the client's goal is *enough* if it meets the established clinical criteria.

Community forums are sessions in which several people come together to discuss a topic of interest to all of them. Participants are likely to belong to the same community or neighborhood, and the topic is likely to be an issue that has communitywide implications.

Condition is a property of a *measurable objective* that identifies prior circumstances or conditions required before a performance can be expected.

Correlation test is a bivariate statistical test used to determine whether there is a statistically significant association between two variables. A correlation test can be used only when both variables are at the interval/ratio level of measurement.

Criteria is a property of a *measurable objective* that is a standard of acceptable performance, reflected in such things as speed, accuracy, or quality.

Descriptive statistics are statistics used to summarize responses or scores for each variable. These statistics are also referred to as *univariate statistics* because they analyze one variable at a time.

Ecomaps are an assessment tool in practice that visually describe the client's person-in-environment constellation, including relationships with friends and family members who are significant to the client, agencies and schools that are involved, jobs, and other social supports.

Effectiveness refers to interventions being successful in bringing about the expected changes in clients' lives.

Efficiency refers to interventions concerned with channeling available resources to the intended target problem or concern without any waste.

Effort refers to what staff members, volunteers, and administrators put into a program or practice area when implementing an intervention.

Elements of programs and practice are distinct entities critical to their functioning. Several elements can exist in each of the stages. For example, input elements could be the target goals or purposes of a program/practice area. Process elements during the implementation stage could be the theoretical approach that is being used. Outcome elements can be the measures of client progress in reaching their goals.

Empowerment models refer to concepts, techniques, and findings that help specific oppressed groups or communities develop their self-determining ability and improve programs. Program participants are sometimes helped to conduct their own evaluations and use outside evaluators and other experts as coaches, facilitators, expert consultants, and critical friends.

Evaluation design is the plan for carrying out an evaluation. It includes a set of study questions and/or hypotheses to explore or test, a source from whom the data is gathered, a specific method of collecting the data, and a data analysis plan. A plan to protect human participants of the study is also an important component to complete and have approved.

Evidence-based interventions are interventions in which there is the best available external evidence that they are effective. Sources of evidence come mostly from research studies using quasi-experimental or experimental designs and practice experience. Evidence-based sources should also be consistent with the values and expectations of the clients receiving these interventions.

Experimental designs are longitudinal group designs that can be used to test whether there is a causal relationship between an intervention and a client outcome variable. These designs are the strongest designs for proving causality and have two groups, a group that receives the intervention and a control group that does not. Participants are selected and randomly assigned to the two groups. The control group is considered identical to the group receiving the intervention, except that it does not receive the intervention.

Experimental models are evaluation perspectives that posit that experimental and quasi-experimental designs are superior to other evaluation designs because they deliver scientifically credible evidence of the impact of programs on clients' welfare. The perspective posits that experimental designs and randomized samples are feasible and ethical, and the only way to rule out other influences such as other sources of help.

Family genograms are an assessment tool in practice that provide a visual display of a family across two or more generations and offer insights into and understanding of the patterns evident in the client's family.

Feminist perspectives on evaluation are defined both by the research methods that feminists prefer and the substantive areas they choose to study. Most feminist researchers prefer qualitative over quantitative methods because of the flexibility built into the method and the value it places on uncovering new knowledge at deeper levels of meaning. This evaluation focus tends to be concerned primarily with studying the relative positions and experiences of women in relation to men and the effects that gender issues have on both sexes, such as gender discrimination in hiring, the low representation of women in administrative and other leadership roles, and salary inequities based on gender.

Focus groups are a special type of group in which participants are invited to discuss a particular topic. Focus groups can be used to find out the views of several people on an issue of importance to a needs assessment. Members of focus groups are usually selected because they have personal knowledge on or expertise in a particular topic. The leader of a focus group facilitates a group discussion by asking members several general questions on the topic.

Formative evaluations focus on planning for a program and improving its delivery of services. Such evaluations are usually initiated and conducted by the agency sponsoring the program/practice area and are driven internally by staff of the agency and outside consultants whom they select.

Fourth-generation evaluations refer to a new approach for this millennium that strives to redress power imbalances and expand the repertoire of data gathering and analysis methods used in evaluations. Someone with this perspective distrusts all methods equally and can recognize and admit the situational limitations of the knower, whether based in science, literature, or another vantage point. This perspective particularly seeks to hear and value the often unheard indigenous voices of other societies in the world.

Frequency distribution is a statistic that describes the number and percentage of times that each of the values of a variable is observed in a sample.

General study questions for evaluations serve two purposes. First, they provide parameters for an evaluation, limiting what will be investigated. Second, they provide enough specificity to know what is to be explored in a specific sense. In other words, they are not too broad to be unrealistic and not too specific to be too restricting.

Goal is an end result intended for an intervention. Goals are important because they provide an intervention with a direction to pursue and an outcome to reach. Without goals, an intervention may be an aimless effort that does not seem to go anywhere important. Goals are often not in a measurable form and need measurable objectives.

Goal Attainment Scale (GAS) is a practice evaluation tool that can be used to evaluate the extent to which the worker's interventions affect the client's goals in a favorable way. It is an incremental scale that can be used to measure degrees of progress.

Informed consent means that the participants of an evaluation are thoroughly *informed* about the study before they are expected to *consent* to participate.

Institutional review boards (IRBs) are a group of people at an agency or university who have been designated to promulgate ethical standards and to approve and monitor the ethical provisions of all studies sponsored by the institution. Evaluators and other researchers are required to submit a formal statement to their IRB that describes their study, its procedures, benefits, and how it protects research participants from risks of harm and invasion of privacy.

Logic model is a tool to theoretically analyze a program. The logic model helps highlight how the stages and elements of a program can be logically linked to one another in an organic whole. Using this model, the sequence of steps in a program's development are important to examine, beginning with the problems of prospective clients and culminating in anticipated client outcomes.

Mapping is a computerized approach that visually locates specific groups or clusters of people or problems in a particular geographic area.

Mapping helps the user recognize where there are concentrations of problems and their association with other relevant factors.

Measurable objectives are statements that identify indicators of whether a client or group of clients reaches a goal. Usually each goal has more than one measurable objective.

Mixed methods are quantitative and qualitative methods of data collection and analysis that can be used in combination with each other in evaluations. Use of mixed methods offers several advantages, including use of the respective data to complement one another in evaluation findings and in triangulating the collected data.

Needs assessment is an organized and systematic effort to assess the need for something, in this case the need for a new program or practice area. Executing a needs assessment of some or all prospective recipients of a program is often the wisest way to conduct an assessment. The specific ways to conduct a needs assessment can take many forms, including use of existing data, construction and administration of a questionnaire, conducting of interviews or focus groups, arranging of public forums, observations, or a combination of these methods.

Overt indicator is a word or phrase added after a performance to help make the performance more observable in a *measurable objective*.

Performance is a property of a *measurable objective* that identifies what a person is expected to do.

Practice refers to the interventions of an individual social worker or human service worker. This is in contrast to a program that involves the interventions of all staff members in that program.

Practice evaluation is a study of one social worker's interventions with clients. Like a program evaluation, it uses the methods of research. However, in contrast to program evaluation, it focuses on how well an individual social worker implements his or her client interventions.

Pre-experimental designs are group designs that can be used to explore a causal relationship between an intervention and a client outcome variable. These designs have only an intervention group. They are the weakest group designs and have limited use, but they are often considered initially because they can be implemented more easily and take less time than experimental and quasi-experimental designs.

Program is an organizational entity in an agency that offers a set of goods and/or services with common goals. The goods and services are typically provided to a target population of clients who either seek them out or are selected to use them. A program typically employs more than one and usually several staff members.

Program evaluation is a study of a social program that uses the methods of scientific research. It concerns itself with the practical needs of an organization, not theoretical issues, and it focuses on how well an overall program implements its services.

Quality refers to a program and practice area being delivered as intended and being done very well at a very high standard.

Quality assurance, also sometimes referred to as quality improvement or quality control, is a set of evaluation activities implemented to gather information about the processes of programs. Its distinguishing characteristics include peer reviews, heavy reliance on client records, observation of small samples of the services, ensuring that minimal standards are met, and immediate incorporation of useful results to improve the program.

Quasi-experimental designs are longitudinal group designs that can be used to explore a causal relationship between an intervention and a client outcome variable. These designs have features that control for some of the extraneous influences by using a comparison group or having multiple measures of the outcome variable.

Regression tests are statistical tests that can predict a client outcome from more than one intervention.

Relevance refers to an intervention meeting the clients' need and solving the larger social problem that clients are experiencing.

Results-oriented models are evaluation perspectives that focus on performance, outcomes, and accountability. Advocates of the results-oriented model believe that it is important to convince various stakeholders that the outcomes they achieve are the ultimate reason why they are in business.

Secondary research additionally analyzes data from a previous study. Many research firms offer their data sets to interested people for secondary analysis, often for a reasonable fee.

Sequencing blocks are an exercise that helps clients explore the causal relationships among prior behaviors that have resulted in a positive or negative outcome. In this case, the outcome behavior is known and the behavior that caused it is to be discovered.

Services are the activities offered by programs. Services focus mostly on the processes that help clients reach their program goals. Helping processes are the major focus of practice courses in social work programs and draw from a broad range of practice theories, such as cognitive behavioral, person-centered, and solution-focused therapies. In-service training programs are also valuable to prepare staff members and volunteers with the skills to assist in the helping processes that are the most effective.

Single-system design (SSD) is a practice evaluation tool that determines the impact of one or more interventions introduced by a social worker on a client system. An SSD uses a graph with the changes that a client makes plotted over time to observe whether the interventions are responsible for improvements in that behavior when they occur.

Stakeholders are the people invested in a program or practice intervention in some way. Examples include representatives of a funding agency, an agency board of directors, staff members, and clients. The success of these stakeholders is, in some way, likely to depend on the program's performance, so they have an obvious stake in what happens.

Statistical significance is a way to determine whether enough improvement occurred in the client's outcome variable after implementation of the intervention. Statistically significant associations can be calculated by applying a statistical test, which determines whether the probability of an association between the intervention and the outcome measure are high. Usually a claim of significance is made when the probability of being in error is less than 5 percent (expressed as $p < .05$).

Summative evaluations focus on the outcomes of programs and attempt to answer the ultimate question: did the intervention reach its goals? These evaluations have a finality to them in that they attempt to measure whether a program was effective. Summative evaluations are typically conducted by an external agent, such as an independent evaluator or a governmental agency, to ensure that they are objective. Funding and regulatory agencies are most interested in summative evaluations because they provide the kinds of information they need to make major decisions around future funding.

***t*-test** is a bivariate statistical test used to determine whether two groups are significantly different on the basis of a particular characteristic. One variable in this statistical formula is the group variable (group 1 or group 2). The second variable is the characteristic being compared.

Target Problem Scale (TBS) is a practice evaluation tool that can be used particularly when client goals are difficult to identify. A TBS is helpful if clients remain focused on their problems and are not prepared to pursue goals beyond these problems.

Theme analysis is a type of qualitative data analysis that involves identifying common themes or patterns prevalent in several cases.

Variability measures are statistics that summarize how the responses to a question vary or disperse away from their central tendency. These statistics complement measures of central tendencies because they provide information about the variability of scores away from the clustering point(s). Two common statistics that measure the variability of scores are range and standard deviation. Both can be used with interval/ratio level variables only.

Appendix C

Answers to Discussion Questions

Chapter 7

Example of Performance, Condition, and Criteria

Can you identify the performance, condition, and criteria in each measurable objective?

Goal: Clients will increase compliance with medication appointments.

Objective A: If clients wish to remember the dates and times of medication appointments, they will write the time of their next appointment on a calendar. [Performance is "write the time," condition is "If clients wish to remember the dates and times of medication appointments," and criteria are "next appointment" and "on a calendar."]

Objective B: If transportation is needed to appointments, clients will call to arrange for it at least two days prior to the appointment. [Performance is "call," condition is "If transportation is needed to appointments," and criteria is "at least two days prior to the appointment."]

Objective C: If clients are ill or otherwise cannot come to their medication appointment, they will call and reschedule their appointment more than twenty-four hours before the missed appointment. [Performance is "call and reschedule," condition is "If clients are ill or otherwise cannot come to their medication appointment," and criteria is "more than twenty-four hours before the missed appointment."]

Exercise Regarding a Short-Term Goal and Its Measurable Objectives

Goal: Clients will decrease their depressive symptoms.

Measurable Objective A: When feeling depressed, clients journal their feelings, thoughts, and behavior 80 percent of the time. [Performance is "journal," condition is "When feeling depressed," and criteria are "feelings, thoughts, and behavior" and "80 percent of the time."]

Measurable Objective B: At the outset of depressive feelings, clients demonstrate (carry out) one positive coping skill one out of three times. [Performance is "demonstrate (carry out)," condition is "At the outset of depressive feelings," and criteria are "one positive coping skill" and "one out of three times."]

Exercise

What's wrong with each of the following measurable objectives?

1. Clients will meet with their counselor and take their meds. [There are two performances rather than one. Also criteria describing how many times they will meet with their counselor and the specific meds and correct dosage need to be specified.]
2. The social worker will meet with the client for five counseling sessions to help the client express his or her anger verbally. [This measurable objective focuses on the social worker's performance, not the client's.]
3. The father will spend nurturing time with his three-year-old son. [Nurturing needs to be defined so that it is observable. Criteria are needed indicating how often he spends such time with his son.]

Discussion Questions

1. What is needed to improve these measurable objectives?
   A. The clients will be monitored by the appropriate staff while at the group home at all times. [Improvements: This objective focuses on staff behavior not client behavior. It also needs an overt indicator for the performance ("will be monitored")]
   B. After ten to twelve therapy sessions, the client will engage in negative self-talk 10 percent of the time. [Improvements: After ten to twelve sessions, the client will engage in (state) positive self-talk nine out of ten times.]
   C. When arriving for her appointment, the client will wait fewer than fifteen minutes to see the doctor 90 percent of the time. [Improvements: This objective focuses on the doctor, not the client.]
   D. During the school year, my client will turn in a progress report completed by teachers every week. [Improvements: During the school year, my client will turn in every week a progress report with at least five of six items graded as As.]
   E. While at X agency, the mother will spend nurturing time reading to her child 100 percent of the time. [Improvements: While at X agency, the mother will spend thirty minutes each day reading to her child.]

3. Identify the performance, conditions, and criteria in measurable objectives A and B:

Goal: Clients with a mental retardation label will strengthen their socialization skills.

Measurable Objective A: *When introduced to a new person, the client will shake hands nine out of ten times.* [Answers: Performance is "shake hands," conditions are "When being introduced to a new person," and criteria are "nine out of ten times."]

Measurable Objective B: *After breakfast, the client will make his bed before leaving for work.* [Performance is "make his bed," conditions are "After breakfast" and "before leaving for work." There are no criteria.]

4. Identify the performance, conditions, and criteria in measurable objectives A, B, and C:

Goal: Mental health clients will achieve optimum mental health.

Measurable Objective A: If prescribed, clients will take (swallow) the correct amounts of medication daily for six months. [Answer: Performance is "swallow," conditions are "If prescribed," and criteria are "correct amounts" and "daily for six months."]

Measurable Objective B: After ten to twelve sessions, clients will state four out of five techniques to control anxiety taught in sessions. [Answer: Performance is "state," conditions are "After ten to twelve sessions," and criteria are "four out of five techniques."]

Measurable Objective C: When experiencing thoughts of self-harm, clients will ask for help from their identified support system within twenty-four hours. [Answer: Performance is "ask," conditions are "When experiencing thoughts of self-harm," and criteria are "from their identified support system" and "within twenty-four hours."]

5. Identify the performance, conditions, and criteria in measurable objectives A, B, and C:

Goal: John Doe will have stronger interpersonal skills.

Measurable Objective A: John will say "good morning" to six out of ten coworkers when arriving at work each morning. [Answer: Performance is "say 'good morning,' " conditions are "when arriving at work each morning," and criteria are "six out of ten coworkers."]

Measurable Objective B: After six sessions, John will talk for ten minutes to one or two coworkers each week. [Answer: Performance is "talk," conditions are "After six sessions," and criteria are "ten minutes to one or two coworkers each week."]

Measurable Objective C: When talking to others, John will look at the person's face 75 percent of the time. [Answer: Performance is "look at the person's face," conditions are "When talking to others," and criteria are "75 percent of the time."]

6. Identify the performance, conditions, and criteria in measurable objectives A, B, and C:

Goal: Clients will develop assertiveness skills in a group on assertiveness.

Measurable Objective A: After three group sessions, the clients will circle assertive comments and cross out aggressive comments on a worksheet and be correct eight out of ten times. [Answer: Performance is "circle assertive comments" and "cross out aggressive comments," conditions are "After three group sessions," and criteria are "on a worksheet" and "correct eight out of ten times."]

Measurable Objective B: After five group sessions, the clients will write two ways they were assertive. [Answer: Performance is "write," conditions are "After five group sessions," and criteria are "two ways they were assertive."]

Measurable Objective C: At the conclusion of treatment, the clients will tell the social worker two things they liked and two things they did not like about group therapy without raising their voices. [Answer: Performance is "tell the social worker," conditions are "At the conclusion of treatment," and criteria are "two things they liked and two things they did not like about therapy" and "without raising their voices."]

Chapter 9

1. Review the six group designs summarized on pages 212–220. Then answer all of the following questions:
   A. Which design seems ideal? Why do you think so? [Answer: One-group pretest/posttest design with a control group, because it controls for all extraneous variables.]
   B. Which design is the easiest and least expensive to use? What can be concluded from this design? [Answer: One-group posttest-only design; the only conclusion that can be drawn from this design is that the intervention may have had an impact.]
   C. Why are *multiple* measures of the client outcome variable obtained when conducting a time-series design? What are the benefits of these multiple measures? [Answer: The multiple measures provide data trends that can help determine the extent to which the intervention as opposed to other factors external to it is the causal agent.]

D. Which design may be the most practical for determining whether the program intervention was responsible for positive changes in the outcome variables? Why? [Answers: One-group pretest/posttest design with a comparison group or time-series design, because they do not involve the ethical dilemmas that the experimental designs impose and have features that control for extraneous variables.]

E. What is useful about a pretest/posttest design? [Answer: The design can determine whether there was any change in the client outcome measure between the pretest and posttest.]

F. Under what circumstances would you consider a posttest-only control group design? [Answer: This design is preferred over the pretest/posttest design with a control group if there is concern that administering a pretest measure could have an influence on the outcome.]

Index